Real-Time

JAVA™

Platform Programming

PETER C. DIBBLE

Sun Microsystems Press
A Prentice Hall Title

ISBN 0-13-028261-8

90000

9 780130 282613

The publisher offers discounts on this book when ordered in bulk quantities.
For more information, contact Corporate Sales Department, Prentice Hall PTR ,
One Lake Street, Upper Saddle River, NJ 07458. Phone: 800-382-3419; FAX: 201- 236-7141.
Email: corpsales@prenhall.com.

Editorial/production supervision: *Jan H. Schwartz*
Cover design director: *Jerry Votta*
Cover designer: *Anthony Gemmellaro*
Cover illustration: *Karen Strelecki*
Manufacturing manager: *Alexis R. Heydt-Long*
Marketing manager: *Debby vanDijk*
Associate editor: *Eileen Clark*
Editorial assistant: *Brandt Kenna*
Sun Microsystems Press Publisher: *Michael Llwyd Alread*

10 9 8 7 6 5 4 3 2 1

ISBN 0-13-028261-8

Sun Microsystems Press
A Prentice Hall Title

Contents

Preface

Real-time computing—computing with deadlines—is a field that involves every programmer, but almost nobody gives it serious attention. The machine tool that controls a flying saw blade is a real-time problem. So is a web site that guarantees to respond to queries within two seconds, or the text editor that must respond to each keystroke within a tenth of a second to keep its user comfortable. In the broadest sense, even the biweekly payroll run is a real-time system.

To the extent that typical programmers worry about timeliness, they think in terms of high-performance algorithms, optimizing compilers, and fast processors. Those are important considerations, but they ignore the question of consistent performance. There are a whole family of things that can make timing undependable, and avoiding those problems is the province of real-time programming.

Over the years I've been working on this book, the fastest Java Virtual Machines have improved to the point where the performance of the Java platform can reliably match or exceed the performance of C++, but that is material for a different book. A real-time programmer is certainly interested in the time it takes to complete a computation, but the important question is whether it will *always* complete on time. Are all the factors that could delay completion properly accounted for?

The Real Time Specification for Java (RTSJ) focuses on the factors that matter to systems that must meet deadlines, primarily time itself and things that could cause unexpected delays. This book focuses on the same things.

This book has to be dedicated to the other members of the real time for Java Expert Group. Others contributed—family, editors, employers, and friends—but the six other "experts" who saw the effort through are special. Thank you Greg Bollella, Ben Brosgol, Steve Furr, James Gosling, David Hardin, and Mark Turnbull. Without you the spec would not be there, this book would not be here, and I would have missed what may have been the most exciting spec-writing exercise in history. By my count, we spent more than a thousand hours together arguing, problem solving, building concepts and tearing them down. Greg (our spec lead for most of the effort) was demanding and a tireless example for us. We worked hard, but we had glorious fun. What could be more fun than working with a group of supremely-qualified friends to complete a difficult piece of work?

I found one aspect of the process particularly interesting. We were all sent as representatives of companies. Nevertheless, in almost every case, we operated as if our companies had instructed us to ignore all commercial motivations and build a good specification. Perhaps it is Sun's fault. They sent us James Gosling. Not only is he highly qualified, and revered in the Java world, he is also a scrupulously honest scientist. Did that example motivate other companies to send similar people? Or perhaps we can trace it back to IBM, who set the ground rules that selected us all. However it was done, it was good. All specifications should be created this way!

The main players on the reference implementation team also deserve special mention. Doug Locke, Pratik Solanki, and Scott Robbins wrote lots of code and participated in Expert Group conference calls in the last year of the specification's development. Not only did they bring the spec to life in code, they also helped us redesign some facilities.

I started writing this book long before the specification was complete. The original goal was to have a set of books ready near the time the specification became final. There would be a specification, a reference implementation and a selection of "how to use it" books all at about the same time. This required a big head start, but things did not work exactly as planned.

The specification grew in a fairly organized way until the release of the preliminary specification. Then the work got bumpy. The implementation of the reference implementation and my experiences writing this book caused major upheavals in the most complex parts of the specification. The Expert Group had been uncertain as to the implementability of our designs for scoped memory management, physical memory, and asynchronous transfer of control. We agreed to put fairly aggressive designs in the preliminary specification, and see how the reference implementation team dealt with them. It turned out that we had to tighten the rules for asynchronous transfer of control slightly, and increase the constraints on scoped memory a lot. Then we discovered that interaction between scoped memory and threads made starting threads in non-heap memory painful nearly to the point of uselessness. We fixed these problems, and I wrote and rewrote chapters.

Every specification that is released before it has been used extensively needs an author who tries to explain the specification, and write code that uses the specification. That person finds problems that are invisible to implementers and the test suite. But the author had better love the specification. A chapter about a feature that is broken will naturally get long and complicated as it tries to show the power and rationale behind the design. Finally it reaches the point of, "this is not complex and wonderful. It is broken!" Then the chapter becomes trash, and a new chapter appears to explain the new design.

Happily, the Expert Group and the reference implementation team were with me. The final specification went up on *www.rtj.org* in late 2001, the reference implementation appeared there in early 2002, and this, the "how to use it" book should be on the shelves in March 2002. We did OK.

Introduction

You can treat this book as two closely-related books. Chapters 1 through 7 are background that might help understand the RTSJ. The remainder of the book is about the RTSJ itself. If you already understand real-time scheduling, or you don't care about scheduling and want to get directly to the code, you can start at Chapter 8 and read from that point on. Other than possibly skipping the first seven chapters, I do not recommend skipping around. Few of the chapters can stand by themselves. After you've skimmed the book once, it can work as reference material, but I suggest that you start by reading the book sequentially.

This book is intended to serve as part of a set comprising three elements: the RTSJ specification, the reference implementation, and this book. You can find the specification and the reference implementation through *www.phptr.com/dibble* or *www.rtj.org*. The preliminary RTSJ document is part of the Addison-Wesley Java Series. It is available in hard copy through your favorite book store. However, the preliminary RTSJ has been superseded by the final, version 1.0, version. At this time, the final specification is only available as downloadable PDF and HTML.

The reference implementation is a complete and usable implementation of the RTSJ for Linux. Almost every example in this book was tested on the reference implementation. I have used the reference implementation on PCs running Red Hat Linux and TimeSys Linux, and it should work with other versions of X86

Linux as well, but the reference implementation relies on the underlying operating system for scheduling, so you will find that features like priority inversion avoidance will depend on the version of Linux you use.

The source code for the reference implementation is available. Some of it is descended from the Sun CVM. That is available under the Sun community source license. The parts of the reference implementation that are not related to Sun code are covered under a less restrictive open source license.

Although the reference implementation is excellent for experimentation, it is not designed for commercial use. It does not take the care with performance or memory use that you'd expect from a commercial product.

You can find links to important web sites, corrections and extensions to this book, and probably other useful things like source code at *www.phptr.com/dibble*.

Landscape

The Java platform seems an unusual choice for real-time programming: garbage collection freezes the system whenever it likes, giving Java technology terrible timing behavior, and performance from one to 30 times slower than the same program written in C++, depending on the program and the details of the Java platform. If the real-time community were not desperate for better tools, the Java platform would be summarily rejected.

The benefits of Java technology are attractive enough that the standard Java platform has been used in a few real-time systems, and its promise justified the effort to design and build real-time extensions—the RTJava platform.

Java Technology and Real Time

Programmers of embedded real-time systems are the most obvious members of the real-time community, but nearly every programmer deals with real time some of the time. Everybody who codes user interfaces should worry about consistent

1

response time. Telecommunication equipment has deadlines imposed by regulations. Trains, airplanes, elevators, trucks, packages in a delivery system, programming on television, packets flowing through a network, children preparing to meet the school bus—all of these systems involve timing constraints, and all of them (except, probably, getting children to the bus on time) are likely to involve computers.

Real-time programming is like any other kind of programming, but arguably harder. Like an ordinary program, a real-time program must produce correct results; it also has to produce the results at the correct time. Traditionally, real-time programming has been practiced in antique[1] or arcane[2] languages. Real-time Java gives real-time programmers access to a modern, mainstream language designed for productivity.

Java puts programmer productivity before everything else. The famous Java slogan, Write Once, Run Anywhere, is just a specialization of programmer productivity—it is clearly inefficient for a programmer to rewrite a program for each target platform.

Those who criticize the willingness of the designers of the Java platform to sacrifice performance for productivity face two arguments.

1. A compiler should be able to optimize out much of the cost of Java's programmer-friendly features.

2. Moore's law has processors speeding up so fast that any reasonable constant-factor overhead introduced by Java will quickly be covered by processor improvements.

If you feel that strongly about performance, use C or assembler, but a Java application would be designed, written, and debugged before the C application is coded. Real-time Java is designed with the same theme.

Note: For this book, we stipulate that the Java platform is slow and has garbage collection delays. These problems are not necessarily permanent. Tricks in the Java virtual machine (JVM) make execution faster and garbage collection less intrusive, but those workarounds are not the focus of this book.

---

1.   Assembly language itself may not be antique, but the practice of programming in assembly language is being obsoleted by RISC processors and sophisticated optimizing compilers.
2.   FORTH is a relatively popular arcane language. The defense department has a whole stable of other arcane languages for real-time systems.

Real time does not necessarily mean "real fast." Computing speed is not the problem for a computer that controls a needle that zips into a $200 glass test tube and stops abruptly a millimeter before it slams through the bottom of the tube. If the system is slow, the solutions are well known: profile, improve the algorithms, tweak the code, and upgrade the hardware. Inconsistent behavior is harder to address. It can only be fixed by finding and removing the underlying cause, which, by definition, appears sporadically. Boosting performance until the problem disappears often does more harm than good. The system may stop failing under test but still fail after it is deployed.

Real-Time Programming Requirements

The real-time programmer needs predictability. If the program stops the needle in time under test, it must never smash the tube unless there is a hardware problem. The worst debugging problem is software that works correctly almost every time. Removing a timing bug that won't appear reliably during testing is an exercise in imagination. Convincing yourself that the repair worked is an exercise in faith—you cannot make the defect appear in the defective software, and it still doesn't appear after you apply the fix. It must be gone. Right?

Real-time programmers work in the usual engineering environment. The design has to optimize several goals: correctness, low cost, fast time to market, compelling feature set. Real time is not the only concern. Predictability helps to achieve a correct implementation quickly. That helps with correctness and time to market, but cost is also an issue. Speed and low memory footprint amount to efficiency. They contribute to cost reduction and expanded feature set. If some tool or technique makes the software faster, it can do the following as a result:

- Let the system use a lower-performance (less expensive) processor
- Let some operations move from dedicated hardware to software
- Free some processor bandwidth for additional features

When the cost of a faster processor or special-purpose hardware is prohibitive, the real choice is to optimize the software or quit. Prohibitive cost is a flexible term. In some fields, it is sensible to expend years of engineering to reduce hardware costs by a few cents per unit. In other fields, it is normal to spend hundreds of thousands of dollars on hardware to save months of engineering time for each software project.

How Big Is Java?

Based on implementations at Microware, the minimum RAM and ROM required for a JDK-style runtime environment is more than 16 megabytes of ROM and 16 megabytes of RAM.

A PersonalJava system with an e-mail client, address book, and other similar applications can run with four megabytes of ROM and four megabytes of RAM. This is enough memory for applications, class libraries, the JVM, the operating system, and supporting components.

EmbeddedJava can be configured much larger and smaller than PersonalJava, but its lower limit would be hard to push below half a megabyte of ROM and half a megabyte of RAM.

The KJava virtual machine promises to run in less than 128 kilobytes.

RTJava doesn't do anything for Java's performance. If anything, RTJava is a little slower than ordinary Java, and ordinary (interpreted) Java is slower than C. (see *The Case for Java as a Programming Language,* by Arthur van Hoff in Internet Computing, January 1997 and *An Empirical Comparison of Seven Programming Languages,* by Lutz Prechelt in IEEE Computer, October 2000.) For now, that shortcoming has to be accepted: Java is slower than the alternatives, and it requires a daunting amount of memory to run a trivial program. (see sidebar, "How Big Is Java?").

Java and Embedded Real Time

Java is not likely to drive C out of the traditional embedded market soon. Embedded programmers are as conservative as cats. This caution is well founded. Software defects in embedded systems can have spectacular, physical effects manifested in fire and crushed metal, and updating embedded software is usually expensive.

Embedded programmers feel uncomfortable shipping technology that hasn't been thoroughly tested in many deployed systems. The barrier to adoption of new technology is subject to a minor tunneling effect. A few adventurous groups will try Java in embedded real-time systems. They will talk about the results. If real-time Java proves that it is a good tool for embedded real time, it could become a common embedded programming tool in five to ten years.

Definition of Real Time

Real-time problems are those for which timeliness, "Occurring at a suitable or opportune time,"[3] is a correctness criterion. If the process finishes late, it is wrong, or at least noticeably less satisfactory than a process that completes on time.

---

3.   *The American Heritage Dictionary of the English Language,* Third Edition, Houghton Mifflin Company, 1992.

Timeliness *always* matters. Few people would call a word processor, a compiler, or a payroll system a real-time system, but perhaps they should. If a word processor takes more than a few tenths of a second to echo a character, its user may become concerned about the competence of the programmers. If a compiler takes much longer than expected to compile a program, its user will fear that it has seized up. Timeliness is especially important for payroll. Late paychecks cause fear and anger in the people waiting for them.

The set of real-time problems is large and diverse, but a few standard tools and techniques work across them all: tools that are optimized for predictability, schedulers that optimize timeliness (instead of throughput), and analysis techniques that consider time constraints.

The space of real-time problems has at least three useful dimensions: the precision with which time is measured, the importance of consistency, and the shape of the utility curve around the deadline.

Precision of Measurement

The precision of the units a real-time system design uses to measure time helps characterize the system (see Figure 1–1). Does it express a second as one second, a thousand milliseconds, or a billion nanoseconds?

Submicrosecond

Some computer problems are expressed with times measured in units smaller than a microsecond (a millionth of a second.) That level of precision can be attained by a general-purpose processor dedicated to a repetitive task or by special-purpose hardware. Someday we may be able to handle such problems on a general-purpose system, but not today. (See Chapter 3 for reasons why it is hard to predict the execution time of a few instructions without tightly controlling the environment.)

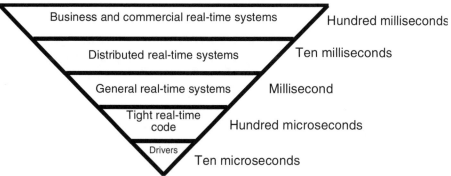

Figure 1–1 Time-scale pyramid

Ten Microseconds

Software commonly handles specifications expressed in tens of microseconds, but coding to specifications this precise requires care and deep knowledge of the underlying hardware. This level of precision coding often appears in carefully written device driver code, and contrary to general principle, the goal is usually to complete a computation in a precise and *short* interval.

Millisecond

General real-time software usually deals with time measured in milliseconds. Most well-known real-time systems fall into this range. These systems can be programmed with normal tools, provided that the programmer demonstrates healthy caution about timing artifacts of the hardware, the compiler, and the system software.

Hundredths of a second

Distributed real-time programming sees time in hundredths of a second. The atomic unit of time is network communication, and the network environment is dynamic. If you cannot tolerate timing that jitters badly at the millisecond level, don't distribute that part of your application.

Tenths of a second

Programs that interact with people see time specified in tenths of a second at the command and response level. This is the precision of the specification for response when a user strikes a key, clicks a mouse, pushes a button, crosses a photodetector, touches a touch-screen, or gives a computer directions in some other way. These systems are usually programmed without any consideration for real-time discipline. Performance problems are fixed with faster hardware or by normal profiling and tuning methods. In a real-time sense, these systems routinely "fail" under load.

Consistency

We're dealing with computers. Although there is randomness at the subatomic level, the electrical engineers have eliminated most of the unpredictable behaviors before the computer ships. Any random behavior that remains is a hardware bug. If we assume bug-free hardware, everything is predictable. However, it may be so difficult to account for all the factors influencing execution time that on many processors and software platform systems, execution time is effectively unpredictable.

In the real-time field, the term *determinism* means that timing is predictable at the precision required by the problem without heroic effort. Determinism is a good thing. Part of the design process for a real-time system involves drawing timelines with events and responses to those events. Without a *deterministic* operating system and processor, the analyst cannot even predict whether an event will reach the event handler before its deadline, much less whether the event handler will complete a computation before the deadline.

Consistency is better than mere determinism. It is useful to know that an urgent event will reach your program at sometime between 10 and 200 microseconds. It is better to know that the time interval will be between 50 and 70 microseconds. A real-time system can be designed to operate in any deterministic environment, but it has to assume that the system will always deliver the worst possible performance. Designing to that assumption is wasteful since typical times are usually near the best case. A consistent system reduces the difference between the expected performance and the worst possible performance, ideally by improving the worse-case performance instead of only degrading the typical performance.

Consistency costs performance. A system that needs to bring its *best-case* (the fastest it can go) and *worst-case* (the worst possible) performance as close together as possible cannot use hints or heuristics and cannot rely on the "80/20" rule. A dynamically constructed binary tree can degenerate into a structure with linear search time. A quicksort can take $O(n^2)$ time. Hints can be wrong, forcing the program to check the hint, then execute the fallback strategy. The real-time approaches to these problems are as follows, respectively: use a self-balancing binary tree, use a different sorting algorithm (mergesort is slower than quicksort on average, but predictable), and do not use hints. The resulting software's typical performance is at least 15 percent worse than the performance of a system that is designed to optimize typical performance, but its worst-case performance may be orders of magnitude better than such a conventional design.

Utility Function Curve

What happens when the real-time system is late? It misses its deadline ... then what? The answer to that question determines where the system falls on the continuum from *hard real time* through *soft real time* to *not real time*.

Hard real-time systems cannot tolerate late results. Something unrecoverable happens: a person dies, a wing falls off the airplane, a million barrels of hot petroleum squirt onto the tundra, or something else unspeakable occurs.

Hard real-time systems are difficult to code but simple to specify. You have to establish that they will meet all their deadlines, but you do not have to decide what to do when the systems miss a deadline. It is like the question, "In the computer that sits in a bomb and tells it when to explode, what instruction do you put after the one that explodes the bomb?"

There are two questions when a system misses a deadline:

1. Should we bother to produce the result even though it will be late?

2. Should we execute a recovery routine?

If the result of the computation is worthless after the deadline, it makes no sense to waste computer time on it. Since the system might have missed the deadline because it was overloaded, wasting time could cause the system to miss other deadlines and convert the failure to meet a single deadline into a total shutdown.

A missed deadline might require a response. Failing to shut off the valve that fills a water tank on time could call for another valve to let some water out of the tank. Not responding to a database query on time could put up a "please wait" message on the user's screen. A mistake in milling a part could call a human supervisor or kick the part into a scrap bin.

Utility is the economists' term for how valuable something is. Economists like to draw graphs, for example, the utility of a commodity as a function of how much you have of it. A graph (Figure 1–2) showing the utility of completion around the deadline characterizes some classes of real-time systems.

The first graph in Figure 1–2 shows a utility function that would represent a non-real-time system. The value of completion declines slowly after the deadline, but there is barely a difference between completing on deadline and being seri-

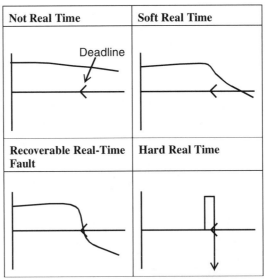

Figure 1–2 Punctuality utility functions

ously late. Think of mowing the lawn. Getting it done earlier is better, but there isn't any point at which it suddenly becomes urgent.

The second graph shows a utility function for a soft real-time system. The value of completion has an inflection point at the deadline. Late completion is worse than on-time completion, but the value stays positive for a while after the deadline. Think of fixing lunch for your children on a relaxed summer day. The children know the time they should be fed, and if you are late, they get fussy. The level of hungry complaints gradually increases after the deadline, but nothing really bad will happen. On time is best, and the value of the computation drops significantly when the deadline is missed.

The third graph represents a real-time problem with a serious time constraint. After the deadline the value of completion quickly goes negative, but it does not become catastrophic. In this case, the slope of the curve decreases because the system can take remedial action. Think of a child flushing a T-shirt down the toilet. The deadline for action is the moment before the child flushes. You would much rather stop him before he flushes. If you are late, you might be able to reach in and snag the shirt; that is unappealing, but not disastrous. Still later there is a good chance you can recover the shirt with a plumber's snake, but we are deep in negative utility. Still, nothing terrible has happened.

The last graph represents classic hard real time. A tiny interval after the deadline, the utility of completion goes to negative infinity. There probably is a utility value for a late result, but it is so negative that the creators of the system requirements don't want the engineer to consider the option of occasionally missing the deadline. Sticking with the children analogy, this is grabbing the child before she runs into traffic. Late is not an acceptable alternative.

Note: The utility function graphs in Figure 1–2 show various behaviors before the deadline. The utility of early results is a whole different question. The functions show that early is the same as on time, early is a little worse than on time, and early is much worse than on time. Since it is easy to delay the effect of an early computation, worrying about early results is generally not interesting.

Java's Problem Domain

The Java programming language is not the language for problems that require plain speed. In an academic world that assertion would not matter, but many real problems push the performance limits of their hardware. Some programming tools and practices are focused on performance. Good optimizing compilers and profiling tools are prized because they wring better performance out of a system, and brute assembly optimization is still practiced.

From the real-time perspective, Java's biggest problem isn't its performance, but its garbage collector. Unless you use it carefully, Java will pause at unpredictable moments and collect garbage for milliseconds. Better garbage collectors make long garbage collection pauses much less frequent or make the pauses shorter, but even with the best technology, only Java code that pays careful attention to the garbage collector can give predictable performance (see Figure 1–3).

The execution of programs on Java platforms is slow, and garbage collection makes it effectively nondeterministic, but it is still useful in real-time systems. The simplest way to manage Java's problems is to avoid them. Most real-time systems have large components with loose deadlines. A system that has to service interrupts in 30 microseconds or lose them and must respond in 2 milliseconds or suffer serious degradation probably uses a few thousand lines of code for that part of the system. Another 50,000 lines might support a user interface, a logging system, system initialization, and error handling. Those components need to communicate with the serious real-time components, but they are soft real time. They can probably tolerate nondeterministic delays of a second or more.

Java technology needs at least a medium-performance processor and a few megabytes of memory to run well.[4] This makes it particularly well suited to systems that have aggressive deadlines with long intervals between them. The sys-

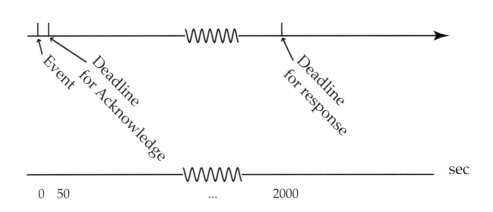

Figure 1–3 Timelines

4.   Java Card and KJava can run satisfactorily on less powerful processors and in less memory than ordinary Java.

tem designers will select a powerful processor to let it meet the deadlines, and in the intervals between deadlines it will have lots of time to run Java programs.

It is inconvenient to use multiple languages to build a system. Using C for the demanding real-time components and Java for the bulk of the components justifies the inconvenience with productivity.

1. Java code is unusually portable. This portability lets most of the development cycle take place on the engineer's workstation.

2. Programmers seem to be more productive in the Java language than in other common languages.

3. The Java class libraries contain many prewritten classes.

4. The Java platform works well in heterogeneous distributed systems.

5. Java applications on the real-time system communicate easily with Java applications in other systems, such as management, supervisory, and diagnostic systems.

Java probably cannot do all the work in a real-time system, but it can do the bulk of the work. See Chapter 8 for an overview.

Real-Time Java's Problem Domain

Real-time Java (RTJava) *can* handle some real-time systems by itself. It is not the best language to use for an MPEG decoder or an image processing system, but it should nicely fit less demanding real-time applications. For applications that leave enough spare processor time to cover the JVM's overhead, real-time Java promises to make real-time programming easier.

RTJava is designed to stretch the platform slightly in the direction of real time without losing compatibility with existing Java code. The design does not make Java faster—it probably makes it a little slower (see "Consistency" on page 6)—but faster hardware or improved algorithms can compensate for Java's fixed overhead. This is the standard Java tradeoff extended to real time: processor overhead for robust software and faster development.

The class of embedded real-time systems that are stamped out like pennies are not likely early adopters of RTJava. Per-unit costs on those systems are reduced mercilessly. The companies that build them would rather spend years of extra engineering than upgrade the processor or pay the license fee for a JVM.

RTJava is more attractive for systems where the cost of the processor is a small part of the total cost. This set includes commercial and industrial applications. The cost of adding Java to the system that controls a scientific instrument, a manufacturing system, or an ATM could be lost in the noise. When the product costs tens of thousands of dollars and ten thousand units would be a good year's production, the advantages in flexibility and time to market of RTJava can justify the cost of a faster processor.

RTJava may prove most useful to programmers who write interactive applications. There is an informal, but important, deadline when a person is waiting. Handling customer service, processing insurance claims, validating credit card transactions, and similar systems account for millions of programmer years of TSO, CICS, Complete, VMS, CMS, UNIX, ACP, Mac, and Windows interactive programs. Fast response is important, but fast and consistent is better. An interactive system that responds in half a second most of the time but sometimes takes five seconds is maddening. Non-real-time tools and methodologies can improve all performance by some factor, but that misses the point. Improving the typical response to three-tenths of a second and the occasional glitch to three seconds is nice, but the problem is still there. The accountable administrator wants to be able to summon a programmer and say "A customer told me that it took more than two seconds to validate a credit card this morning. Check the error logs. Tell me why it happened and how to make sure it doesn't happen again." with the same confidence he'd tell the programmer to check into a division by zero error.

Systems handling money may be even more constrained to consistently meet deadlines than are systems handling people. Real-time software might make it reasonable for a stock brokerage to promise that all trades will complete within 100 milliseconds.

Summary

All real-time systems need consistent performance. They differ in the precision they require and how offended they are at a missed deadline. The Real Time Specification for Java does not require that a conforming Java platform be unusually fast. It adds tools to Java to make it possible for a programmer to get consistent performance.

Nearly all systems benefit from consistent performance. This generalization includes the usual real-time systems. It also includes most commercial, industrial, recreational, and personal systems.

Chapter 2

Architecture of the Java Virtual Machine

▼ WRITE ONCE, RUN ANYWHERE—MAYBE

▼ JVM COMPONENTS

▼ INTERPRETER IMPLEMENTATION

The *Java virtual machine* (JVM) is a software implementation of a computer architecture. Since Java programs target the JVM, compiled Java programs should be portable. They execute the same instructions and use support libraries with standard APIs and identical (or at least similar) behavior whether they execute on an embedded system with an arcane processor or on a multiprocessor server.

Write Once, Run Anywhere—Maybe

In some respects, the JVM specification has done an admirable job. All the basic operations do the same thing on every correct JVM. That is not a small achievement; for instance, every processor or floating-point support library seems to have slight differences in the way it implements floating-point arithmetic. Even implementations of IEEE standard floating point turn out to be subtly different. The JVM puts a consistent interface over such differences. Simple programs run, and give the same results, on all JVMs.

Parts of the specification for the JVM are peculiarly loose. The specification seems to be a compromise between strict specifications to support portable code, and loose specifications to make it easy to port the JVM to diverse architectures. For instance:

- The *Java Language Specification*, JLS, does not insist that the JVM have multiple priorities. It requires—

  > When there is competition for processing resources, threads with higher priority are generally executed in preference to threads with lower priority. Such preference is not, however, a guarantee that the highest priority thread will always be running, and thread priorities cannot be used to reliably implement mutual exclusion.[1]

  —which can be interpreted to mean that higher priorities are scheduled exactly like lower priorities.

- Garbage collection is not required anywhere in the JLS. It is perfectly acceptable to create a JVM with no garbage collection system provided that you don't add an explicit way to free memory.

- The specifications for Java's drawing primitives are similarly loose. They permit Motif-style or Windows-style rectangle borders and fills, which give noticeably different results.

Even the real-time Java extensions are not magic. The JVM may let an MC68000 execute the same Java programs as an Alpha, but it does not make them run at the same speed. Technically, a real-time program should not depend on the performance of the platform once the platform is fast enough to meet all its deadlines, but blind reliance on write-once-run-anywhere is a mistake. For real time it is better to think WOCRAC (Write Once *Carefully*, Run Anywhere *Conditionally*).[2]

JVM Components

A given JVM might be implemented as a monolithic program, but it is designed as a set of components. The coarse-grained components are class loader, bytecode interpreter, security manager, garbage collector, thread management, and graphics. Each of these components—except perhaps graphics—has a significant influence on the real-time performance of the JVM.

---

1. *The Java Language Specification*, James Gosling, Bill Joy and Guy Steele, Addison Wesley, 2000, page 415.
2. This phrase was coined by Paul Bowman at the 1999 Mendocino, California meeting of the Real Time Java Expert Group.

Class Loading

The first time a Java program uses a class, the JVM finds the class and arranges to have it integrated with the rest of the Java environment.

Class loading includes the following steps.

1. Find the class in a file with a name derived from the fully qualified name of the class by converting dots to file delimiters (slash on UNIX, backslash on DOS-descended systems) and adding the suffix *class* to it. The JVM can search extensively for the file. It looks in each directory named in the CLASSPATH environment variable and possibly in every directory in the trees rooted in a directory on the class path.

2. Read the class file into a buffer.

3. Digest the class file into JVM internal data structures that reflect the data defined by the class file, the constants used by it, the classes in it, and the methods in it.

4. Run the *verifier* over the class. The verifier is a "theorem prover" algorithm that proves that the bytecode in the class obeys various rules; for instance, the verifier will not permit the JVM to load a class that includes code that uses uninitialized data.

Note: Things that the verifier can guarantee don't need to be checked at runtime. It is better to check as much as possible once at load time than to repeat checks every time the code is used. The verifier uses a relatively long time to make powerful general guarantees, but the bytecode interpreter gains considerable efficiency when problems like uninitialized data cannot happen.

---

5. Before the first use of the class, the JVM must initialize static data for the classes in the file. It does not actually have to initialize the static data when the class is loaded; it could initialize the static data any time before the static data is accessed.

6. The JVM is allowed to load classes that can be used by the classes in this file. This can cause the first reference to a class that is not built into the JVM to load all the classes that could possibly be used by the transitive closure of that class.

7. The JVM may choose to compile some of the newly loaded methods.

How it's done and how the time consumed by the load operation (and the time it happens) can vary among JVM implementations. Ordinary JVMs are optimized for throughput and can choose to defer potentially expensive operations like initialization as long as possible—perhaps until a method that uses the field in question is actually called. A real-time JVM cannot use that class of optimization because the programmer would have to assume that each method call would incur initialization costs unless he could prove that the initialization had already taken place; for example, it was the second call to the method in straight-line code.

Bytecode Interpreter

The JVM uses one-byte operation codes called *bytecodes*. The maximum possible number of one-byte codes is 256, and the JVM defines nearly the full set. The set of standard opcodes is given in Table 2–1.

Table 2–1 Java opcodes

Code	Op	Code	Op	Code	Op
0	noop				
		Push specific constants			
1	aconst_null	2	iconst_m1	3	iconst_0
4	iconst_1	5	iconst_2	6	iconst_3
7	iconst_4	8	iconst_5	9	lconst_0
10	lconst_1	11	fconst_0	12	fconst_1
13	fconst_2	14	dconst_0	15	dconst_1
		Sign extend and push literal			
16	bipush	17	sipush		
		Push item from constant pool			
18	ldc	19	ldc_w	20	ldc2_w
		Push item from local variable			
21	iload	22	lload	23	fload
24	dload	25	aload	26	iload_0
27	iload_1	28	iload_2	29	iload_3
30	lload_0	31	lload_1	32	lload_2
33	lload_3	34	fload_0	35	fload_1
36	fload_2	37	fload_3	38	dload_0
39	dload_1	40	dload_2	41	dload_3
42	aload_0	43	aload_1	44	aload_2

Table 2-1 Java opcodes (Continued)

Code	Op	Code	Op	Code	Op
45	aload_3				

Push item from array

Code	Op	Code	Op	Code	Op
46	iaload	47	laload	48	faload
49	daload	50	aaload	51	baload
52	caload	53	saload		

Pop and store in local variable

Code	Op	Code	Op	Code	Op
54	istore	55	lstore	56	fstore
57	dstore	58	astore	59	istore_0
60	istore_1	61	istore_2	62	istore_3
63	lstore_0	64	lstore_1	65	lstore_2
66	lstore_3	67	fstore_0	68	fstore_1
69	fstore_2	70	fstore_3	71	dstore_0
72	dstore_1	73	dstore_2	74	dstore_3
75	astore_0	76	astore_1	77	astore_2
78	astore_3				

Pop and store in array

Code	Op	Code	Op	Code	Op
79	iastore	80	lastore	81	fastore
82	dastore	83	aastore	84	bastore
85	castore	86	sastore		

Stack manipulation

Code	Op	Code	Op	Code	Op
87	pop	88	pop2	89	dup
90	dup_x1	91	dup_x2	92	dup2
93	dup2_x1	94	dup2_x2	95	swap

Arithmetic and logic

Code	Op	Code	Op	Code	Op
96	iadd	97	ladd	98	fadd
99	dadd	100	isub	101	lsub
102	fsub	103	dsub	104	imul
105	lmul	106	fmul	107	dmul
108	idiv	109	ldiv	110	fdiv
111	ddiv	112	irem	113	lrem
114	frem	115	drem	116	ineg
117	lneg	118	fneg	119	dneg
120	ishl	121	lshl	122	ishr

Table 2-1 Java opcodes (Continued)

Code	Op	Code	Op	Code	Op
123	lshr	124	iushr	125	lushr
126	iand	127	land	128	ior
129	lor	130	ixor	131	lxor
132	iinc				

Conversions

Code	Op	Code	Op	Code	Op
133	i2l	134	i2f	135	i2d
136	l2i	137	l2f	138	l2d
139	f2i	140	f2l	141	f2d
142	d2i	143	d2l	144	d2f
145	i2b	146	i2c	147	i2s

Simple flow control

Code	Op	Code	Op	Code	Op
148	lcmp	149	fcmpl	150	fcmpg
151	dcmpl	152	dcmpg	153	ifeq
154	ifne	155	iflt	156	ifge
157	ifgt	158	ifle	159	if_cmpeq
160	if_cmpne	161	if_cmplt	162	if_cmpge
163	if_cmpgt	164	if_cmple	165	if_acmpeq
166	if_acmpne	167	goto	168	jsr
169	ret	170	tableswitch	171	lookupswitch
172	ireturn	173	lreturn	174	freturn
175	dreturn	176	areturn	177	return

Operations on objects

Code	Op	Code	Op	Code	Op
178	getstatic	179	putstatic	180	putfield
181	getfield	182	invokevirtual	183	invokespecial
184	invokestatic	185	invokeinterface	186	*no op assigned*
187	new	188	newarray	189	anewarray
190	arraylength	191	athrow	192	checkcast
193	instanceof				

Miscellaneous

Code	Op	Code	Op	Code	Op
194	monitorenter	195	monitorexit	196	wide
197	multianewarray	198	ifnull	199	ifnonnull
200	goto_w	201	jsr_w		

Java specifies a fascinating mix of bytecodes. Most of them are nearly trivial. Many opcodes are expended on load, store, and basic operations for each supported data type. The JVM instruction set also optimizes the use of small constants with shorthand operations that push constants, and load and store from small offsets in local storage.

Some JVM instructions are wildly complex: create an array of objects, invoke a method, and two different single-instruction switch statements.

A typical bytecode interpreter is structured as a loop:

```
op = byteCode[pc]
switch(op){
   case 0: /* noop */
      pc += 1;
      break
   case 1: /* aconst_null */
   ...
}
```

There are many ways to accelerate this interpreter. First, brute force: almost all interpreters have been rewritten in hand-coded assembly language. Sometimes the assembly language is generated by hand-tuning of the output of a C compiler. Sometimes it is written from scratch. In either case, a careful, but uninspired, assembly language implementation of the interpreter usually gets about a 30 percent performance improvement over the C implementation of the interpreter.

There are probably hundreds of tricks that go beyond "uninspired" and yield a better than average performance improvement. Three are presented below.

Deep Processor-Specific Optimization. Modern high-performance processors have multiple functional units that can execute concurrently. These processors work best if the instruction stream is organized so the processor can keep all the functional units busy. Some processors can reorder the instruction stream to keep their units busy, but even those processors work better if the instruction stream is organized to help them.

Keeping the state of each functional unit in mind while writing code is tedious, but that level of craftmanship can generate big performance improvements.

This isn't generally a good investment for the bytecode interpreter. First, the optimizations are specific to a particular version of the processor. An interpreter tuned for the PowerPC 604e might run worse than an untuned interpreter on a PowerPC 603. Second, the available performance improvement depends on the number of functional units, and the processors with the most functional units are often the ones with the most ingenious systems for reordering their own instruction streams.[3] Third, most Java opcodes require only a few machine instructions. There is not much room for reorganization.

Cache Optimization.   Processors run faster when their code and data are in the cache, but cache is a limited resource. It is possible to write the bulk of the Java interpreter in less than 64 kilobytes, but a 64-kilobyte instruction cache is huge (in 1999) and the interpreter should share the cache with other code.

The amount of acceleration available for cache optimization depends on the difference between cache speed and memory speed. Cache could be more than 10 times faster than main memory on systems with slow memory.

The trick to this optimization is to track which memory falls into the same *cache line* or *way*. These addresses will contend for the same cache line or small group of cache lines. Code that has "hot" cache lines will frequently wait while the processor loads the cache with data from a new address.

Cache optimization is particularly appropriate for real-time systems because cache faults are a major cause of nondeterministic timing behavior. Systems that control cache faults reduce this nondeterminism—but they cannot eliminate time variations caused by the cache unless they completely control the cache.

Register Optimization.   A simple port of the Java bytecode interpreter from C to assembly language usually gets much of its performance improvement by using registers for nonlocal context that C compilers cannot easily track. An inspired port goes to the next step in register usage.

The Java virtual machine is a stack machine. That means that it doesn't have general-purpose registers, but keeps all its work on a stack or in various types of named fields. The bytecode interpreter that is part of the Sun Java platform distribution and simple assembly language interpreters keep the Java stack in memory, but this approach is inefficient. Nearly every bytecode accesses the stack once or twice. If the top few entries on the stack were usually in registers, the interpreter could run about twice as fast.[4] It would be easy to treat a group of registers as part of the stack if processors let you index through registers the way you can index through an array in memory, but that would be an unusual architectural feature.

One viable approach is to dedicate some registers to a window on the top of the stack and to code separate implementations of each opcode for each feasible arrangement of the stack in that window. If four registers are dedicated to the top

3.   Very Long Instruction Word (VLIW) processors are an exception to this rule. They have several functional units and insist that the instruction stream schedule them all.

4.   Expected speedup figures like this are wildly approximate. They depend on how good the interpreter is before the optimization and how well suited the hardware architecture is to the optimization. In this case, *approximately two* means that 1.5 and 4.0 are equally likely.

of the stack, the top of the stack could be at any of those four, and the window could contain from zero through four stack entries. That gives 20 possible arrangements and 20 implementations of each opcode.[5]

The opcode dispatcher changes from a lookup of the handler function in a single-dimensional table with the opcode as the index, to a lookup in a two-dimensional table with the opcode as one index and the register arrangement as the other.

Security Manager

The SecurityManager class can prevent untrusted code from violating security constraints. The best-known security manager is the *sandbox*, which wraps a security wall around applets. Every time an applet uses a Java platform service that might impact the security or integrity of the underlying system, the service asks the security manager for permission. Many services include code snippets like:

```
SecurityManager security = System.getSecurityManager();
if (security != NULL)
  security.checkXXX(...)
```

where checkXXX is replaced with the name of one of the methods in SecurityManager. The security manager either returns normally or it throws SecurityException to signify that the operation violates security constraints.[6]

The current security manager is determined by the class loader that loaded (or more precisely, defined) the executing class. Applets are the standard example. They are loaded by a special loader that loads applets from a web site, so they always operate in the sandbox, which is the security manager associated with the applet loader.

Every class loader can be associated with a security manager that protects the system from nefarious operations attempted by classes it brings into the system.

Security Checking Methods. The security checking methods in the security manager are summarized in Table 2–2.

Real-Time Issues. The security manager makes the performance of applications depend on the class loader that brings them into the system. Every checked operation includes a path through the security manager, and the security manager depends on the class loader that loaded the real-time code. The possibility that the security manager might reject an operation is not a uniquely real-time issue, but

---

5.   There is little point in letting the stack window go empty, so a 4-register window would probably implement cases for a depth of two, three, and four.

6.   To be painfully accurate, the checkTopLevelWindow method in the security manager returns a boolean. All other checkXXX methods in the Java 2 security manager return void.

Table 2–2 SecurityManager check methods

Method Name	Arguments
checkCreateClassLoader	None
checkAccess	Thread t
checkAccess	ThreadGroup g
checkExit	Int status
checkExec	String cmd
checkPropertiesAccess	None
checkPropertyAccess	String key
checkLink	String libName
checkRead	Int fd
checkRead	String file
checkWrite	Int fd
checkWrite	String file
checkDelete	String file
checkConnect	String host, int port
checkListen	Int port
checkAccept	String host, int port
checkSetFactory	None
public boolean checkTopLevelWindow	None
checkPackageAccess	String packageName
checkPackageDefinition	String packageName

the time it spends deciding whether to permit an operation matters to real-time programmers.

Applications under development are normally loaded by the default class loader. That class loader normally uses a trusting security manager that checks nothing and consequently uses little time. If the system can be deployed under a less credulous security manager, it may execute checked functions more slowly than it did under test.

It's difficult to predict timing for the checked operations even without the contribution of the security manager. Only a few of the check functions are associated with operations for which timing might normally be easily characterized:

- *checkAccess* — Checks operations that modify a thread.

- *checkPropertyAccess* — Checks security on operations that get the value of a system property.

- *checkPropertiesAccess* — Checks security on operations that get or set the system properties data structure.

- *checkPackageAccess* — Checks whether the caller is allowed to access a package. Since the default implementation of `checkPackageAccess` always throws `SecurityException`, the performance of this method should not be an issue.

The other check methods implemented by the security manager are associated with I/O or other similarly complex operations.

Garbage Collector

Java does not *technically* require a garbage collector, but it is painfully restricted without one. If there is no garbage collector, the JVM cannot detect memory that is no longer in use, and the programmer has to adopt a coding style that creates only objects that should exist "forever." For general use, a JVM requires a garbage collector that detects objects that are no longer in use and returns them to the free pool.

It would be nice if the Java garbage collector would collect all forms of garbage—memory, open I/O paths, other I/O resources, and classes that cannot be reached without a major effort—but most JVMs just collect unused memory.

Garbage collection is not a new idea. Languages like LISP and SmallTalk have used garbage collection for decades. There are even a few tools that add garbage collection to C and C++. If the language runtime can identify pointers and chunks of allocated memory (in an object-oriented language all those chunks are objects), it can go through each allocated chunk and see if any other chunk points to it. If a chunk of memory can be reached by following pointers from something the runtime knows is in use (like a variable on the stack), it is alive. If it cannot be reached, it is dead and can be freed. Stated like that, garbage collection looks like it takes time proportional to the square of the amount of memory the program is using.

Advanced garbage collection algorithms use heuristics to run much faster than $O(n^2)$, but worst-case performance drops back here. The impact of garbage collection on real-time performance is enough to take Java completely out of consideration for many real-time projects. Rejecting Java for real time because it includes a garbage collector is not always justified.

Note: Big O notation is a common notation for algorithm analysis. Technically it means "at most some constant times." Informally it works pretty well to think of it as "order of."

For instance, the code fragment

```
for(i = 0; i< n; ++)
   for(j = 0; j < i; ++j)
      <stuff>
```

executes <stuff> exactly $n \times (n-1)$ times. Execution takes some amount of time that depends on the quality of the compiler and the underlying architecture, but it is often enough for us to simply characterize the execution time as $O(n^2)$.

The JVM collects garbage at three times:

- *On request* — The `System.gc` method suggests to the JVM that this would be a good time to collect garbage. It does not require garbage collection, but, in fact, it generally causes collection to start immediately. The exact operation of the method is JVM dependent.

- *On demand* — The only thing that *demands* garbage collection is the new function. If new needs memory, it calls the garbage collector with a request to free at least enough memory to satisfy the current allocation request.

- *Background* — The JVM has a low-priority thread that detects idleness. It spends most of the time sleeping. Each time it runs, it sees whether other threads have run since it last looked. When the JVM has been idle for a few periods, the idle-detection thread triggers garbage collection. The assumption is that if nothing but the idle detector has run for a while, nothing important will want to run for a while. This approach is also called *asynchronous* garbage collection.

On-demand garbage collection is always a problem because it runs when the JVM is nearly out of memory. If the JVM could postpone demand garbage collection, it would be operating with a partially crippled ability to allocate objects. As a rule, the JVM stops everything until demand garbage collection frees some memory. Incremental garbage collectors may free some memory fairly soon (see Chapter 4), but in the worst case they fall back to a roughly $O(n^2)$ algorithm. Garbage collection time depends on the exact algorithm, the number of objects in the system, and the speed of the processor, so there is no specific time penalty, but systems that otherwise run Java at a reasonable speed can take a large fraction of a second to complete garbage collection.

Background and request garbage collection run when the system can survive if they don't complete. Under these circumstances, any garbage collection can be preempted whenever preemption will leave the JVM's data structures consistent. The delay before a garbage collector can be preempted (see "Mark and sweep is not preemptable" on page 50) can be as much as an order of magnitude less than the delay before it completes.

On-request garbage collection is the programmer's weapon against on-demand collection. A programmer presumably knows when the system will be idle for at least a few milliseconds and can request garbage collection at that time. If the program requests garbage collection frequently enough, garbage will not accumulate and the JVM will never be forced to demand garbage collection.

Background garbage collection is the JVM's attempt to automate on-request collection. The JVM doesn't have any way to know when the system has time to pause for garbage collection, so it guesses. A real-time programmer would worry that background garbage collection would run at exactly the wrong time, but fortunately it can be disabled when the JVM is started. When background garbage collection is disabled, the JVM is left with on-demand and on-request garbage collection. The program must request collection often enough to prevent on-demand collection; otherwise, it has to assume that every new will include a full garbage collection.

Finalizers. Garbage collection must run finalizers on objects that have them before it disposes of them. This is a serious problem. Finalizers are designed as a tool to clean up resources associated with an object. They can close an I/O path, change a GUI element, release a lock, or any other housekeeping chore that needs to be executed when an object is no longer in use. If they are used this way, finalizers should execute quickly and should not reanimate the object.

The JVM enforces only one rule for good behavior by finalizers. A finalizer can execute for a long time and even add a reference to its object from some other object. Finalizers are run at the end of garbage collection, and their effect on performance is an important real-time issue; for example, see Example 2–1.

- First, any finalizer will cause the garbage collector to reevaluate the liveness of the object and every object it references. That could cost $O(n^2)$ time since the finalized object could reanimate itself, which would reanimate all the objects referenced by it, etc., traversing a reference graph that could have as many as n^2 edges.

- If there are slow finalizers, they could run during any garbage collection; the system design must allow for that extra time on every garbage collection.

- The Java platform protects itself from objects that reanimate themselves in their `finalizer` by storing a reference to themselves. Reanimation is permitted, but only once. The next time the system garbage collects the object, it does not run the finalizer.

Example 2–1 A finalizer with bad real-time behavior

```
protected void finalize() throws Throwable {
    class IDontWantToDie extends Thread {
        public void run() {
            System.out.println("Reanimating");
        }
    };
    //  Burn lots of time
    IDontWantToDie th = new IDontWantToDie();
    th.start();
    try {th.join();} catch(InterruptedException e){}
    KeepAlive.ref = this; //  Bring me back to life
    super.finalize();
}
```

The best strategy is to avoid finalizers if possible and absolutely avoid finalizers that could execute at any length.

Defragmentation. The garbage collector operates on live memory while it frees unreachable memory. The memory that remains allocated after the garbage collector finishes might be *defragmented*.

If memory is obliviously allocated by new and freed by the garbage collector, it will soon leave free memory fragmented into numerous small extents. There may be tens of megabytes of free memory, but if it has been fragmented such that the largest contiguous free chunk is 24 kilobytes, then no object bigger than 24 kilobytes can be allocated no matter how aggressively the garbage collector works.

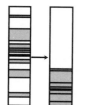
The drawing on the left shows an extent of memory before and after defragmentation. Before defragmentation, the largest possible allocation was about a quarter the size of the total amount of free memory. The defragmentation process packs all allocated memory together. After defragmentation, all the free memory could be used by a single object.

The trick to defragmentation is how to update every reference to the objects that are moved. If the system just moves an object, every pointer (reference in Java) to that object will point to the old address. It can be time consuming to track down every reference to an object, but during garbage collection the JVM has already done just that. It can move objects such that all free memory is contiguous for a cost O(number of references to all objects + size of memory) .

Thread Management

A thread encapsulates concurrency. On a multiprocessor system, each thread can execute on a separate processor. If there is only one processor or if the JVM doesn't support multiple processors, all the threads will execute on one processor. Threads will act nearly the same whether they are actually executing concurrently on multiple processors or sharing one processor. The software that supports threads puts the same interface around concurrency whether it is real or virtual.

Threads are conceptually simple. The data for a thread is little more than an *execution context*; that is, a set of CPU registers, a processor stack, and a Java stack. Java APIs start threads, stop them, change their priority, and interrupt them. The *dispatcher* switches control from one thread to another (when there aren't enough physical processors to run all of them), and the *scheduler* decides when to run each thread. The locking mechanism hidden under the synchronized keyword gives programs more precise control over concurrency than does adjusting priorities. A vast body of wisdom has grown up concerning proper use and implementation of threads, but the principle is simple.

The mechanism that supports threads can be included in the *operating system* (relatively sophisticated system software) or *kernel* (relatively simple system software), or it can be implemented in a library that is linked directly to the JVM.

Kernel Threads. Threads or processes are a basic service of the system software. Since simple kernels are often linked directly to application software and never provide protection domains like processes, the distinction between kernel and library threads is only meaningful for operating systems. Nevertheless, threads implemented in the operating system are usually called kernel threads.

If the operating system provides threads that meet the JVM's requirements, it makes good sense to use them. The major advantages of this approach are these:

- It can easily extend to multiple processors.

- Threads become visible outside the process that forks them. This may make them possible targets of signals from other processes and lets thread priorities change independently of the priorities of other threads in their process.

- Kernel scheduling mechanisms can be complex and wonderful. If the JVM uses kernel threads, it gets "free" access to these services.

Library Threads. If the system software doesn't provide thread support or if the support doesn't meet the JVM's requirements, the JVM can provide the support itself or use an existing library to support threads.

Note: The Sun JVM comes with a threads package called Greenthreads. This package was originally implemented because although Sun's UNIX supported threads, it did not meet the JVM's requirements. The Solaris JVM no longer uses Greenthreads, but it is still part of the JVM source distribution from Sun.

The major advantages of library threads are the following:

- The threads do not necessarily need to call the operating system for every thread operation. This is particularly significant for context switching. Kernel threads need to enter and leave the OS for every context switch. Library threads can context-switch with a function like `longjmp`.

- Java priorities are contained within a single process. This helps prevent rogue Java applications from interfering with other activities in the system.

- The garbage collector has to freeze all the threads in the JVM before it can operate on memory. Ordinary threading implementations may not include a way to selectively freeze threads, but it is severely antisocial to freeze threads that are not involved with the JVM. An operating system keeps code in one process from interfering with other processes; this mechanism makes it impossible for library threads to freeze unrelated threads.[7]

Input/Output

Java programs have two paths to I/O. The usual path runs though the JVM to libraries that bind it to the operating system's I/O services. The performance of these services is similar to that of the same services from C. Most of the elapsed time for I/O passes while the system is in control. It makes little difference that the JVM adds another layer of wrapping around the basic service.

The standard JVM is imperfectly adapted to asynchronous I/O. The base Java specification supports asynchronous user interface I/O through AWT, and asynchronous network I/O through the networking packages. These sources of asynchronous I/O are specifically handled in the JVM. The mechanisms for handling

---

7. Kernel threads don't automatically lock the entire system for each garbage collection, but it is possible to lock up the system during garbage collection if the JVM is carelessly implemented.

this asynchrony are tightly bound to the glue code that uses it. It is not accessible from Java applications.

If a program wants to support asynchronous I/O from a new device, it has a choice of finding a way to push it through AWT or appointing a service thread to wait on the device.

Some Java implementations, notably JavaOS, use Java code for most OS services. They even write device drivers in the Java programming language.

Note: Device drivers cannot be written in pure standard Java programming language. The registers that control and monitor I/O devices are mapped into either regular memory or a special I/O address space. In either case, they are accessed with pointers to primitive data types. References to objects supported by the Java bytecode instruction set do not suffice. Interrupts are also commonly used for I/O, and the Java platform has no direct access to interrupts or interrupt masking.

Java device drivers either include a layer compiled to native code or they use an "extended" JVM instruction set that adds limited support for pointers.

Graphics

The abstract windowing toolkit (AWT) is the Java platform's graphics API. Swing and Truffles extend AWT toward greater functionality and a touch-screen interface, respectively. Nobody would characterize AWT as fast, but like many real-time systems, it is an event-driven system. It has pushed improved event handling facilities into the Java programming language and libraries.

Polling. Programs with user interfaces need to know when something like a mouse click or a key press happens in the real world. These events don't happen when an application asks for them; they happen when the user chooses to move something. The program *could* keep checking (or *polling*) for each event that interests it, but doing so would be tedious, and since users are slow compared to computers, it would waste time.

Imagine yourself sitting at a traffic light. If it is a long light, you might consider reading a newspaper or catching up on e-mail while you wait for it, but if you get involved in another activity, you need to remember to check (or poll) the light every few seconds. If you check it too often, you don't get much reading done. If you leave too long an interval between polls, you may not respond to a green light promptly and the cars behind you may (um …) notify you shortly after the light changes.

Software has the same dilemma. If it polls frequently, it does not accomplish much else; if it polls infrequently, it is unresponsive.

Events. Wouldn't it be nice if the traffic light made a polite noise when it was about to turn green? You could then give most of your attention to e-mail and only switch attention to the light when it is about to change color. That is what events do for software.[8]

The Java event system allows a program to register an object, called a *listener*, with the event system, as shown in Example 2–2.

This tiny AWT application puts up a little window with a button in it, then it loops forever, sleeping. When the user asks the window to close, AWT calls the `windowClosing` method in the listener object registered for that frame. In this case, the `windowClosing` method just shuts down the whole application.

The important thing is that AWT reaches in and calls `windowClosing` while the test object is busy sleeping. The application doesn't need to poll the frame while it waits to see a "closing" flag asserted.

Events are tied to AWT. The event system classes are part of the AWT package, but the tools are in the Java programming language. Other specialized event systems can be implemented outside the AWT, but it is sometimes easier to feed all real-world input through AWT (forcing hardware like switches, valves, and thermocouples to conform to an interface designed for keystrokes and mouse movements).

Interpreter Implementation

The core of the JVM is a loop that interprets the Java bytecodes. There are between 200 and 256 bytecodes, depending on how the JVM has enhanced the standard set with optimizing extensions. Most of the operations are nearly trivial: pushing literal values, performing simple arithmetic and logic on stacked data, and flow control. Other operations are complex; it takes only one opcode to allocate an array of objects, execute a switch statement, or invoke a method.

Standard Interpreter

A completely untuned JVM uses a bytecode interpreter written in C. Such implementations are nicely portable, but such JVMs established that Java programs run up to 40 times slower than do C++ programs. These JVMs are no longer taken seriously as anything but a hack to get a quick JVM port.

---

8.   The full treatment of real-world events requires the real-time Java enhancements to events
     and asynchronous interrupts discussed in Chapters 11 and 17.

Example 2–2 AWT events

```
import java.awt.*;
import java.awt.event.*;     // This brings in WindowAdapter

public class test {
    public static void main(String [] args){
        Frame fr = new Frame("test frame");
        /*
            Create an anonymous class that implements
            the WindowListener interface.
            Use Frame's addWindowListener to register it.
            AWT will now call methods in WindowAdaptor whenever
            something interesting happens to the frame.
        */
        fr.addWindowListener(new WindowListener() {
            //  Exit when the window starts closing
            public void windowClosing    (WindowEvent e){
                System.exit(0);
            }
            //  Ignore all other events.
            public void windowOpened     (WindowEvent e){}
            public void windowClosed     (WindowEvent e){}
            public void windowActivated  (WindowEvent e){}
            public void windowDeactivated(WindowEvent e){}
            public void windowIconified  (WindowEvent e){}
            public void windowDeiconified(WindowEvent e){}
        });

        //  Put a button on the frame and make it appear
        fr.add(new Button("button"), BorderLayout.CENTER);
        fr.setSize(100, 100);
        fr.setVisible(true);
        fr.setLocation(200, 200);
        //  Wait until killed by an "outside force"
        while(true){
            try {
                Thread.sleep(100);
            } catch (InterruptedException e) {}
        }
    }
}
```

Optimized Interpreter

Recoding the bytecode interpreter into assembly language is fruitful. Humans make better decisions about global register conventions than do compilers. A simple job of recoding keeps a global instruction pointer and stack pointer. More careful work will keep at least the top entry in the stack in a register, and perhaps the top four or more. (See "Bytecode Interpreter" on page 16.) The most highly optimized interpreter is still slower than code that is compiled to native machine instructions, but the gap might be closed to less than a factor of four.

From the real-time point of view, optimized interpreters are nearly entirely a good thing. Optimizations that don't keep more than one stack position in a register give a performance improvement without making performance hard to predict. Interpreters that keep the top few stack entries in registers are still predictable, but the execution time of a single instruction depends on whether it is able to execute entirely from registers, and that depends on the instructions that are executed before it. This complexity makes performance prediction difficult, but it is still under control, and the speedup is worth the added difficulty in predicting the performance of small groups of instructions.

JIT

A JIT is a just-in-time compiler. Classes are loaded into the JVM in bytecode form, but the JIT compiles the bytecodes into native code some time after they are loaded. A JIT might compile all the methods in the class as part of the loading process, or it might not compile a method until it has established that the method is "hot" by calling it a few times.

A JIT generates native code. In theory, a JIT can execute benchmarks at least as fast as code that is compiled with a conventional compiler, but a JIT poses serious problems for real-time programs. Under a JIT:

1. a method runs zero or more times, using the standard interpreter,

2. then it is compiled, and

3. then it runs much faster.

Under a JIT, the longest execution time for a method is probably the time to compile the method, plus the time to execute the compiled code. A fast compiler will lessen the damage, but it will probably generate poorly optimized code.

Every JIT is designed on two related compromises:

1. Compile early and get the speed of compiled code immediately, or compile late and lessen the risk of compiling a method that will seldom be used.

2. Optimize compiled code carefully to maximize performance on code that calls compiled methods frequently, and maximize the pause while each method is compiled.

If the JIT uses a simple rule—for example, compile each method the first time it is executed—the program can control the point at which it subjects itself to the JIT overhead. The system has to be designed to compile all methods before they are needed for real-time operation. Such a design requires care, and the code that calls each time-critical method before it is needed surely needs explicit documentation to keep some future programmer from removing the superfluous calls.

Note: A JIT is often a less expensive way to increase performance than a faster processor. A simple JIT generally gives applications roughly five times better performance than does an interpreter. Systems for which a few dollars in production cost are worth a struggle may find it less expensive to add a JIT license and RAM to hold compiled code than to upgrade the CPU.

All common JITs share a problem. They compile methods to native code and put the compiled code in a buffer, but they are not good at removing compiled code from the buffer. With a static environment, all the live methods are soon compiled and the system runs in a steady state. If the system runs different applications over a span of days, a compost of old methods will build up in the native code buffer until the system runs out of memory and chokes.

Most JITs are written for desktop systems. That class of hardware has plenty of memory for a big code buffer, and the JVM seldom runs for more than a few hours at a time. On such systems, overflowing the code buffer is unlikely and JIT builders concentrate on performance.

Many real-time systems are short on memory, but they are still expected to run smoothly until the hardware wears out or power fails. Fortunately, most real-time systems also run the same set of methods for their whole lifetime. Such systems do better with a JIT that never loses the output of the JIT. A JIT that flushed old code out of the compiled code buffer would make it hard to control the time at which methods were compiled.

Snippets

Early versions of Sun's Hotspot JVM used a snippet compiler. Snippet compilation is well suited to dynamic code like the collections of classes that make up a Java application. A snippet compiler is hard to drive to worst-case behavior, but that worst-case behavior is abysmal.

A snippet compiler compiles blocks of Java bytecode much smaller than a method. It uses insanely aggressive assumptions when converting the bytecodes to native code. For instance, it feels able to inline *nonfinal* methods. Those methods could be wrong the next time the snippet is used, but chances are they will be right. The snippet includes code which verifies that the snippet is still valid. If it is not, the snippet is discarded and execution reverts to the original bytecode. The same type of trick works for any code that has variable behavior; for example, locking and conditional branches. It also lets the compiler freeze the addresses of objects into code. When the garbage collector relocates those objects, it discards snippets that might refer to them. The JVM regenerates the snippets with new addresses when it needs them.

With a carefully contrived benchmark, snippets can give arbitrarily good speedup. Build a nest of accessor methods as deep as you like; the snippet compiler will convert *n* method invocations and one field reference into one field reference. Since the speedup is proportional to the number of nested accessor methods, this trick can generate any speedup you want to claim, but the speedup is not totally specious. Real Java code sometimes includes deep nests of trivial methods. A conventional compiler cannot inline ordinary methods, so a snippet compiler can easily outperform optimized C++ on a benchmark that features virtual method invocation.

The basic assumption of a snippet compiler is that the cost of compiling tiny bits of code is small and the likelihood of needing to recompile any particular snippet is low enough that the ongoing cost of maintaining the snippets is far less than the speedup they offer. It is a demonstrably good assumption. The Sun Hotspot JVM gives good performance without obvious JIT performance glitches.

Real-time performance analysis asks how bad it can get: every snippet could become invalid immediately. If the JVM makes snippets aggressively, the worst-case performance is a little worse than a JVM that works by generating native code for every block of bytecode, executing it, and discarding it. That situation would probably result in performance less than a quarter as good as an ordinary interpreter. Using that rough guess and assuming that a JVM with a snippet compiler runs about 20 times faster than an "ordinary" interpreter, the worst-case performance of a JIT is 80 times worse than its typical performance.

Many real-time applications can tolerate the worst-case behavior of a normal JIT because they can control it. They don't need to design for worst-case behavior because they can force the compilation to take place when it suits them. The same trick is possible for a snippet compiler, but the rules for generating and discarding snippets are comparatively subtle and depend on aspects of the Java environment that programmers like to ignore. Worse, the rules are undocumented and likely to change at each release of the JVM.

The real-time parts of an application could be written so no reasonable JVM would need to discard snippets. It takes more effort, however, than controlling a conventional JIT, and the performance improvement for moving from a conventional JIT to a snippet compiler is not as great as the improvement for moving from an interpreter to a JIT.

Compilation to Independent Process

Adding a JVM to a system does not suddenly eliminate the system's ability to run native code, and Java programs have several facilities for interacting with processes outside the JVM. These separate processes might be legacy applications, highly tuned code to handle some tight timing situation, or code that uses low-level hardware facilities that cannot easily be reached from Java classes.

The important observation here is that the JVM is just a process. Operating systems can run many processes and manage interactions among them. This is old technology. Although handling real-time constraints in a mix of high-level languages and assembly language is sometimes difficult, real-time programmers can do it. The Java language and JVM add new tools to this collection.

A native process can be coded in the Java language. Several Java compilers[9] can create binary images that execute without the services of a JVM. A programmer can use these compilers to capitalize on many of the strengths of the Java language without accepting the overhead of an interpreter or even a JIT.

Native Methods

A native method is native code that is bound into the Java environment. It is invoked from Java code and can call back into the JVM. If it avoids references to Java objects, a native method can perform like any other native code except that it is subject to the Java runtime (including garbage collection.)

Compilation to a Native Method

Compilers that compile Java classes directly into native code have been developed. If these binary objects are to be used by ordinary Java applications running in a JVM, the obvious path is JNI, the *Java Native Interface.*

The native method interface, JNI, is designed to be used by programmers. It does not require the programmer to make heroic efforts to bring parameters from the Java stack to the programmer's environment or to access objects that were cre-

9.   A few examples of Java compilers that can generate stand-alone programs are the Java compiler from the Free Software Foundation, the cooperative Java effort between Edison Design Group and Dinkum Software, and Symantic Visual Café.

ated by the JVM. The usability features of the JNI slow it down. The cost of moving between the JVM and a native method depends on the hardware architecture and the implementation of the JVM, but it is typically equivalent to dozens of lines of C. Furthermore, every time a native method wants to reference an object controlled by the JVM, it must first tell the JVM to tie down the object. Some garbage collectors might free objects that are only referenced by a native method and not tied down, and any garbage collector might relocate such objects.

This all amounts to a significant performance penalty for native methods. They will give good performance for a length function that does not need much access to objects maintained by the JVM. They may perform worse than interpreted bytecode for short methods that use objects maintained by the JVM.

Compilation to the JIT Interface

The JIT interface can also call native code, but it assumes the native code was generated by a JIT attached to the JVM. The JVM has no qualms about asking a JIT to generate code that carries the load of operating with JVM internal conventions. This interface is relatively undocumented, unforgiving, and tedious to use, but it is relatively efficient.

Chapter 3

Hardware Architecture

▼ WORST-CASE EXECUTION OF ONE INSTRUCTION

▼ MANAGEMENT OF TROUBLESOME HARDWARE

▼ EFFECTS ON THE JVM

The software engineer for a real-time system should not ask how fast a processor can go, but how much it can be slowed down by unfortunate circumstances. From this point of view, it is unfortunate that modern processor architecture optimizes for throughput. It makes excellent sense for most systems to trade a rare factor of 100 slowdown for a performance doubling everywhere else.

This design philosophy is a major part of the reason you are probably using a desktop computer several hundred times faster than a departmental minicomputer built ten years ago, but it leaves real-time programs with a choice of obsolete processors or processors with scary real-time characteristics.

Many hardware architects' tricks are aimed at making the best of slow memory. Memory can be made very fast, but lightning-fast memory is expensive. Slower memory is orders of magnitude less expensive than the stuff that nearly keeps up with modern processors. The clever trick is to keep a copy of the most recently used memory in high-speed memory cache, and have the processor look there before it goes to slow memory. It turns out that just a few kilobytes of cache are enough to satisfy most memory loads and stores from the cache. So how long does a load instruction take? If it is loading from cache, the instruction might take one cycle.[1] If the load is not satisfied from the cache, we have what is called a *cache miss*, and the processor will have to go to slow memory. It might even have to write some data from the cache to make space for the new data. It could take a hundred cycles or more before the load instruction completes. If the processor went directly to the memory, all memory access would take about a tenth as long as a cache miss. A real-time programmer would like the opportunity to choose a factor of ten slowdown everywhere over a factor of 100 slowdown at hard-to-predict intervals.

Note: Seymour Cray solved the cache problem the other way. He didn't put cache into Cray computers. He made all the memory run at cache speeds.

Demand paging is another memory optimization that everyone but real-time programmers love. Demand paging makes disk space behave like stunningly slow memory. All the computer's RAM acts as a cache for the disk-based memory. Provided that the software running on the computer acts like typical software, the system's throughput will degrade slowly as it needs more and more memory until it hits a point where it starts to *thrash* and suddenly slows to a crawl. It is a fine thing to be able to effectively buy RAM for the price of hard-disk space, but a real-time programmer sees that memory access has now slowed from one cycle for a cache access to about 10 milliseconds for a disk access.

Memory access is a particularly rich vein of performance variation, but the CPU itself can cause trouble. Branch prediction causes the processor to execute a branch instruction faster if it goes the same way it has been going in the recent past. This gives the instruction a significant variation in execution time, depending on its past history.

---

1. Talking about a one-cycle instruction is an oversimplification. It may take three or five or even seven cycles to work its way through the processor pipeline, but it is called a single-cycle instruction because it doesn't need more than one cycle at any stage of the pipeline.

Worst-Case Execution of One Instruction

Consider

```
ld r0,r7,12
```

—an assembly language instruction that means load register r0 from the memory 12 bytes off the address in register r7. To give us a starting point, let's say that the processor is rated at 100 MIPS. We would expect this instruction to take about a hundredth of a microsecond, or 10 nanoseconds.

Most of the time the instruction will take about 10 nanoseconds, but if everything conspires to hurt the performance of this single instruction, it could take as much as 100 milliseconds to get to the next instruction. That represents a performance difference of about a factor of ten million between the most likely execution time for the instruction and the longest time it could take.

Worst-Case Scenario

First, the processor reads the instruction.

> If the processor is lucky, the instruction will be in the instruction cache. Reading the instruction from the instruction cache takes just a cycle or two.

If the instruction is not in the cache, the processor must read it from memory.

> Reading from memory takes much longer than reading from the cache. In the best case, it can take just a few cycles. In the worst case, the processor finds that the instruction falls in a page that is not in its address translation cache (also called a translation lookaside buffer, or TLB).

An address translation cache miss requires more memory accesses.

> To discover how it should treat the address of the instruction, the processor has to find a page table entry in the page table. A CISC processor would find and read a page table entry invisibly—except that it would read memory several times as it found the data in a search tree. Many RISC processors generate an exception when a page table entry is not cached and let the TLB fault exception handler find the page table entry and make a place for it in the address translation cache.

> At least the exception handler will not generate a translation fault. That would cause recursion that would quickly crash the system. The OS ensures that the code and data for handling address translation faults will not cause translation faults.

> A typical address translation fault handler might be around 30 instructions long. Each of those instructions has some execution time. All of them have to read the instruction from cache or memory. Some of them also read data, and some of them write data.

The instruction might be in demand paged memory.

The page table might indicate that the page is not in RAM but rather in secondary storage, probably a disk file.

The OS has to read the page from disk into RAM, and it may have to write a page to the disk to free a place to read the page into. Disks are getting faster, but a disk read takes on the order of 10 milliseconds. The instruction execution and memory access times up to this point have been measured in nanoseconds.

Next, the processor reads the data.

The procedure follows the same path as reading the instruction except that when the processor loads the instruction cache, it can simply replace other instructions in the cache. Since the data cache holds data that may have been changed since it was loaded, the processor may have to store data from the cache to make space for the new data.

Both the store of the cache line and the load of the cache line can generate address translation cache faults and even demand paging.

Exceptions happen.

We don't have to worry about software exceptions. They indicate things like division by zero. You can predict when that will happen, and we'll make sure it doesn't. (Furthermore, division by zero would be remarkable for a load instruction.)

Hardware interrupts will occur from time to time. An interrupt could occur directly before or after this instruction. Another interrupt could take place before the first one is fully serviced, then another and another…. Control might never return to this instruction stream.

It is safe to assume that things will not get that bad. An interrupt load so heavy that the system spends all its time servicing interrupts is either a sign of a serious defect or an unusual system design. The intervals between interrupts are usually distributed in a bell-curve-like fashion. The likelihood of getting even one interrupt between two instructions is low. The chance of getting two is much lower. Unless one of the interrupt sources can generate interrupts as fast as you can service all the system's interrupt sources, the worst case is that every device in the system that can generate an interrupt will choose this moment to raise its interrupt.

On a 100 MIPS RISC machine, interrupt service tends to take about 10 microseconds if the cache behaves terribly for the interrupt code. If we have a system with ten sources of interrupts, all the interrupts together will use 100 microseconds.

Memory timing is worse than it looks.

The specified access time for a memory chip is the best you can do. If the memory is DRAM, it needs to be refreshed from time to time. Many systems use direct memory access (DMA), which uses memory bandwidth and gets in the way of the processor. If you let it, DMA can use all the memory bandwidth. Then, the processor will not be able to access memory until the DMA completes. A big DMA across a bus could take 10 milliseconds

If our processor is rated at 100 MIPS, we would expect the typical instruction to take 10 nanoseconds. When we've considered all the major factors that can slow the instruction down, the time could be worse than 30 milliseconds.

Table 3–1 summarizes this horror story in nanoseconds.

Table 3–1 Worst-case instruction timing

Event	Time Estimate (nanoseconds)
Execute instruction	10
Instruction cache miss	50
Instruction ATC miss	500
Data cache miss	100
Dirty data cache write ATC miss	500
Data cache read ATC miss	500
Demand paging for instruction read (write dirty page)	20000000
Demand paging for dirty data cache write (read page)	10000000
Demand paging for data cache write (write dirty page)	20000000
Demand paging for data cache write (read page)	10000000
Demand paging for data cache read (write page)	20000000
Demand paging for data cache read (read page)	10000000
Interrupts	100000
One big DMA	10000000
Total	100101660

Figure 3–1 represents the numbers in Table 3–1 graphically.

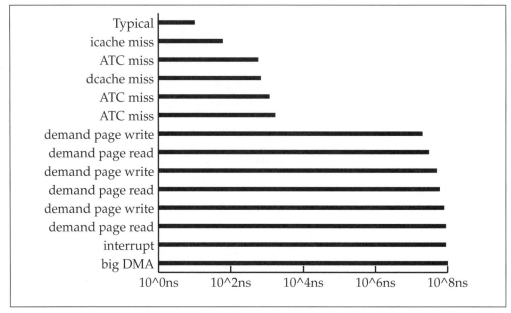

Figure 3–1 Factors in nondeterminism for one instruction (log scale)

Practical Measures

You can prevent the worst case from getting this bad. To start with, real-time systems usually try to keep time-critical code in page-locked memory. That means that the operating system will always keep those pages in real memory, not off in the page file on disk. That cuts 90 million nanoseconds off the worst-case time.

Getting DMA under control reduces worst-case degradation by another two orders of magnitude. Systems designed for real time usually have tunable DMA. The DMA can be throttled back to a percentage of the memory bandwidth and even made to stop entirely while the system services interrupts. We can still slow the completion of a single instruction from 10 nanoseconds to 203,310 nanoseconds, a factor of twenty thousand, even after throttling DMA down to 50 percent of bus bandwidth and page locking the instruction and data memory.

This kind of worst-case scenario is an exercise in balancing risk. Every possible type of system overhead has to land on a single instruction to degrade its performance as shown in Table 3–1. Bad luck on that scale is extremely unlikely for a single instruction and approaches impossibility for two instructions in a row. At some point, you have to say that it is more likely for the processor to spontaneously disassemble into a pinch of sand than to degrade a substantial piece of code by more than 50 percent or so. The careful programmer worries about it; most others just assume that everything will continue to work fine.

Massive performance perturbation is like Brownian motion. It is visible and sometimes significant in the microscopic frame of reference. At a large scale, it is so unlikely that it is universally ignored.

The rule-of-thumb figures in Table 3–2 seem to work well for normally careful code on modern 32-bit processors with fast memory. Oddly, the performance variability on a processor doesn't seem to depend strongly on the performance of the processor. Note that you should never assume better than 10-microsecond precision unless you understand and control the entire state of the machine. Performance variability (measured in microseconds) worsens with execution time for intervals longer than 100 microseconds, but the effect diminishes rapidly enough that ordinary engineering care should be enough to accommodate likely variation.

Table 3–2 Timing jitter with no interrupts, translation faults, or demand paging

Typical Time	Worst-case degradation
Up to 10 µs	10 µs
Up to 100 µs	factor of 2
Above 100 µs	200 µs

Management of Troublesome Hardware

Programmers who are willing to exert themselves need not be troubled by any of the factors in the previous section.

Managing Demand Paging

The huge performance degradation caused by demand paging is the first to go. Real-time programmers avoid demand paging. Real-time programs run in either *pinned* or *page locked* memory, which the operating system leaves in real memory. Often the memory used by a real-time program is page locked by default because the program is running under an operating system that does not support demand paging.

Managing DMA

Direct memory access is too useful for real-time systems to ignore, but it can be controlled. Many DMA controllers can be throttled such that they use no more than a specified fraction of memory bandwidth, or they can be configured to get off the memory bus entirely when the processor is servicing interrupts. Depending on system requirements, these mechanisms can convert DMA from a crippling problem to a minor inconvenience.

Some systems have multiple memory buses. One bus is used for DMA and the other is reserved for high-performance memory access. Sometimes entire pools of memory are isolated to prevent unexpected interference with access to the memory.

In any case, DMA hurts a program's performance only when the program attempts to access memory, not when the program is run from the cache.

Managing Cache

Cache is usually hidden from application programmers. At most, they are given instructions that flush or invalidate caches. These instructions are required if the program deals with DMA or self-modifying code.

Processors are beginning to support caches whose contents can be controlled by software. The simplest such mechanism just lets part of the cache be configured as cache-speed memory. The address and size of the high-speed memory can be set with system configuration registers. Of course, the cache that has been configured as memory no longer behaves as cache, thus slowing down everything except the code that uses the cache-speed memory. This is a bad plan for most systems, but real-time programmers should know what code needs to have consistent high performance.

More sophisticated caches allow chunks of the cache to be dedicated to specified processes or regions of memory. All the cache continues to operate as a cache, but some of the cache is taken out of the general pool and dedicated to code or data that needs predictable performance. The dedicated cache may still fault, so its performance is not consistent, but access to the dedicated part of the cache is controlled. It can be analyzed and each cache fault can be predicted. Code that uses a dedicated cache partition may take cache faults; although its performance is not consistently optimal, it knows when the faults will occur, so its performance is predictable.

The operating system can take some measures to make the cache more predictable. For instance, on processors that support it, the cache can be considered part of a process state and preserved across context switches.

Managing Address Translation Cache

The address translation cache (ATC, also called a translation lookaside buffer or TLB) is a cache. It would make no sense to convert an ATC to memory, but dedicating parts of the ATC to software components is common practice, and preloading the ATC at process startup and context switch time is not common, but it is done; e.g., Microware's OS-9 operating system preloads the ATC on most processors that support it.

Managing Interrupts

Some systems just don't use interrupts. That removes the timing uncertainty caused by interrupts, but it surrenders a powerful tool.

To some extent interrupts can be predicted—not exactly when they will occur, but about how often they should be expected. This predictability lets the designer for a real-time system calculate how likely a block of code is to experience a given number of interrupts.

In desperation, a program can mask interrupts. Interrupts can only be masked by *system privileged* code, and it increases interrupt response time (which is a critical performance figure), but interrupt masking absolutely prevents interrupt overhead while the mask is in place.

Effects on the JVM

A JVM can do little to control its worst-case performance. Like all real-time programs, a JVM running real-time software should not use demand paged memory. The most efficient JVMs also take cache residency into account. They can keep in the cache the parts of the bytecode interpreter that the JVM designer expects to be most popular. Beyond this, Java programs are helpless.

Even if a Java program could control the way hardware details affect their performance, Java religion (Write Once, Run Anywhere, or WORA) dictates that they shouldn't try. There is a contradiction in even trying to use hardware-aware techniques to control the performance of a Java program without introducing hardware dependencies.

Java programs are software. If the programmer is willing to sacrifice enough, Java software can surely achieve time precision like that of similar C programs, but it would require heroic efforts, and it is the wrong approach.

1. It is hard to document hardware dependencies in Java programs. How do you express cache line alignment of data when Java won't even expose the size of data structures?

2. The programmer is left using low-level inspection tools or "tweak and benchmark" techniques for hardware-dependent optimizations. These techniques work, but imagine the documentation required to explain a field inserted in a class to adjust the alignment of subsequent fields.

3. Just thinking about it is enough to make a committed Java programmer feel sweaty and a little faint.

There are several ways to escape from Java into native code. These mechanisms are included specifically to enable programmers to connect code written in other languages to Java programs. It is relatively easy to perform machine-dependent optimization on C or assembly language code, and native methods and processes are inherently machine dependent.

Further discouraging news: native methods look like they let machine-dependent optimizations work, but like all timing work on advanced processors, micro-scale optimizations that work reliably are harder than they seem. Native code supports optimization for throughput, but performance cannot be predictable on the microsecond scale unless the code can control the cache and the other factors mentioned in "Worst-Case Execution of One Instruction" on page 39.

The RTSJ does not try to micro-optimize the performance of the JVM. It targets problems that cause programs to miss deadlines by tens or hundreds of milli-seconds such as:

- Garbage collection

- Priority inversion

- Uncontrolled asynchronous events

Predictability on the microsecond scale is a hardware problem.

Chapter 4

Garbage Collection

▼ REFERENCE COUNTING

▼ BASIC GARBAGE COLLECTION

▼ COPYING COLLECTORS

▼ INCREMENTAL COLLECTION

▼ GENERATIONAL GARBAGE COLLECTION

▼ REAL-TIME ISSUES

The Java specification does not require garbage collection; it just provides no other mechanism to return to the free pool the memory that is no longer in use. Like the base Java specification, the RTSJ does not require a garbage collection. It does require the implementation to include the class GarbageCollector which formalizes communication with the garbage collection mechanism, but no garbage collection works fine with GarbageCollector.

The two obvious choices for managing unused memory in a JVM are to dictate that no application may allocate objects that it does not intend to keep around forever, or to find unused objects and recover their memory.

The process of identifying unused objects and recovering their memory is called *garbage collection*.

The JVM will recover garbage when it thinks the system is idle, when the program requests garbage collection, and when there is not enough free memory to meet the memory request for a new object allocation.

Reference Counting

If each object contains a counter that tracks the number of references to that object, the system can free an object as soon as the reference counter goes to zero. This forces every operation that creates or deletes a reference to an object to maintain the reference count, but it amortizes the cost of garbage collection over all those operations and it frees memory at the earliest possible moment. Garbage collection by reference counting is simple and reliable, except for one problem.

Reference counting cannot easily detect cycles. If A contains a reference to B, and B contains a reference to A, they both have a reference count of one. The garbage collector will not be able to free them even though there is no way to reach A or B. If reference counting were inexpensive it would be a nice primary garbage collection algorithm backed by another system that could run occasionally to free cycles that reference counting left behind. Unfortunately, garbage collection is expensive in both time and space. It adds complexity to every operation that can store a reference, and it adds a reference count field to every object.[1]

Basic Garbage Collection

If you have some way to find all the objects in a system and some way to identify object references, garbage collection is simple.

- You select a *root set*, the set of objects and scalar references that you know the program can reach. This contains static fields, local variables, parameters, and other data such as JVM internal pointers.

- The root set and every object that can be reached on a path from the root set is *live*. All the other objects are *dead* and can be freed.

---

1.   Since all of memory could be full of objects that reference a single object, the reference count must be able to accommodate reference counts comparable to the size of memory.

History of Garbage Collection

The LISP language is a well-known early application for garbage collection. It has no memory management facility other than the ability to create a cell, so like Java it needs garbage collection.

There is a strong connection between LISP and Java. The primary inventor of Java, James Gosling, is also the person responsible for Gosling emacs, an implementation of emacs that is interpreted by a built-in LISP interpreter.

The Reference Classes

The Reference classes were added to the standard Java class library at version 1.2. They give the programmer an interesting level of interaction with the garbage collector.

All the classes derived from the abstract Reference base class contain a special reference to another object.

The reference in a PhantomReference will not prevent the garbage collector from deciding that an object is unreachable. If an object has a PhantomReference, the garbage collector will place that PhantomReference object on a special queue when it cannot be reached except through phantom references. This allows the application to respond to the object's release in more elaborate ways than a finalize method could support.

The reference in a WeakReference object will not prevent the referenced object from being garbage collected, but the garbage collector sees the reference and makes it null when the referenced object is ready to finalize. It may also place the WeakReference object in a queue. This is good for data structures like the WeakHash structure. It makes it easy to find objects, but the application does not need to remove objects from a weak hash. When objects cannot be reached except through the hash table, they are automatically removed.

A SoftReference object is like a WeakReference object except that the reference in a SoftReference object will discourage the garbage collector from freeing the referenced object. The garbage collector will only free objects that are softly referenced if it would otherwise be out of memory. This is good for caches. The application can cache objects in memory with the understanding that the cache will only use memory that would otherwise go unused.

Mark and Sweep

The simplest algorithm for garbage collection is mark and sweep. It is a straightforward conversion of the preceding outline into an algorithm.

Algorithm 4–1. Mark and Sweep

```
Mark:
add every object referenced from the root set to the work queue
and set the "live" flag on those objects
while the work queue is not empty
        dequeue an object from the work queue
        for each reference in the object
                if the referenced object is not "live"
                        set the "live" flag
                        add the object to the work queue
Sweep:
for every object in the system
        if the "live" flag is not set
                the object is garbage, free it
        else
                clear the "live" flag
```

That is it. It takes time proportional to the number of live object references in the system plus the number of objects (live and dead) in the system.

Mark and sweep is simple, but it is hostile to real time. You can implement mark and sweep to be preemptable at many points, but it cannot be preempted and resumed. (See Demonstration 4–1 and Figure 4–1.)

Imagine what could happen if mark and sweep were preempted and resumed:

Initial conditions:
  Let field x in object D contain the only reference to object B.
  Object D is alive, but the garbage collector has not reached it yet.
  Object A contains no reference to B, and the garbage collector has already reached A and cleared its dead flag.

Garbage collection is preempted by thread t.
  Thread t assigns the value in x (from D) to a field in A.
  Thread t clears x.
  Thread t allows the garbage collector to resume.

The garbage collector completes its scan of live objects.
  It sees no reference to B.
  (Thread t moved the only reference to B from object D to an object that the garbage collector had already processed.)

The garbage collector sees that B is still flagged as dead and frees it.

This is an error.

Mark and sweep is not preemptable.

Demonstration 4–1 Mark and sweep is not preemptable

Since the algorithm does not free any memory until control reaches the last `for` loop, it makes no progress if it is preempted.

The net effect of all this is that mark and sweep must grab complete control of the JVM for an amount of time that depends on the number of objects in the system, the number of links between objects, the performance of the processor, and the quality of the garbage collector's code. This shuts down execution of everything but garbage collection for an interval somewhere between a tenth of a second and several seconds.

These long pauses are terrible for real-time computation, and there is no known way to escape garbage collection's time cost without paying a high price somewhere else. There are garbage collection algorithms that greatly decrease the cost of garbage collection except for pathological cases (see the discussion on page 54), but the pathological cases happen and they take as long as conventional garbage collection. If the application is willing to commit to a memory budget (e.g., "I will allocate no more than 10 kilobytes per second"), garbage collection can be made part of each memory allocation request. The problems with the budgeting strategy are that it falls apart if a thread exceeds its budget and that it degrades the performance of memory allocation substantially.

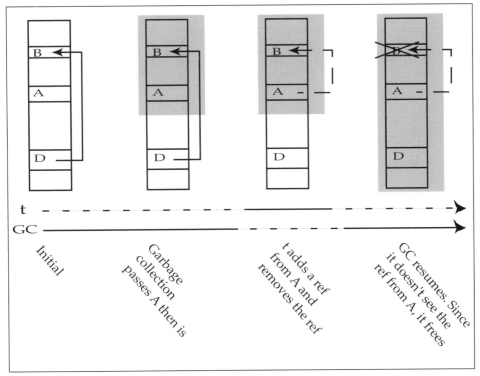

Figure 4–1 Garbage collection preemption timeline

A JVM that supports the Real Time Java specification may support advanced garbage collection, but for real-time performance it allows code to avoid garbage collection altogether. (See Chapter 13.)

Defragmentation

After allocation and garbage collection proceed for a while, memory will tend to be a stable state with blocks of allocated memory scattered between blocks of free memory. This is called fragmentation because the free memory is in fragments instead of one contiguous extent.

Fragmentation causes two problems:

1. The memory allocator has to search for an extent of free memory big enough to accommodate the allocation request. Popular allocation algorithms either use the first chunk they find (that algorithm is called *first fit*) or look for the free extent that most nearly fits the allocation (*best fit.*) The worst-case performance of both first fit and best fit is $O(n)$, where n is the number of fragments. If there was just one extent of free memory, allocation time would be $O(1)$.

2. Allocation requests can only be satisfied if the allocator can find an extent of free memory big enough to satisfy the request. You cannot satisfy a request for 200 bytes with two 100-byte extents.

Moreover, once memory is fragmented, the standard fix is drastic: shut everything down, free all memory, and restart the best you can. Just moving allocated objects around so free memory is contiguous would require the system to locate every reference to each object it moves, and update them. With a normal C-based system, this can only be done with the classic computer programmer's trick of "adding one more level of indirection."[2] This technique is best known for its heavy use in the Mac OS and is common for disk file systems.

If programs are not allowed to hold pointers to memory, but only pointers to pointers to memory, defragmentation can move memory objects and only update the single system pointer to the object. That sounds wonderfully simple, but an actual implementation requires more infrastructure. The program must be able to hold pointers to objects at least briefly unless it has an instruction set that lets it handle double indirection as easily as single indirection.

Garbage collection has a convenient interaction with defragmentation. A garbage collector must be able to identify pointers, and by the end of most garbage collection algorithms, all the pointers to live objects have been followed. The gar-

---

2. I don't know where the saying originated, but it is commonplace among programmers (at least the operating systems type) that almost every algorithm problem can be solved with one more level of indirection.

bage collector has already accomplished the work that makes defragmentation difficult. It would be sad to waste all this good information by not defragmenting memory as part of the garbage collection process.

Defragmentation is not a natural part of mark and sweep collection, and it is not generally attached to it since it would make a protracted process even longer. Other garbage collection algorithms defragment as part of the process.

Copying Collectors

Copying collectors find garbage like mark and sweep collectors do but take a fundamentally different approach to returning unreferenced memory to the free pool. Mark and sweep garbage collection works by identifying live data, then freeing everything else. Copying collectors copy all live objects out of a region of memory, then free the region. An outline of the algorithm is shown in Algorithm 4–2.

As each live object is identified, it is copied into the new region. The old version of the object is given a forwarding address. As the garbage collector traverses the graph of live objects, it gives objects with forwarding addresses special treatment:

1. It updates the reference in the current object to point to the new copy of the target object.

2. The forwarding address marks the object as the beginning of a cycle, so the traversal moves to another branch.

When the traversal completes, every live node has been copied to the new region and every reference has been updated to point directly to the copied instance of its target.

The region that objects have been copied into contains only live objects, and the live objects are all allocated from contiguous memory. There is no fragmentation.

The region that objects have been copied from contains no live objects. It is ready to be the target for a future iteration of collection.

Copying collectors have four advantages over mark and sweep:

1. Every cycle through the collector defragments memory at no additional cost.

2. Allocation is trivial. Free memory is never fragmented, so allocation involves no searching. The allocator just returns a pointer to the beginning of the free extent and moves the beginning of the free extent by the size of the allocated object.

3. It is easier to make a copying collector preemptable.

4. All the residue in a region can be freed in one operation.

The last advantage doesn't apply unconditionally to the Java environment. Java objects may have finalizers that are expected to run before objects are freed.

A region can still be returned to free memory in a single block, but any finalizers in the region have to be found and executed first.

A copying collector needs a free region as big as the region being collected. The system can never use more than half of its total memory. For large-scale real-time systems this might be an ineligible cost, but for many systems it is enough to rule out a simple copying collector.

Algorithm 4–2. Cheney's copying collection algorithm

```
void * FromSpace;
void * ToSpace;

void flip() {
        void * scan, free;
        swap FromSpace and ToSpace pointers

        scan = ToSpace;
        free = ToSpace;

        // Copy all the objects in the root set into the new space
        for each RtPtr in root set
                RtPtr = copy(RtPtr);

        //      while there is anything in the new region that we
        //      haven't looked at
        while scan < free {
                x = object at offset scan in the new region
                for each reference p in x
                        *p = copy (*p)
                scan += sizeof(x);
}

void * copy(void *ptr) {
        //      if the object has already been copied, it has to be zapped with
        //      a forwarding address
        if ptr is forwarded
                return forwarding address of ptr
        else
                void * tmp = free;
                copy *ptr to *free;
                free += sizeof *ptr;
                mark *ptr with a forwarding address of tmp;
                return tmp;
}
```

Incremental Collection

Long pauses while garbage collection completes are painful. Even systems that are not normally considered real time appear broken if they stop responding for noticeable intervals.

Any garbage collector can be made slightly preemptable. The collector notices a preemption request, proceeds backward or forward to a point where the memory system is consistent and there is no resource leakage, and allows itself to be preempted. If garbage collection makes some progress when it is preempted, it is an incremental collector. Unfortunately, when it is preempted, the reference graph that the garbage collector works from becomes obsolete and invalid.

If a garbage collector were able to concentrate on finding garbage directly instead of finding live objects (everything that is not alive is dead) it would be easy to make it incremental. *A dead object cannot come back to life,*[3] so each time the garbage collector finds a piece of garbage, it can immediately free it and make progress.

Consider the following (hideously inefficient) garbage collector:

Algorithm 4–3. Trivial incremental collector

```
for each object x in the system {
        referenced = false
        for each object y in the system {
                if (y contains a reference to x){
                        referenced = true
                        break
                }
        }
        if (referenced == false)
                free object x
}
```

This algorithm can be preempted with no delay, though it has to restart at the beginning. Unfortunately, it permits garbage to survive through many iterations of the entire algorithm, and cycles are never reclaimed.

Imagine a linked list of 1000 nodes that has just been made inaccessible. The nodes in this list happen to be ordered such that the collector sees the tail of the list first, then iterates back to the head.

---

3. To make a dead object Y come back to life, routine X would have to place a reference to it in the root set or in some live object. But, routine X cannot place a reference to Y anywhere unless it has that reference. If routine X is holding a reference to Y, then Y is not dead.

The trivial incremental collector will reclaim one node of the list each time it executes.

Algorithm 4–3 fails because it has to restart each time it is preempted. A high priority thread that wakes up every millisecond or so would never let this algorithm get beyond the beginning of its list of objects.

Here's a completely different approach:

Algorithm 4–4. Different trivial incremental collector

```
Loop:
    Atomically copy all collectable memory to GC_Private memory.
    Run any garbage collection algorithm on the GC_Private copy.
    Instead of freeing the copies of memory, free the originals.
    Clean the GC data structures.
    Repeat.
```

The insight behind Algorithm 4–4 is that a garbage collector can do all its computation on a snapshot of memory. Any object that was garbage when the snapshot was made will still be garbage when the garbage collector detects it. Each time the garbage collector detects a dead object, it tells the system to free the corresponding object in active memory. It doesn't matter whether it frees the object in the snapshot. When the garbage collection algorithm terminates, the entire buffer used for the memory snapshot is cleared and used for the next cycle.

Except for the long lock while it makes a private image of collectable memory, this algorithm is even more preemptable than Algorithm 4–3. After the copy operation, it can be preempted and resumed at any point. Copying all memory is a $O(n)$ time operation, where n is the size of memory, but it can still be quite fast. First, this is a straightforward copy. It should run as fast as memory can handle the loads and stores. Second, on a machine with an MMU, the memory can be copied with MMU lazy-copy techniques. The MMU can be used to map the pages to two addresses and mark them read-only. It need only actually copy pages that are written after it "makes a copy."

Algorithm 4–4 is in most ways an attractive incremental collector. Its only serious problems are its heavy memory requirement for its working buffer and the way it shuts down writes to memory while it makes its working copy.

Incremental Garbage Collection in Practice

There are many incremental garbage collection algorithms, most of them developed for multiprocessor LISP machines.[4]

Incremental garbage collection uses some new terms:

Mutator

> Incremental garbage collection is analyzed like a concurrent algorithm. The garbage collector is faced with a *mutator*, a thread that allocates, accesses, and modifies memory. A correct algorithm must behave correctly no matter what the mutator does.

Conservative

> A garbage collector must never free memory that is still live. It is less harmful if it fails to recognize some garbage; especially if the failure is timing related and the *floating garbage* will be collected on the next pass. The more conservative a garbage collection algorithm is, the more likely it is to leave floating garbage.

Accurate

> In the context of garbage collection, accuracy is the opposite of conservatism. An accurate garbage collector will collect all objects that are unreachable at the time the garbage collector completes.

Read barrier

> This mechanism informs the garbage collector when the mutator reads an object. Barriers are generally attached to specific objects, not used to monitor all reads.

Write barrier

> This mechanism informs the garbage collector when the mutator writes into an object. The garbage collector generally cares only about writes of references, so the barrier can safely ignore all write operations except the operations that store references.

A correct garbage collector must never free a live object. The collection algorithm can guarantee this if it ensures that a mutator never writes a reference to an object the garbage collector has not considered into an object that the garbage collector will not visit again.

---

4.   A garbage collection running on a second processor is the ultimate in incremental garbage collection. Interleaving between the garbage collector and the mutator cannot get finer. If no locks are required, interleaving is at the level of references to memory.

> **There is no other dangerous operation.**
> Incremental garbage collection must prevent reclamation of live objects. Retention of garbage is bad, but not harmful.
> The garbage collector will only reclaim a live object if it has seen no reference to the object.
> This is only possible if the mutator changes the reference graph.
> There is no way a read from the mutator can change the reference graph by reading.
> There is no way the mutator can change the reference graph by writing anything but references.
> Writes to nodes the garbage collector has not yet considered cannot cause harm.
> That leaves only writes of references to objects the garbage collector has already considered as potentially harmful.

Only operations that store object references can cause the garbage collector to free a live object. Figure 4–1 at the beginning of this chapter illustrates how freeing a live object can disrupt garbage collection. The garbage collector can choose from two methods to prevent this disruption:

1.   When the mutator references an object the garbage collector has not yet considered, immediately add it to the garbage collector's pending list. This is done with a read barrier around all unconsidered objects.

2.   When the mutator writes a reference to an unconsidered object into an object that has been considered, cause the garbage collector to revisit the object the reference was stored into. This technique uses a write barrier around all the reference fields the garbage collector has already traversed.

Algorithm 4–4 is an extreme instance of method two. A garbage collector that implements Algorithm 4–4 either locks out writes from the mutator during its copy stage or uses a write barrier to capture all writes during the copy and reflect them in the snapshot. Other garbage collection algorithms combine barriers with mark and sweep or copy collectors to get more complicated, but highly preemptable, garbage collectors.

Generational Garbage Collection

Typical performance benefits if the garbage collector, the allocator, and the language share information. The size, contents, and history of an object influence the type of garbage collection that should be used on it. For instance, copying takes time proportional to the size of an object to move the object to the live set. The performance of mark and sweep does not depend on the size of objects.

The classic generational garbage collector is based on the observation that most objects die shortly after they are created. The older an object is, the more likely it is to remain alive. The garbage collector capitalizes on this heuristics by creating new objects in a special area called an *eden*. Frequent execution of a copying collector moves objects out of the eden into *tenured* memory regions. A complex implementation might have a hierarchy of tenured regions to separate adolescent objects from middle-aged ones.

A simple generational collector saves the cost of copying the tenured data every time the collector runs, but it still has to consider references, called *intergenerational references*, from tenured objects. It does this by including all the objects in the tenured regions in the root set. Since the graph traversal to determine liveness in the eden has to consider whether each object is in the eden before it copies it and since there may be many tenured objects, generational collectors struggle to hide tenured regions when they collect the eden.

Intergenerational References

Instead of scanning the entire set of tenured objects for references to the eden, the garbage collector would like to just add a list of references from tenured to untenured to its root set.

Two mechanisms can create a reference between objects in different generations:

1. The garbage collector can cause an intergenerational reference by moving either the object containing the reference or the target of the reference to a new generation. It is reasonable to ask the garbage collector to track these references.

2. Application code can store an intergenerational reference. These references have to be tracked by the code that makes the change. This code uses a mechanism called a *write barrier*. If static and local fields are made part of the root set, the only writes that need to be tracked are reference stores to instance fields. The write barrier can be enforced by code added to the routines that implement the op codes that store references into instance fields. It might also be done by using the MMU to write-protect tenured storage and call a check for stores of intergenerational references when the MMU detects a write fault.

The collector need not track references from the eden to tenured objects unless it wants to avoid the overhead of scanning the eden when it collects a tenured region. Since the eden is expected to be active, tracking references from it would be a relatively expensive job, and since the eden is small, requiring the garbage collector to collect the eden when it collects tenured regions is a minor addi-

tion. On the other hand, if it is expensive to exclude collection of intergenerational references from the eden, it does no harm to collect them.

Large Object Store

Large objects cause trouble for a simple generational scheme. The eden is kept small to keep down the cost of collecting it, but that leaves it too small for many objects. Large objects that fit into the eden fill it too quickly and cause too much collection. To solve this problem, the memory allocator uses a *large object store* for large objects. The large object store keeps large objects from fouling the eden, and it can use a mark and sweep collector, which works better than a copying collector on large objects.

Real-Time Issues

Without a processor dedicated to garbage collection, the JVM cannot guarantee that garbage collection will not disrupt the timing of any code that includes object creation. All nonconcurrent mechanisms are based on heuristics and operate by deferring expensive garbage collection. They may run for days without a significant garbage collection pause, but they do occasionally pause.

Chapter 5

Priority Scheduling

▼ SCHEDULING TERMS

▼ EXECUTION SEQUENCES

▼ PREEMPTION

▼ FIXED VERSUS DYNAMIC PRIORITY

▼ PRIORITY INVERSION

▼ WHY 32 PRIORITIES?

▼ PROBLEMS WITH PRIORITY SCHEDULING

The central issue of real-time programming is getting things done on time. That breaks down into two separate issues:

- Designing, coding, and analyzing real-time code so it predictably executes in the required interval.

- Ensuring that the resources such as CPU time are allocated so real-time activities get enough time and resources to meet their deadlines.

Chapters 2 and 3 dealt with issues that affect predictable performance. Scheduling addresses the allocation of resources.

Scheduling Terms

The part of an operating system that switches between tasks has been decomposed with an elegant separation of policy and mechanism. The component that

61

actually saves one task's state and starts the next task executing is called the *dispatcher*. The component that decides which task to run next is called the *scheduler*.

Dispatchers are traditionally simple and fast. When the system is in a hurry to get something done (stop calculating pi and open the door before Bones smashes his nose into it), it starts by switching to the task that will do the urgent work. The time used by the dispatcher looks like pure overhead. Real-time system software struggles to push that overhead toward zero. There is nothing clever in a dispatcher. A real-time programmer wants it fast and trivial.

A scheduler is different. A non-real-time system might be content with a scheduler that hands out CPU time in FIFO order; most real-time systems use a fixed-priority scheduler.[1] A simple fixed-priority scheduler "just" ensures that the system is always executing the highest-priority task that is ready to run. Priorities express an "importance" measurement for real-time systems: how important each task is at a given moment. The major alternative for real-time systems is deadline scheduling, which schedules tasks according to the time when they must complete the current computation instead of according to their priority.

Execution Sequences

Execution sequences are a convenient representation for concurrency. Table 5–1 is a textual version of what an execution sequence looks like.

Table 5–1 Execution sequence

Task$_1$	Task$_2$
sort(a)	sort(b)
getInput()	doOutput()
load x int t$_1$	
	load x into t$_2$
add 1 to t$_1$	add 1 to t$_2$
store t$_1$ into x	
	store t$_2$ into x

If the order of execution of Task$_1$ and Task$_2$ does not matter or if they actually execute concurrently, they can appear in the same row. When ordering between two tasks matters, they do not share a row.

---

1. Fixed priority preemptive scheduling is the minimum required by the RTSJ.

In the previous example, $Task_1$ and $Task_2$ both do sorts, then $Task_1$ does input and $Task_2$ does output. The order of those operations does not matter, except that the execution sequence asserts that $Task_1$ finishes receiving input and $Task_2$ completes its output before $Task_1$ loads x into t_1. After $Task_1$ finishes loading x, $Task_2$ loads x into t_2. Then $Task_1$ adds one to t_1 and $Task_2$ adds one to t_2 in no particular order. After those operations complete, $Task_1$ stores t_1 into x and then $Task_2$ stores t_2 into x.

This execution sequence illustrates a classic *race condition* (a sequence of instructions in multiple instruction streams where the execution sequence can change the final results.) Both $Task_1$ and $Task_2$ think that they are incrementing x, and they will. Unless they get tangled as shown above. That execution sequence illustrates that $Task_1$'s increment can be lost.

The execution sequence can be made more graphical and rotated, as shown in Figure 5–1.

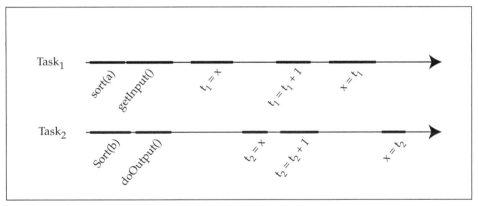

Figure 5–1 Example execution sequence

Preemption

Unless a system has at least one processor per concurrent task, the operating system may occasionally *preempt* a task to give another task access to the processor. Some operating systems permit preemption only at certain points; others have various sections where preemption is deferred. Real-time operating systems take great pains with *preemption latency* (the maximum duration preemption is deferred) and *preemption service time* (the length of time it takes to complete preemption after it is enabled).

Any system with real-time pretensions will preempt a task to start a higher-priority task that has become runnable. For instance, a task that is waiting for a switch to be moved will start executing very soon after the switch moves unless another task of the same or higher priority is already executing. This sounds almost like the definition of priority, but unless a scheduler specifically says it is preemptive or supports preemption, it probably uses priority only to select the next task when the current task offers preemption (usually by blocking.)

The Seductive Charm of Nonpreemptive Scheduling

Every competent operating system provides preemptive scheduling, but preemption is not an unmitigated good thing. Without preemption, a system of tasks cannot suffer a race condition unless the programmer almost literally asks for it. With a preemptive scheduler (or multiple processors), every time a task uses a shared resource it must assume that other tasks are using it at the same time. Unless cooperating tasks use exotic algorithms or locks, race conditions will occur. With a nonpreemptive scheduler (on a single processor), each task executes until it uses a system service that offers preemption. Control will *never* switch from task to task between two arbitrary instructions.

Figure 5–2 is the nonpreemptive analog of Figure 5–1. It shows the execution sequence for a system where getInput, doOutput, and Yield offer preemption. Notice that where Figure 5–1 illustrated a race condition that caused the corruption of value of *x*, Figure 5–2, with no preemption, shows no race condition.

Compared to fully preemptive or concurrent systems, a nonpreemptive scheduler almost removes the complexity of designing and debugging multitasking systems.

Even for desktop systems, preemption has proved to be important. Nonpreemptive scheduling works well enough if every task offers preemption frequently. Unfortunately, it is easy to forget to put a yield in every computation loop. The program works fine without the yield; in fact it runs a little faster. Other

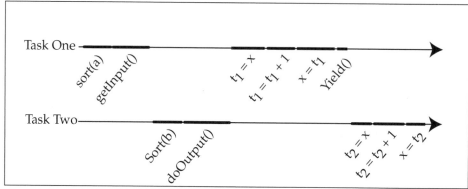

Figure 5–2 Nonpreemptive scheduling

programs suffer, but maybe that is acceptable for a fraction of a second. One thing leads to another, and you get an annoying system lockup. Then there is the problem of system crashes. What if a task encounters a bug that causes it to enter a tight infinite loop? The system locks up. There is no way for the operating system to take control away from the buggy task. Early versions of Microsoft Windows and Apple's Mac OS were nonpreemptive; they suffered terribly from user interfaces that froze for long periods and from frequent system crashes.

Fixed versus Dynamic Priority

A fixed-priority scheduler schedules strictly according to the priorities assigned by the programmer. The alternative is a dynamic-priority scheduler, which allows the scheduler to modify the priorities of tasks. Strictly fixed priority schedulers are becoming rare. They suffer from priority inversion. Consequently, fixed priority has come to mean "fixed except for priority inversion avoidance."

Priority Inversion

The family arrives home and suddenly realizes that grandma is scheduled to visit in fifteen minutes. The parents ask the older child, June, to tidy and vacuum the front hall. William, the younger, and rather inefficient, child is assigned the playroom. As it happens, William moves fast enough to take possession of the vacuum cleaner before June finishes tidying the front hall. When she goes for the vacuum cleaner, she finds it in use. She has to wait until William finishes vacuuming the playroom. Grandma arrives long before William is finished vacuuming the playroom. The front hall cleaning task does not meet its deadline, and the parents are deeply embarrassed.[2]

Literal-minded children would probably behave exactly as specified. More creative (or even cooperative) children would realize that William could let June borrow the vacuum cleaner for a few minutes (which turns out to be difficult in the computer analog), or June could have helped William vacuum the playroom and freed the resource to clean the front hall much sooner—maybe early enough to meet the deadline.

This problem and its "obvious" solution are common in real-time systems. The problem is called *priority inversion*, and techniques for solving the problem are called *priority inversion avoidance protocols*. The standard priority inversion avoidance protocols are two variants of June helping William: *priority inheritance protocol* and *priority ceiling emulation protocol*.

---

2.   Since the time June will wait for the vacuum is bounded by the time William can spend working on the playroom, this is bounded priority inversion. If we involved a third person who did not want the vacuum, but was able to prevent William from working, then we would have unbounded priority inversion.

First, the problem in computer terms. There are three tasks:

Task	Priority
A	low—10
B	medium—15
C	high—20

and one resource, X.

1.   Task *A* acquires a lock on X.

2.   Task *B* preempts *A* and starts a long computation.

3.   Task *C* preempts *B* and attempts to lock X, but it cannot get the lock. Task *A* holds a lock on X.

C is the highest-priority activity in the computer, but it cannot progress until task A releases X, and A cannot release the resource until B lets it have some processor time. This scenario effectively gives task C the same priority as task A. (Otherwise, why does it have to wait for task B to finish its computation?) This priority inversion is illustrated by the timeline in Figure 5–3.

This situation is called priority inversion because a high-priority process is scheduled as if it has a lower priority than a low-priority process.

Priority inversion can be controlled by a careful programmer, but only if it is anticipated and designed around. Unfortunately, priority inversion is easy to overlook and terribly difficult to find in a deployed system. It occurs only when a particular sequence of events causes a low-priority task to hold a resource when a

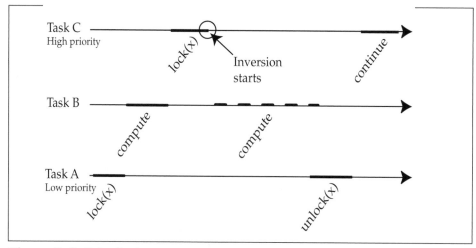

Figure 5–3 Priority inversion

high-priority task wants it. That situation may require an improbable combination of events. It can lie dormant in a system through the testing period and emerge as an intermittent bug in the deployed system.

The Martian Lander

The priority inversion problem that troubled the Martian lander transformed priority inversion from an esoteric topic for real-time engineers to a well-known near disaster.

A high-priority watchdog task had to acquire a lock on a bus. Occasionally it would find that lock held by a low-priority task. When that happened, the watchdog would time out and the system would conclude that it had a serious problem and reboot. This made the lander so unreliable that it made national news.

Fortunately, the engineers at the Jet Propulsion Laboratory were able to enable priority inheritance for the lock by patching its control block.

The priority inversion occurred at least once in the lab while the software was under development, but it was not reproducible so it was classified as a hardware glitch.

If any task waiting for a lock has a higher priority than the task that holds the lock, a lock that implements the priority inheritance protocol assigns the priority of the highest-priority waiting task to the task holding the lock until that task releases the resource. In our example, priority inheritance protocol would give Task A the priority of Task C from the time Task C attempted to lock X until the time Task A unlocked X. This would let Task A execute the block of code between the lock and then unlock without waiting for Task B. (See Figure 5–4).

The advantage of the priority inheritance protocol is that application interfaces to locks that implement priority inheritance protocol are no different from those to conventional locks. Thus, one can upgrade a system without changing any application source code.

Priority inheritance has the following problems:

- Its implementation is slightly complex. Under priority inheritance, a task sometimes temporarily alters the priority of another task when it attempts to acquire a lock. This may happen several times as higher-priority tasks join the wait queue. The system must then arrange to restore the original priority of the task when it releases the lock.

- The execution sequence through a lock is less likely to cause mysterious problems, but it is still peculiar. The priority of a task is raised, not because of anything it does, but by another task that is not specifically designed to change any other task's priority.

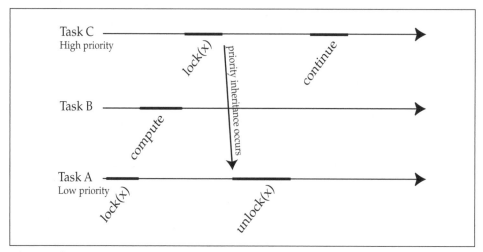

Figure 5–4 Priority inheritance

The most common alternative to priority inheritance protocol is the priority ceiling emulation protocol. This protocol temporarily raises the priority of the task holding the lock above the priority of the highest-priority task that will *ever* attempt to acquire the lock. Under the priority ceiling protocol, a task always sets its own priority when it acquires a lock and returns to its previous priority when it releases the lock. This behavior simplifies the implementation of the priority inversion avoidance protocol and makes it easier to understand the execution sequence through the lock. The section of code that holds the lock executes indivisibly with respect to other tasks that might want to acquire the lock, as shown in Figure 5–5.

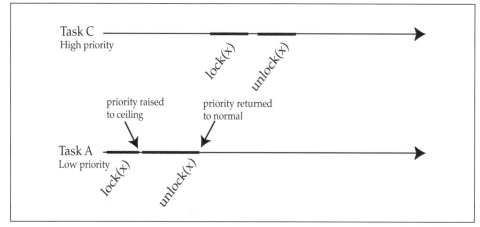

Figure 5–5 Priority ceiling emulation

Why 32 Priorities?

"Rate monotonic scheduling requires at least 32 priorities." That assertion has become almost part of real-time folklore. The POSIX real-time specification calls for no fewer than 32 distinct priorities, and the Real Time Specification for Java requires at least 28. Most real-time operating systems support at least 256 distinct priorities, and OS-9 supports 65,535! There *is* a theoretical basis for the assertion. The paper, "Real-Time Computing with IEEE Futurebus+" by Lui Sha, Ragunathan Rajkumar, and John Lehoczky, in *IEEE Micro*, June 1991, shows that given certain assumptions, the benefit of additional bus arbitration priorities diminishes rapidly above about 32. The paper addresses bus arbitration, but the computation applies without alteration to task priorities.

History

Doug Locke, a member of the RT Java Consultants Group and a hard-working member of the working group that defined the POSIX real-time specification, is the common thread from the discovery of the significance of 32 priorities, through POSIX to the RTSJ. As a new Ph.D. he helped write the IEEE Micro paper by supplying practical constant values for equations that the authors had worked out, and he supported the idea of 32 priorities as an academically respectable number for POSIX and the RTSJ.

It is not practical to compute the value of additional priorities for application-specific assignment of priorities, but rate monotonic analysis defines a rule for assigning priority to tasks. Rate monotonic analysis (see Chapter 7) assigns each task a priority according to how frequently the task needs service (see Chapter 5).

Simple application of rate monotonic analysis falls apart if there are not enough distinct priorities to go around. Tasks have to share priorities. A good strategy for sharing is to assign priorities in groups according to *constant ratios*; for instance, given a constant ratio, r, of 2, this algorithm would give tasks with a period less than one millisecond priority n (the highest priority), tasks with periods between one and two milliseconds priority $n-1$, tasks with periods between two and four milliseconds priority $n-2$, and so forth.

Lehoczky and Sha[3] have computed the loss in efficiency caused by folding priorities together this way:

$$Loss = 1 - [\ln(2/r) + 1 - 1/r]/\ln 2 \quad when(r < 2) \qquad \textbf{Eq 1}$$

$$Loss = 1 - 1/(r \bullet \ln 2) \qquad\qquad when(r \geq 2) \qquad \textbf{Eq 2}$$

where r is the constant ratio.

The next step is to determine the ratio r that will give just enough groups of periods to exactly cover the available priority values. This involves two assumptions:

1. Assume that the system contains more different periods than there are priorities. This is just a restatement of the point of this exercise. We're trying to figure out how few priorities we can get away with. Strict rate monotonic scheduling wants separate priorities for each period, but we're hoping that we'll find that fewer priorities are almost as good.

2. Assume that periods range from 1 millisecond to 100,000 milliseconds. This choice was based on the range of periods in systems that Doug Locke was implementing at that time.

Now we calculate the loss in scheduling efficiency we get by squeezing the priority assignments down to 256 priorities.

1. Priority zero will be assigned to activities with a period of one millisecond, or $L_0 = 1ms$.

2. Priority 255 will be assigned to activities with a period of 100,000 milliseconds, or $L_{255} = 100000ms$.

3. Other periods will be distributed across the other 245 priorities such that the ratio, r, of the range of each priority to the one before it is a constant.

4. Starting from L_0 we have $L_1 = L_0 \bullet r$, $L_2 = L_1 \bullet r$ or $L_2 = L_0 \bullet r^2$ and finally $L_{255} = L_0 \bullet r^{256}$.

5. So $r = (L_{255}/L_{0(0)})^{1/256} = 1.046$.

6. Filling this value for r into Eq 1 gives $Loss = 0.0014$.

So, cramming a wide range of periods into only 256 priorities gives about a tenth of a percent loss in scheduling efficiency. Figure 5–6 demonstrates that the range of periods changes the way scheduling loss increases as the number of pri-

---

3. J. P. Lehoczky and L. Sha, "Performance of Real-Time Bus Scheduling Algorithms," *ACM Performance Evaluation Review,* Special Issue, Vol 14, No. 1, May, 1986.

orities decreases, but even for large changes in the range of periods, about 32 priorities allows efficient scheduling.

Fifty or sixty priority levels would be better, but 32 priorities is comfortably before the point in the graph that indicates rapid loss in scheduling efficiency.

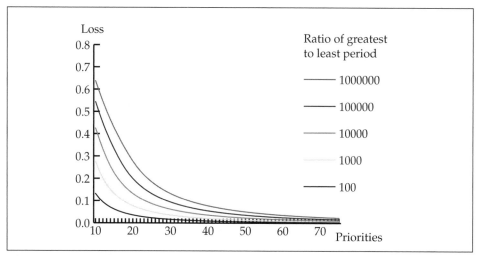

Figure 5–6 Change in scheduling efficiency with number of priorities

Problems with Priority Scheduling

Priorities can be a good scheduling paradigm if they are not loaded with meaning beyond their design. A task with higher priority will be given preference over lower-priority tasks when competing for system resources. If a system has to update a status display, log historical information, and control the feed rate into a band saw, the priority assignments are clear:

Control   high

Display   medium

Logging   low

The intuition here is that seriously bad things happen if the control function does not complete on time, that it is inconvenient if the status display is sluggish, and that there is no harm at all if the logging function runs late. The priority attribute expresses how *important* activities are, nothing about the actual timing of the tasks.

This expression of importance is important; if a system is going to fail to accomplish all its tasks, it should fail in the least harmful way. For real-time systems, priority is an odd choice of scheduling parameter. In a theoretical sense, priority is only a useful parameter if the system is trying to minimize the damage from failing to meet deadlines. If the system is not failing, priority is, at best, an obscure way of telling the scheduler about deadlines.

It might be life-or-death important to load the dishwasher between dinner and bedtime, but it only takes five minutes and it can be done any time between 6:30 and 9:00 P.M. There is no need to fail to answer the telephone at 6:30 (which is not nearly as important as loading the dishwasher but has a much narrower time window). A priority scheduler would load the dishwasher first and miss the telephone. A better scheduler would answer the telephone at 6:30 and defer loading the dishwasher until 6:35. It would complete both tasks in plenty of time.

A skilled real-time programmer can do amazing things with priorities and locks. We are surrounded by systems that use priorities and locks to display marvelous feats of real-time programming, but scheduling should not be that hard.

It seems more sensible to tell the system when a task needs to complete and what resources it needs. Those are the facts that matter to a real-time system. Meeting deadlines is the goal, not doing the most important thing first.

An entire real-time scheduling discipline is based on this idea. The basic idea is *dynamic priority,* or *deadline* scheduling. Deadline schedulers have nearly magical potential, and the Real Time Specification for Java enables, but does not require, support for these advanced schedulers. See Chapter 6 for a more detailed discussion of deadline scheduling.

Scheduling with Deadlines

▼ UNDERLYING MECHANISM

▼ SCOPE OF THE SCHEDULER

▼ SOME SYSTEMS

▼ TIMING IS USUALLY PROBABILISTIC

Since a real-time system is driven by deadlines, perhaps programmers should communicate those deadlines to the operating system. That is the basic idea behind deadline scheduling. It is a good idea. Scheduling using deadlines works beautifully when

- The program's scheduling is primarily driven by deadlines;

- The programmer can accurately characterize the processor time requirements of the application;

- The scheduler can meet all deadlines.

Scheduling with deadlines gets harder to use and harder to implement if it is expected to help the system degrade gracefully under overload.

Deadline scheduling is a form of *dynamic priority scheduling.* This term distinguishes the fixed priority scheduling algorithm where priority is controlled by the programmer from algorithms where priority is controlled by the scheduler.

Underlying Mechanism

Real-time tasks must meet deadlines. Sometimes the deadline is expressed in terms of a time sequence that includes program events and real-world events— the control program must turn the current off before the wire overheats. Those are certainly deadlines in a strict sense of the word, but deadline scheduling requires deadline *times.*

First, applications need a way to communicate their timing requirements to the scheduler. The scheduler must know the next deadline for each task. This communication could use function calls like this:

```
setDeadline(time);
```

If all applications pass the scheduler the time of their next deadline and a ceiling on the processor time required to reach that deadline, the scheduler can tell the application whether it can guarantee that it will meet the deadline. This is called *feasibility analysis.* In the extreme case, the scheduler may refuse to accept a deadline unless it can guarantee to meet it; this is called *admission control.*

```
if(setDeadline(deadlineTime, cpuBudget) != SUCCESS)
    handleAdmissionControlFailure();
```

If the scheduler is going to make guarantees, it needs accurate information. A task that asked for two milliseconds, then computes for five milliseconds may use processor time that was intended for another task. If a task uses more than its allotted time, the scheduler's plans are no longer useful, and other tasks may fail to meet their deadlines because of the overrun. A scheduler with *enforcement* can preempt the overrunning task when it exceeds its budget.

Enforcement could take the form of simple preemption: on overrun a task would be preempted in favor of other tasks, but when the preempted task is next scheduled, it continues as if it were not interrupted. This is easy for the scheduler and the application, and it is harmless if the preempted task is rescheduled in time to meet its deadline. If the preempted task does not meet its deadline, it becomes an example of a more general problem. Should the scheduler tell tasks when they fail to meet their deadlines, and if so, how?

- It might be fair to say that real-time programs should be able to tell through their interaction with physical reality when they miss a deadline. By definition, something seriously bad will happen if a task in a hard real-time system misses a deadline, so tasks should simply look to the "real world" for notification of failure.

- The program can poll the scheduler from time to time asking whether it has missed its deadline yet.

- The scheduler can asynchronously execute a *deadline miss handler* on the task's behalf—like a UNIX-style signal.

- The scheduler can permanently alter the task's control flow. It could, for instance, stop execution and restart it back at the beginning of some main cycle in the task.

None of these are faultless solutions, but in this kind of failure-recovery strategy, the goal is a usable solution that does not cost so much that it overloads a system into cascading failures.

The scheduler accepts requirements from the system and builds the best schedule it can. The schedule can be viewed as a timeline showing when each task will run (or use resources other than the processor), but the role of the scheduler in a system is specifically to tell the dispatcher which task to release from a wait queue.

Scope of the Scheduler

The scheduler does not control everything. It is surrounded and filled with nonschedulable entities: interrupt service routines, tasks that aren't scheduled by the deadline scheduler, DMA, and other overhead. The hardware issues identified in Chapter 3 are only a few of the nonschedulable entities a deadline scheduler might have to live with.

A deadline scheduler has to tolerate nonschedulable entities. Deadline scheduling practitioners struggle to bring every activity under the control of the scheduler, then they leave slack in their time budget to accommodate the worst damage they expect.

In the context of the Java platform the garbage collector is a major nonschedulable entity. A programmer can bring it under control by forcing garbage collection at convenient moments, and a scheduler can do something similar, but when the garbage collector needs to run, it is above all rules including those of the scheduler.

> There is a deep similarity between garbage collection and "rest" stops for children on a road trip. You schedule them at convenient moments, but additional stops are required at the least convenient moments ... and they are **not** optional.

Preview

The Real Time Specification for Java escapes the garbage collection nonschedulable entity by letting the programmer take certain threads out of the garbage collection domain. See Chapter 13.

Some Systems

Real-time scheduling is the chosen field of a whole subcommunity of the computer science systems discipline. Its adherents have invented dozens of deadline scheduling algorithm variants. This section touches on a few representative algorithms.

Earliest Deadline First (EDF)

If a schedule can meet all deadlines, then the schedule that always runs the task with the earliest deadline will succeed.

> Earliest Deadline First
> Consider just the interval, a, between the current time and the next deadline.
> The task for the next deadline, task A, must be executed in that interval or it will not meet its deadline.
> Executing task A at the beginning of the interval gives it the best chance of meeting its deadline.
> If there is time left over in interval a, it doesn't matter to the following deadline where in interval a it is allowed to execute.

Earliest deadline first does not care about CPU time budgets. This is a wonderfully simplifying factor, but simple earliest deadline first is not a serious scheduling algorithm. It is mainly a good demonstration that deadline scheduling can succeed.

The following are faults of earliest deadline first scheduling:

1. It has no admission control.

2. It works if there is a successful schedule, but it may fail spectacularly if no schedule will meet all deadlines. EDF has no way to know a schedule will fail or to search for the least damaging way to fail when failure is inevitable.

The simplicity of earliest deadline first can lead it to total failure. Any execution sequence that fully utilizes the CPU is fragile. Such schedules are certain to miss at least one deadline if anything takes longer than expected. EDF's blind adherence to policy is illustrated in Figure 6–1, which shows an execution sequence that misses every deadline.

The scheduler could have met all but the first deadline by sacrificing the first computation (which is going to fail anyway) and distributing its time among the other tasks, as demonstrated in Figure 6–2.

Earliest deadline first scheduling has no way to execute this principle. Extended versions of earliest deadline first scheduling, such as Robust Earliest Deadline (see "Handling Overload" on page 82) can handle overload situations if they have enough information to plan for the overloads.

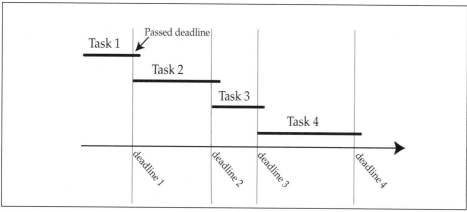

Figure 6–1 Total failure by EDF

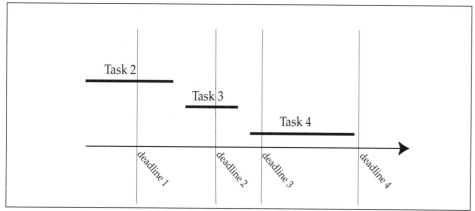

Figure 6–2 Alternate schedule for the problem from Figure 6–1

Least Laxity

Laxity is the amount of time between the time a computation would complete if it started now and the deadline for the computation. *Slack time* is another term for the same thing. Scheduling the task with the least laxity first has many of the same characteristics as EDF scheduling. Least laxity needs both a deadline and compute time for each task, whereas a deadline suffices for EDF. Like EDF, least laxity will generate an optimal schedule for any load that can be scheduled. The basic least laxity algorithm does not explicitly manage overload situations, but it fails less catastrophically.

The major failing of a straightforward implementation of a least laxity scheduler is that the scheduler will rapidly flip tasks in and out of the processor if they have nearly the same laxity. Imagine the situation illustrated in Figure 6–3 where Task A has 50 milliseconds slack time, Task B has 49 milliseconds slack time, and Task C has 47 milliseconds slack time. After Task C has executed for three milliseconds, it will still have 47 milliseconds slack time, but Task A will have 47 milliseconds and Task B will have 46 milliseconds. Since Task B now has the least laxity, the scheduler will switch to Task B. Two milliseconds later, Tasks A and C will both have 45 milliseconds slack time, so the scheduler will switch to one of them. From here on the scheduler will call for a change in control every time it calculates slack times. Assuming that context switching is not free (and it usually takes at least the equivalent of a few dozen instructions), this frantic jittering between tasks will degrade performance.

The solution to this problem is to make the least laxity scheduler a little less mechanical about following the least laxity rule. If least laxity only causes a change in control on some event other than the passage of time or when the change will affect the deadlines that are met, it will let the tasks continue to execute even when another task's laxity passes theirs.

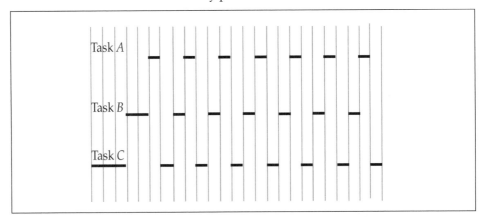

Figure 6–3 Excessive context switching under least Laxity

The major disadvantage of least laxity scheduling when compared to EDF is that least laxity must know the cost of each task. Least laxity's major advantage is that it does not go into total collapse when a task does not meet a deadline. This does not mean that least laxity handles failure well. (See "Handling Overload" on page 82.) It could be argued that ungraceful degradation is acceptable in a real-time system since those systems should never miss *any* deadlines.

Periodic Scheduling

If a large part of a system's load can be expressed as "do x every y microseconds," then the periodic scheduling algorithm may be useful. Constraining the problem to periodic tasks greatly simplifies the scheduling problem. The load can be characterized by a list of tasks, each with its period and cost. Compare this to the aperiodic problem where each event has a deadline and cost.

The most celebrated algorithm for scheduling periodic tasks is not a deadline scheduler or some other form of dynamic priority scheduling algorithm. It is the rate monotonic scheduling algorithm discussed in Chapter 7. Briefly, rate monotonic scheduling depends on a proof that it is optimal to assign static priorities to periodic tasks such that tasks with shorter periods get higher priorities. That means that if it is possible to schedule a set of periodic tasks by means of static priority assignments, a rate monotonic priority assignment will work. The problem with rate monotonic scheduling is that it can not guarantee success unless between about a tenth and about a third of the processor time is left idle.[1]

Dynamic priority schedulers can schedule sets of periodic tasks up to full processor utilization.

Aperiodic Servers

Many inputs from the physical world are *aperiodic*. They do not occur at predictable intervals. At best, occurrences of an aperiodic event may fit a normal statistical distribution. At worst, they are just random. Unless the distribution of aperiodic events is constrained, the system cannot guarantee to meet associated deadlines. This only matters for schedulers that offer feasibility analysis. A scheduler like EDF can schedule service for each aperiodic event when it occurs and work nicely until it reaches overload.

A system with a periodic component and an aperiodic component can use a periodic scheduling algorithm by doing the following:

- Calling the aperiodic tasks "nonschedulable entities" and letting them pre-empt all scheduled activities. The maximum processor consumption by non-

---

1. Normal rate monotonic analysis cannot fully utilize the processor, but an alternate, more complicated analysis technique can reach 100 percent utilization with rate monotonic priority assignments.

schedulable entities in any period has to be determined and subtracted from the time the scheduler is allowed to manage.

- Forcing the aperiodic tasks to fit a period schedule by assigning a period and a cost to them. This kind of system usually handles all aperiodic events with a single task called a *server*, but there could be several servers for aperiodic events with different scheduling characteristics.

Removing aperiodic tasks from the scheduler's control gives service for every aperiodic event higher priority than all periodic tasks. If that is an accurate model of the system, then this strategy is barely acceptable, but it gives terrible processor utilization unless the worst-case load of nonschedulable events is light. If the worst-case load of aperiodic events could hit the system with ten milliseconds of work in twenty milliseconds, then the scheduler can safely build only schedules that use no more than half the processor time. The maximum length of time non-schedulable entities can remove from the scheduler matters too. If a sequence of events can consume ten contiguous milliseconds, the scheduler has to assume that short tasks need at least ten milliseconds more than they've asked for. At a minimum, this means periodic events with periods less than ten milliseconds cannot be scheduled.

Servicing aperiodic events with a periodic server brings service of the aperiodic events under the control of the scheduler. This system lets the scheduler delay service for an aperiodic event while a periodic task completes a scheduled activity. Aperiodic events are serviced on a best-effort basis in the dedicated slots. This technique amounts to polling for events.

Figure 6–4 illustrates the periodic server.

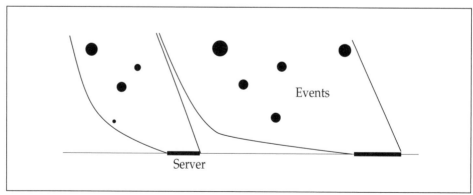

Figure 6–4 Aperiodic server

Deadlines for aperiodic events are measured from the occurrence of the event. The usual measure for this service is response time, the interval between the event and completion of the associate routine. Unless the aperiodic load in any period is known in advance, a server's execution of aperiodic events can only be soft real time. The worst-case response time for aperiodic events will be at least the period of the task that services aperiodic events. If events crowd together beyond what the server can handle in its allocated time slot, response time may exceed a multiple of the server's period.

If the period of the aperiodic server is short and the cost is high, the server delivers good response time but requires a large part of the CPU time. Given the statistical nature of most aperiodic events, most of this huge allowance usually goes to waste. If the period is long or the cost is low, the scheduler will be able to devote more time to periodic tasks, but the response time of the aperiodic server will deteriorate.

Scheduling theorists, naturally, don't like to solve a problem by removing aperiodic events from the control of the scheduler. Their goal has been to build a scheduling model for the aperiodic server that delivers good response time without using an unreasonable share of the schedule.

A strict periodic scheduler is too structured for a high-performance aperiodic server. Imagine that two aperiodic events take place in one period of the aperiodic server, one at the beginning of the period and the other in the middle. If the server is scheduled at the beginning of its period, it will give good response time for the event at the beginning of the period and bad response time for the event in the middle of the period. At first it seems that this problem could be solved if we ran several servers configured so that the aperiodic server time is divided into small, frequent chunks, but that approach makes the problem worse. The numerous executions of the aperiodic server add context switching overhead to the system, and if there is not enough time for an instance of the server to handle the load, it needs to pass some events forward to the next iteration. Those events get poor response time.

Succinctly stated, we need the aperiodic server to work well with ordinary periodic tasks but to use its time as nearly as possible on demand.

Priority Exchange Server. One algorithm, called the *priority exchange algorithm*, lets the periodic server "bank" time in light periods by trading it with another periodic task. The periodic debt is per deadline, so each time a task reaches a deadline, any time debt associated with that deadline disappears.

Take an aperiodic server, S, with period T_S and capacity C_S. At the start of period i with deadline d the scheduler gives the aperiodic server a capacity, or time allowance, of C_S^d. Each periodic deadline d that appears in period i is given an initial aperiodic capacity of zero. Any given periodic task might have no deadlines that fall in this period of the aperiodic server, or it may have many deadlines. No matter. Capacity holders are distributed per deadline, not per task.

The scheduler selects tasks to run in a standard EDF fashion, except that ties are broken in favor of aperiodic service.

If the aperiodic server is scheduled to run and has no work, the scheduler runs the next-most-eligible task and increments the aperiodic capacity, $C_{S_i}^d$, of the computation by the amount of time it uses. Now this computation will carry a debt to the aperiodic server until it reaches its deadline. This exchange of time takes place without changing the deadline (or the corresponding execution eligibility/priority) of either the aperiodic server or the other task. The tasks have not really exchanged processor time, since the aperiodic server may not use the stored capacity. They have exchanged priorities; thus, the name priority exchange server.

Total Bandwidth Server . The *total bandwidth server* puts service for each aperiodic event on the schedule when the event occurs, but it regulates that service so it does not conflict with other commitments already in place.

The total bandwidth server's budget is expressed as a fraction of the total CPU time. For tasks serving asynchronous events, the server must not assign deadlines that would cause the tasks to demand more than the asynchronous server's budget. If an event occurs that would need a millisecond of CPU time to service and the server's budget is one-tenth of the processor, it would assign service for the event a deadline ten milliseconds in the future. Service for asynchronous events cannot be allowed to overlap, so the ten milliseconds is measured from the occurrence of the event or the last deadline assigned by the asynchronous server, whichever is later.

The total bandwidth server assigns deadlines as if the asynchronous server were executing in a fraction of the processor. It can be a little more aggressive at the cost of additional complexity. If the scheduler admits a deadline from the asynchronous server, it has committed to complete the task by the deadline. It may well complete the task before the deadline. If the total bandwidth server can learn the estimated completion time of the last asynchronous event's service, it can schedule the next event's service starting after the estimated completion time instead of after the last event's assigned deadline.

Handling Overload

If a scheduler cannot meet all its deadlines, it is *overloaded*. Hard real-time scheduling theorists might feel justified in ignoring overload since, by definition, missing hard real-time deadlines is unthinkable. Still, a scheduler should have some defined behavior when it cannot meet all deadlines. EDF blindly tries to meet the earliest deadline even if it is impossible and will cause domino failures stretching far into the future. A slack-time scheduler will not waste time on hopeless cases, but it will concentrate on tasks with large processor requirements, using time that could have met many lighter-weight deadlines.

Scheduling algorithms designed for graceful degradation under overload conditions tend to add some measure of importance to the description of each deadline. The most sophisticated algorithms can manage an overloaded schedule for the least damage. For instance, if a traffic control system were given the choice of one of the following—

1. Hanging if the load of airplanes to track becomes too great,

2. Failing to update tracking information on random airplanes at random times, or

3. Losing tracking information on airplanes that are not near other airplanes or the runways,

—the system would probably specify Option 3.

Unfortunately the scheduling algorithms with the most attractive behavior under overload use a lot of processor time. When the system is already short on processor time, it could spend more time computing the schedule than executing it.

We can eliminate one problem from consideration. No optimal *online* algorithm can be constructed for recovering from overload in a system with aperiodic input. If the scheduler were clairvoyant, it would stand a chance, but without knowledge of the future, the scheduler cannot schedule for the least damage. Figure 6–5 through Figure 6–7 illustrate the problem.

The scheduler has two tasks waiting to run:

task a

> has a value of 10, a deadline in 60 milliseconds, and a processor requirement of 20 milliseconds.

task b

> has a value of 30, a deadline in 50 milliseconds, and a processor requirement of 30 milliseconds.

The scheduler will meet both deadlines by running *task a* before or after *task b*. Assume it chooses to run *task b* first, as shown in Figure 6–5. When

task c

> with a value of 100, a deadline in 40 milliseconds, and a processor requirement of 30 milliseconds

appears in 10 milliseconds, the scheduler will be forced to preempt *task b* and run *task c* (as shown in Figure 6–6) Although the scheduler is able to complete *task c* on time, it doesn't meet either of the other two deadlines. If it knew that *task c* was about to be scheduled (as it would if it were clairvoyant), the scheduler would have started running *task a* immediately (as shown in Figure 6–7). That would let it complete *task a* and *task c* before their deadlines. No cycles would be wasted on *task b*.

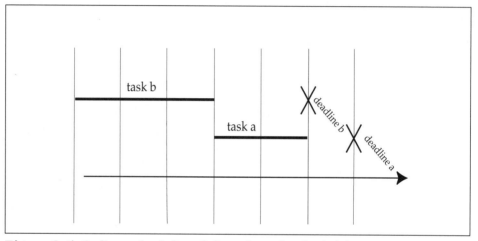

Figure 6–5 Online scheduling failure (initial schedule)

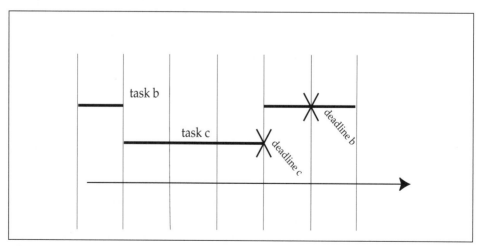

Figure 6–6 Online scheduling failure (disrupted by task c)

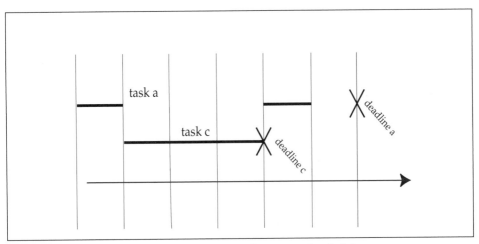

Figure 6–7 Online scheduling failure (better schedule)

If the nonclairvoyant scheduler had chosen to run *task a* first, we could have let *task c* appear at 40 milliseconds and run for 10 milliseconds. That would let *task a* and *task c* meet their deadlines, but *task b*, which has a value three times as high as that of *task a*, would fail to meet its deadline.

The scheduler cannot do a good job if an opponent keeps throwing work into the schedule that is designed to disrupt every scheduling decision. That may not sound fair, but it is enough to prove that the scheduler cannot make an optimum schedule unless it knows all the scheduling events before it builds the schedule.

Timing Is Usually Probabilistic

As this chapter points out, execution time on modern processors is extravagantly variable. Even if demand paging is ruled out, the execution time of a brief routine can occasionally be at least two orders of magnitude worse than its typical time. This is not good news for primitive deadline schedulers. It makes some form of failure inevitable. A primitive scheduler will blindly follow its algorithm, letting important deadlines fail in favor of trivial deadlines or allowing chain reactions that leverage a single missed deadline into a long sequence of missed deadlines.

Reacting to nondeterministic hardware is an issue for every scheduling algorithm, but priority scheduling is inherently tolerant of variable execution time. By its nature, priority scheduling shuffles failure to the lowest-priority tasks, provided that priority means *priority* (e.g., priority has not been overloaded with periods as is the case with rate monotonic analysis). Deadline scheduling focuses on CPU time and as a consequence is relatively delicate.

A scheduler that detects the failure and finds the least harmful damage control can isolate and control the effect of nondeterministic processors. This class of scheduler is harder to use and difficult to test, but any other class of deadline scheduler should be used only in systems that are tolerant of large-scale failures.

Chapter 7

Rate Monotonic Analysis

▼ THEOREMS
▼ RESTRICTIONS

A monotonic sequence of numbers always goes one way. If it is monotonically increasing, it never decreases. Rate monotonic scheduling analysis sorts all periodic tasks by their frequency, then assigns priorities so the lowest frequency task gets the lowest priority and the highest frequency task gets the highest priority. There is never a time when a higher frequency task should get a lower priority than a lower frequency task. For a certain class of systems, this simple rule works at least as well as any other way of assigning fixed priorities.

If the scheduler is fixed-priority preemptive and the load is periodic with independent tasks, rate monotonic analysis applies. Rate monotonic analysis is based on a wonderful little theorem that says you can schedule a load without worrying about how important each task is or without drawing careful timelines. It proves that if a periodic load can be scheduled by a fixed-priority preemptive scheduler, it can be scheduled by assigning priority based on frequency—the higher the frequency, the higher the priority.

Basic rate monotonic analysis requires the right type of scheduler and the right type of problem. It is easy to find fixed-priority-preemptive schedulers. They are the rule for real-time system software, and the Real Time Specification for Java requires one. Problems with an entirely periodic load and independent tasks are not so common. A desire to analyze more realistic problems has caused analysts to stretch rate monotonic analysis into methods for formal analysis of many types of real-time systems.

Theorems

This section describes three theorems for formal analysis of real-time systems. The seminal Liu and Layland theorem is presented first because it can be called the beginning of formal real-time analysis. The other two theorems are for a graphical approach to scheduling heavier loads than Liu and Layland's theorem permit, and a computational approach to scheduling heavier loads.

Liu and Layland's Theorem

This theorem quantifies what might be called the efficiency of rate monotonic analysis. If everything fit together neatly, rate monotonic analysis could schedule work until every processor cycle was full. But what if the tasks have periods and processor demands that interfere with one another? How bad can it get?

Theorem 7–1. Liu and Layland 1

The conditions:
- The scheduler is a fixed-priority preemptive scheduler.
- Tasks are strictly periodic and noninteracting.
- The deadlines are equal to the periods; that is, a task can complete any time in each period. It does not need to meet a more precise deadline.
- Task priorities are assigned such that tasks with shorter periods get higher priorities.

The result: For all cases of task phasing, a set of n tasks will always meet its deadlines if

$$\sum_{i=1}^{n} \frac{C_i}{T_i} \le U(n) = n(2^{1/n} - 1) \qquad \text{Eq 1}$$

Where

C_i The execution time (cost) for task i during one of its periods

T_i The period of task i

C_i/T_i Relative use of task i

$U(n)$ The utilization at which RMA will guarantee a successful schedule

In the perfect case, the sum of the relative uses of all the tasks would give a utilization of 1, but as Figure 7–1 shows, the maximum RMA utilization rapidly drops to about 70 percent (more precisely, 0.779.)

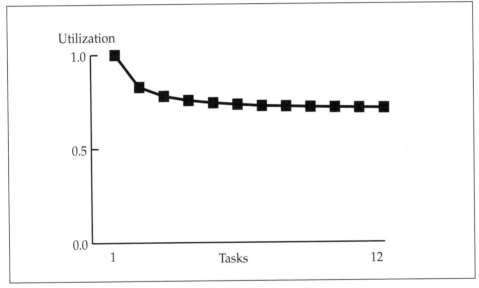

Figure 7–1 RMA efficiency

A Graphical Approach

The Liu and Layland theorem in the previous section sets a utilization bound below which it proves that all conforming loads are schedulable. The analysis is simple, but it could require the analysis to specify about 30 percent too much processor power. That does not mean that assigning priorities according to the rate monotonic algorithm automatically wastes 30 percent of CPU time.

The most intuitive way to prove that a load can be scheduled is to draw the timeline for that load and observe that it all fits. Liu and Layland contributed to this process too.

Theorem 7–2. Critical Zone

If a set of independent, periodic tasks is started synchronously and each task meets its first deadline, then all future deadlines will be met.

The idea is that the worst time to start a task's period is at the same time a higher-priority task is started. If all tasks are started at the same time and each of them meets its first deadline, then all future deadlines will be met because the situation will never be worse than it was at the start.

The critical zone theorem shows that if we can draw a timeline that successfully starts all tasks at the same time and meets all deadlines until every task has met its deadline at least once, the system is feasible. The timeline will have to be as long as the longest task period, but no longer.

The process here is fairly straightforward. You assign priorities according to period, then generate a timeline by simulating the scheduler. Compute the detailed timeline until the first deadline for the lowest-priority task. If that timeline shows that all deadlines are met, then by the critical zone theorem, the set of tasks is feasible under rate monotonic priority assignments.

Example 1.   Three tasks use 96 percent of the processor's capacity, as shown in Table 7–1. This is far more than simple RMA can permit, so we have to resort to somewhat more painful analysis.

Table 7–1 Tasks for Example 1

Task	Execution Time	Period	Priority
1	50	100	High
2	90	300	Medium
3	55	350	Low

The timeline in Figure 7–2 shows these three tasks all completing by their deadlines. Each time a low-priority task is preempted, the timeline shows in parentheses the amount of time it has remaining.

In Figure 7–2, Task 1 meets its deadline three times and is set to meet it again. Task 2 and Task 3 meet their deadlines once. By the critical zone theorem, this timeline is enough analysis. This system is feasible even though it uses nearly all the processor resources.

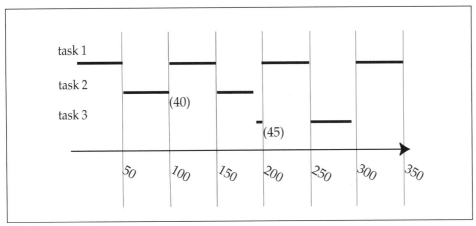

Figure 7–2 Timeline for Example 1

It might seem intuitive that if the lowest-priority task meets its deadline, all the higher-priority tasks must have. That intuition is wrong. You have to check them all.

Lehoczky, Sha, and Ding's Theorem

Lehoczky, Sha, and Ding added a tool (called the scheduling point test) that can show computationally that a particular load can be scheduled even though it is above Liu and Layland's bound.

The scheduling point test is more demanding than Liu and Layland's theorem and less intuitive than the critical zone theorem, but it works all the way to 100 percent utilization and it does not require a timeline.

Theorem 7–3. Scheduling Point Test

A set of independent tasks scheduled by the rate monotonic algorithm meets its deadlines if the following conditions are satisfied:

$$\forall i, 1 \leq i \leq n, \min \sum_{j=1}^{i} C_j \left\lceil \frac{lT_k}{T_j} \right\rceil \leq lT_k \qquad \textbf{Eq 2}$$

$$(k, l) \in R_i \qquad \textbf{Eq 3}$$

$$R_i = \left\{ (k, l) \,\middle|\, 1 \leq k \leq i, l = 1, \ldots, \left\lfloor \frac{T_i}{T_k} \right\rfloor \right\} \qquad \textbf{Eq 4}$$

Where

n	The number of tasks in the set. The tasks are ordered by decreasing priority
j	One of the tasks in the set.
k	Another task in the set. By Equation 4, k must be less than i.
l	The number of periods of task k being analyzed. By Equation 4, l can take on integer values from 1 to the floor of the period of task i divided by the period of task k. (Since the tasks are sorted by decreasing priority and k is less than i, $\lfloor T_i/T_k \rfloor$ cannot be less than 1.)
$\lceil lT_k/T_j \rceil$	The number of times task j executes in l periods of task k.
$C_j \lceil lT_k/T_j \rceil$	The time required for task j to execute within l periods of task k.

For every task, i, you pick values for k and l that obey Equation 4. If there are values for k and l for which $\sum_{j=1}^{i} C_j \left\lceil \dfrac{lT_k}{T_j} \right\rceil \leq lT_k$, then task i passes. If every task passes, the system can be scheduled.[1]

Example 2. We can algebraically evaluate the same system that was attacked graphically in Example 1.

First we check the total load by summing
$$\sum (C_i/T_i) = (50/100) + (90/300) + (55/350) = 0.96$$

This is more than the Liu and Layland bound of 0.779 (see Figure 7–1), so we need to employ a more complicated tool, the scheduling point test.

The procedure for using the scheduling point test runs in three nested loops:

Algorithm 7–1. Scheduling Point Test

```
for i = 1 to number of tasks
        for k = 1 to i
                for l = 1 to lower bound of period(task(i))/period(task(k))
                        if(Equation 2 gives success)
                                break to next value of i
        if we get here
                fail
succeed
```

---

1. Analyzing a system with the scheduling point test is suitable work for a computer.

Since we have three tasks, the outer loop will execute three times:

For $i = 1$:

$$(i = 1), (k = 1), (l = 1)$$

So:

$$\sum_{j=1}^{1} C_j \left\lceil \frac{lT_1}{T_j} \right\rceil = 50 \left\lceil \frac{1 \bullet 100}{100} \right\rceil = 50 \leq (lT_1 = 100)$$

For $i = 2$:

$$(i = 2), (k = 1, l = 1, 2, 3), (k = 2, l = 1)$$

Now we start looking for a combination of k and l that will satisfy Equation 2. For $k = 1$ and $l = 1$, the equation gives:

$$\sum_{j=1}^{2} C_j \left\lceil \frac{lT_1}{T_j} \right\rceil = 50 \left\lceil \frac{1 \bullet 100}{100} \right\rceil + 90 \left\lceil \frac{1 \bullet 100}{300} \right\rceil = 50 + 90 \leq (lT_1 = 100)$$

That relation is not true, so try $l = 2$

$$\sum_{j=1}^{2} C_j \left\lceil \frac{lT_1}{T_j} \right\rceil = 50 \left\lceil \frac{2 \bullet 100}{100} \right\rceil + 90 \left\lceil \frac{2 \bullet 100}{300} \right\rceil = 100 + 90 \leq (2T_1 = 200)$$

which works.

So now we look for value for k and l that will satisfy Equation 2 for $i = 3$.

For $i = 3$:

$$(i = 3), (k = 1, l = 1, 2, 3), (k = 2, l = 1), (k = 3, l = 1)$$

For $k = 1$ and $l = 1$, the equation gives:

$$\sum_{j=1}^{3} C_j \left\lceil \frac{lT_1}{T_j} \right\rceil = 50 \left\lceil \frac{1 \bullet 100}{100} \right\rceil + 90 \left\lceil \frac{1 \bullet 100}{300} \right\rceil + 55 \left\lceil \frac{1 \bullet 100}{350} \right\rceil =$$

$$50 + 90 + 55 \leq (1T_1 = 100)$$

which is not true (since 195 is not less than or equal to 100,) so try $l = 2$:

$$\sum_{j=1}^{3} C_j \left\lceil \frac{lT_1}{T_j} \right\rceil = 50 \left\lceil \frac{2 \bullet 100}{100} \right\rceil + 90 \left\lceil \frac{2 \bullet 100}{300} \right\rceil + 55 \left\lceil \frac{2 \bullet 100}{350} \right\rceil =$$

$$100 + 90 + 55 \le (2T_1 = 200)$$

which is not true, so we try $l = 3$:

$$\sum_{j=1}^{3} C_j \left\lceil \frac{lT_1}{T_j} \right\rceil = 50 \left\lceil \frac{3 \bullet 100}{100} \right\rceil + 90 \left\lceil \frac{3 \bullet 100}{300} \right\rceil + 55 \left\lceil \frac{3 \bullet 100}{350} \right\rceil =$$

$$150 + 90 + 55 \le (3T_1 = 300)$$

which works.

That gives us values of k and l that satisfy Equation 2 for all values of i. By the Scheduling Point Test, the load in Table 7–1 is feasible.

Restrictions

This section describes restrictions that apply to independent tasks, deadlines, and multiprocessors.

Independent Tasks

RMA breaks down if tasks depend on one another. If the specification includes a statement like:

> every twenty minutes, after waiting for the traffic light to turn green, roll a green croquet ball across the street.

the rolling task cannot complete until after the traffic-light control task sets the color of the light to green. Nothing the scheduler does to the croquet task will cause it to complete until the traffic light completes. Simply assigning priorities according to frequency is no longer enough. Fortunately, if the system implements a priority inversion avoidance algorithm that lets us bound the length of time a task might wait for another task, we can adjust Theorem 7–1 and Theorem 7–3. so they account for blocking.

Theorem 7–4. Theorem 7–1 with Dependencies

The conditions:

- The scheduler is a fixed-priority preemptive scheduler.
- Tasks are strictly periodic blocking time bounded.
- The deadlines are equal to the periods; that is, a task can complete any time in each period. It does not need to meet a more precise deadline.
- Task priorities are assigned such that tasks with shorter periods get higher priorities.

The result: For all cases of task phasing, a set of n tasks will always meet its deadlines if

$$\forall i, 1 \le i \le n, \frac{C_1}{T_1} + \frac{C_2}{T_2} + \ldots + \frac{C_i}{T_i} + \frac{B_i}{T_i} \le U(i) = i(2^{1/i} - 1) \qquad \textbf{Eq 5}$$

Where B_i is the maximum time task i is blocked in one cycle.

Theorem 7–5. Scheduling Point Test with Dependencies

A set of tasks scheduled by the rate monotonic algorithm meets its deadlines if the following conditions are satisfied:

$$\forall i, 1 \le i \le n, \min \sum_{j=1}^{i-1} C_j \left\lceil \frac{lT_k}{T_j} \right\rceil + C_i + B_i \le lT_k \qquad \textbf{Eq 6}$$

$$(k, l) \in R_i \qquad \textbf{Eq 7}$$

$$R_i = \left\{ (k, l) \mid 1 \le k \le i, l = 1, \ldots, \left\lfloor \frac{T_i}{T_k} \right\rfloor \right\} \qquad \textbf{Eq 8}$$

Deadlines Equal to Periods

Straight RMA uses deadlines and periods interchangeably. If a task needs to complete 60 times a second, we assume that any time in each sixtieth of a second is a good time to complete a computation. What if the timing requirement is more demanding? Perhaps the data for the computation arrives at the specified frequency, but the computation must complete by seven-eighths of the way through the period.

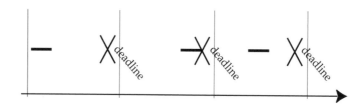

Basic rate monotonic analysis can easily adapt to this new requirement. Instead of scheduling according to rate, schedule according to deadlines:

The shortest deadline gets the highest priority.

If tasks have equal deadlines, the higher frequency gets the higher priority.

In this case, deadlines are not absolute times but are the interval between the start of the period and the deadline.

Since deadline monotonic scheduling is a more general version of rate monotonic scheduling (where the deadline always falls at the end of the period), it is the more powerful tool, but techniques like the scheduling point test only work for rate monotonic priority assignment.

Try assigning rate monotonic priorities, and analyze the system. If feasible, reassign priorities by using a deadline monotonic rule. Since deadline monotonic performs better than rate monotonic, the system remains feasible.

Multiprocessor Systems

Simple RMA doesn't work for multiprocessor systems. If the processors are scheduled independently and their interactions can be characterized, the system can be analyzed piecewise, but if one scheduler (simply) runs the *n* highest-priority tasks, RMA falls apart.

Sorry.

If you want to pursue RMA and advanced real-time scheduling further, try:

Practitioner's Handbook for Real-Time Analysis: Guide to Rate Monotonic Analysis for Real-Time Systems by Mark H. Klein, Ray Obenza, Thomas Ralya, and Bill Pollak published by Klewer Academic Publishers, 1993.

Meeting Deadlines in Hard Real-Time Systems by Loic Briand and Daniel Roy, published by the IEEE Computer Society Press, 1999.

Real-Time Systems Symposium Compendium - CD-ROM, from IEEE Computer Society Press.

Hard Real-Time Computing Systems: Predictable Scheduling Algorithms and Applications by Giorgio C. Buttazzo, and Giorgio Buttanzo, published by Kluwer Academic Publishers, 1997.

Introduction to the Real-Time Java Platform

▼ A BRIEF HISTORY OF REAL-TIME JAVA

▼ MAJOR FEATURES OF THE SPECIFICATION

▼ IMPLEMENTATION

▼ RTSJ HELLO WORLD

A real-time specification for Java is a rather remarkable idea. Java programs running on a JVM are, as a rule, much slower than similar programs written in C and compiled to the target processor. Even worse for real time, garbage collection stops everything else from time to time. These are not the characteristics of a good real-time platform. The promise of the Java platform for real time is that Java specifies a complete platform, and the charter of the Real Time Java Expert Group allowed it a free hand with the entire scope of the Java platform.[1] The Java platform includes aspects of the system from a robust class library and language specification all the way down to the instruction set of the virtual processor and many details of the multitasking runtime.

---

1. The permission to change Java was not as open as it sounds. As James Gosling pointed out at an early Expert Group meeting, if we crossed some undefined line in our changes, it would not matter what we called it. It would not be Java.

Previous attempts at real-time standards have struggled with limited scope. The most significant previous effort was the POSIX real-time specification. That specification had to be UNIX-like, and it could specify only a library API. Its control of the language was limited to "calling out" the ANSI C specification, and POSIX says nothing about the underlying machine's instruction set.

A Brief History of Real-Time Java

Many people contributed to the idea and its realization. Gallons of rhetorical blood and sweat were invested in a brief specification. Kelvin Nilsen deserves credit for starting the process. Years before Java appeared in public, Kelvin invented a garbage collection algorithm with good real-time characteristics. First, he embedded most of his garbage collection system in hardware, then he built software-only implementations. Kelvin promoted his idea at academic conferences and in the marketplace, but it did not catch on. One problem may have been that it required a specially instrumented compiler. Java was just what Kelvin needed, a new language with no legacy code, which generated interpreted bytecode and which needed garbage collection. He could fit his garbage collector into the JVM, and the JVM needed an improved garbage collector. Kelvin started a real-time Java working group to discuss ways to improve Java's real-time characteristics.

IBM and Sun were also interested in a real-time version of Java. They started efforts to build interest in real-time Java about the same time Kelvin did. It all came together in a grand meeting where Sun, IBM, and NIST (National Institute of Standards and Technology) jointly blessed a working group. It commenced meeting under the aegis of NIST and the leadership of Lisa Carnahan. After several months of meetings, the group produced a document called *Requirements for Real-Time Extensions for the Java™ Platform: Report from the Requirements Group for Real-Time Extensions for the Java™ Platform.* The report lists 53 groups as joint authors.

Around September of 1998, Sun announced the Java Community Process, a new process for maintaining and extending the Java specification. IBM promptly submitted a request for a real-time Java specification based partly on the NIST requirements document. The request, the first Java Specification Request (JSR-000001), was accepted in December of 1998.

Greg Bollella from IBM was selected as the JSR-000001 Specification Lead, and he formed an Expert Group with two tiers to help him create the specification. The primary group would do most of the work. Table 8–1 lists the members of the Expert Group.

Table 8–1 Real-Time Specification for Java Primary Expert Group

Greg Bollella	IBM
Paul Bowman	Cyberonics
Ben Brosgol	Aonix/Ada Core Technologies
Peter Dibble	Microware Systems Corporation/ TimeSys
Steve Furr	QNX System Software Lab
James Gosling	Sun Microsystems
David Hardin	Rockwell-Collins/aJile
Mark Turnbull	Nortel Networks

The Consultant Group would provide advice and participate in the major iterations of the specification. Table 8–2 lists the members of the Consultant Group.

Table 8–2 Real-Time Specification for Java Consultant Group

Rudy Belliardi	Schneider Automation
Alden Dima	National Institute of Standards and Technology
E. Douglas Jensen	MITRE
Alexander Katz	NSICom
Masahiro Kuroda	Mitsubishi Electric
C. Douglass Locke	Lockheed Martin/TimeSys
George Malek	Apogee
Jean-Christophe Mielnik	Thomson-CSF
Ragunathan Rajkumar	CMU
Mike Schuette	Motorola
Chris Yurkoski	Lucent
Simon Waddington	Wind River Systems

The combined Expert Groups first met at the Spring 1999 Embedded Systems Conference and started serious work in March 1999.

In September of 1999, the specification was published for "participant review." This is a formal stage in the Java Community Process in which the Expert Group shows a preliminary specification to other people who are involved in the process. In this case, the Expert Group decided to publish the specification on an open Web site. Formally, it was a participant review, but the document was visible to the world. Comments came in and the specification was improved. The official public review stage started in December 1999. More comments arrived and the specification was further improved. Finally, after about a year of steady work, the Expert Group released the preliminary edition of The Real-Time Specification for Java, which was printed and ready to be distributed in June 2000 at JavaOne.

The first edition of the specification was not an official specification. The Java Community Process requires three things before a specification is accepted: the specification, a reference implementation, and a test suite. Not only are the reference implementation and test suite required before anyone can write products that claim conformance, they also serve to prove that the specification can be implemented and is generally sane. The specification book was published before the other tasks were complete, to make it readily available to people tracking the standard and to draw more public interest and comment.

Through 2000 and most of 2001, the Expert Group continued to meet in frequent conference calls. Late in 2000, TimeSys volunteered to create the reference implementation, and they delivered a preliminary reference implementation to the group in April 2001. Naturally, a usable implementation of the preliminary specification focused attention on some areas that needed improvement. The sections of the specification on asynchronous transfer of control and scoped memory, in particular, were carefully studied. A revised specification, a reference implementation that conformed to the revised specification, and a test suite were submitted to the JCP Executive Committee for approval in October 2001.

Major Features of the Specification

The Real-Time Specification for Java enhances the Java specification in six ways:

1. It adds real-time threads. These threads have scheduling attributes that are more carefully defined than is the scheduling for ordinary Java threads.

2. It adds tools and mechanisms that help programmers write Java code that does not need garbage collection.

3. It adds an asynchronous event handler class and a mechanism that associates asynchronous events with happenings outside the JVM.

4. It adds a mechanism called asynchronous transfer of control that lets a thread change control flow in another thread. It is, essentially, a carefully controlled way for one thread to throw an exception into another thread.

5. It adds mechanisms that let the programmer control where objects will be allocated in memory.

6. It adds a mechanism that lets the programmer access memory at particular addresses.

What the Real-Time Java does not change may be as important as the things it changes. Ordinary Java programs will run on an implementation of the Real-Time Specification. They can even run while the JVM is executing real-time code. There is no magic that will cause ordinary Java programs to become more timely when they run on a JVM that implements the Real-Time Specification, but they won't behave any worse than they did.

Furthermore, non-real-time code will not interfere with real-time code unless they share resources.

Threads and Scheduling

Whether it is by priority scheduling, periodic scheduling, or deadline scheduling, the way tasks are scheduled on the processor is central to real-time computing. Non-real-time environments (like a standard JVM) can be casual about the details of scheduling, but a real-time environment must be much more precise. The specification treads a line between being specific enough to let designers reason about the way things will run but still flexible enough to permit innovative implementation of the RTSJ. For instance, there is only one method for which the RTSJ requires every implementation to meet a particular performance goal: allocation from an LTMemory area.

LTMemory Performance

The **RTSJ** specifies a high standard for the performance of LTMemory allocation because that allocation mechanism is intended for use in the tightest time-critical code. The specification is trying to assure designers that allocation of LTMemory is safe for critical real-time code.

Allocation from an LTMemory area must need time that is linear in the size of the allocation memory. That is the best possible allocation performance. Memory allocation in the JVM has several stages: first the right amount of free memory is allocated, then the memory is initialized in various stages under the control of the JVM and the class constructors. Every field in the object must be initialized before that field is used. In some cases, some initialization can be deferred, but ultimately every byte in the object is initialized.

The implementor can use any allocation algorithm that has asymptotically better performance than initialization of the allocated memory.

The RTSJ includes priority scheduling because it is almost universally used in commercial real-time systems and because all legacy Java applications use priority scheduling. The RTSJ requires at least 28 real-time priorities in addition to the

10 priorities called for by the normal JVM specification. The RTSJ calls for strict fixed-priority preemptive scheduling of those real-time priorities. That means that a lower-priority thread must never run when a higher-priority thread is ready. The RTSJ also requires the priority inheritance protocol as the default for locks between real-time threads, permits priority ceiling emulation protocol for those situations, and provides a hook for other protocols.

The RTSJ provides room for implementors to support other schedulers. The specification does not define the way new schedulers will be integrated with the system; it only says that an implementor may provide alternate schedulers and defines scheduler APIs that are general enough to support a wide variety of scheduling algorithms.

Sock Scheduling

While the Expert Group was refining the scheduling interfaces, we, to prevent ourselves from designing interfaces that would only accommodate known schedulers, invented a series of sock schedulers that would schedule according to various properties of socks.

Garbage Collection

The standard JVM specification does not require garbage collection. It requires dynamic memory allocation and has no mechanism for freeing memory, but the Java Language Specification does not require any particular solution for this massive memory leak. Almost every JVM has a garbage collector, but it is not required.

GC-less JVM

David Hardin (on the Expert Group) had extensive experience with the Rockwell Collins JEM chip. It is a hardware implementation of Java and has no garbage collector. Programming with no garbage collector requires discipline, and many standard Java idioms become convoluted, but it works well enough that the JEM has become a modestly successful Java platform.

The RTSJ continues the policy of the original Java specification. The RTSJ discusses interactions with a garbage collector at length, but a Java runtime with no garbage collector could meet the specification.

The RTSJ, although it does not require a garbage collector, specifies at least one API that provides for a particular class of garbage collection algorithm. Incremental garbage collectors that pace their operation to the rate at which threads create garbage are promising for real-time systems. Garbage collection can be scheduled as an overhead charge on the threads that create garbage and execute in brief intervals that do not disrupt other activities. The RTSJ has a constructor for real-time threads; the constructor includes a memory-parameters argument that can specify the allocation rate the garbage collector and scheduler should expect from the thread.

The Expert Group did not feel comfortable requiring a magical garbage collector and relying on it to make all the real-time problems with garbage collection disappear. Instead, we took the attitude that even the best-behaved garbage collector may sometimes be more trouble than it is worth to the real-time programmer. An implementation can provide any (correct) garbage collection algorithm it likes, and users will certainly appreciate a good one, but for real-time programming, the RTSJ provides ways to write Java code that will never be delayed by garbage collection.

The first tool for avoiding garbage collection is no-heap, real-time threads. These threads are not allowed to access memory in the heap. Since there is no interaction between no-heap threads and garbage collection or compaction, no-heap threads can preempt the garbage collector without waiting for the garbage collector to reach a consistent state. Ordinary threads and heap-using, real-time threads can be delayed by garbage collection when they create objects in the heap, and they have to wait for the garbage collector to reach a consistent state if they are activated while the garbage collector is running. No-heap, real-time threads are protected from these timing problems.

Asynchronous Event Handlers

Many real-time systems are event driven. Things happen and the system responds to them. It is easy to code an event-driven system structured so that each event is serviced by a thread created for that particular event, and it makes the scheduling attributes of each event clear to the scheduler. The idea sounds obvious. Why isn't it common practice? The time between an event and the service of the event is overhead on real-time responsiveness. Thread creation is slow. It is a resource-allocation service, and real-time programmers avoid resource allocation when they are concerned about time.

Asynchronous event handlers are an attempt to capture the advantages of creating threads to service events without taking the performance penalty.

Event-driven programming needs events. The standard Java platform has extensive mechanisms for input from its GUI, but no general-purpose mechanism for associating things that happen outside the Java environment with method

invocation inside the environment. The RTSJ introduces *happenings* as a pathway between events outside the Java platform and asynchronous event handlers.

Asynchronous Transfer of Control

Asynchronous transfer of control was a late addition to the RTSJ, and it was much harder to invent than you might think.

Asynchronous transfer of control (ATC) is a mechanism that lets a thread throw an exception into another thread. Standard Java includes a similar mechanism, `thread.interrupt`, but it is weak.

Why is ATC so important?

1. It is a way to cancel a thread in a forcible but controlled way.

2. It is a way to break a thread out of a loop without requiring the thread to poll a "terminate me" variable.

3. It is a general-purpose timeout mechanism.

4. It lets sophisticated runtimes take scheduler-like control of execution. People interested in distributed real time have powerful requirements for this control.

Why is ATC so hard?

1. Code that is not written to be interrupted may break badly if the JVM suddenly jumps out of it.

2. You cannot just jump from the current point of execution to the "right" catch block. The platform has to unwind execution through catches and, finally, clauses in uninterruptible methods until it has fully serviced the exception.

3. Nested methods may be waiting for different asynchronous exceptions. The runtime has to make certain that the exceptions get to the right catch blocks.

Memory Allocation

By itself, support for no-heap, real-time threads would be useless. The thread would be restricted to elementary data types. It would not even be able to access its own thread object. The RTSJ created two new memory allocation domains to give no-heap threads access to objects: immortal memory and scoped memory.

Immortal memory is never garbage collected and would make no-heap threads thoroughly usable even without scoped memory. Immortal memory fits the large class of real-time programs that allocate all their resources in an initialization phase and then run forever without allocating or freeing any resources. Even systems written in C and assembly language use this paradigm. Even without garbage collection, resource allocation often has tricky timing characteristics and nasty failure modes. It makes sense to move it out of the time-critical part of an application.

Immortal memory is simple to explain and implement, but it leads to unnatural use of the Java language:

- The Java Platform does not encourage reuse of objects. In some cases, properties of objects can only be set by their constructor, and the Java language's strong typing makes it impossible to reuse an object as anything other than exactly its original type. (The Java language has no union.)

- The Java class libraries freely create objects. A programmer who called innocuous methods in the collections classes or the math classes could quickly find immortal memory overflowing with throwaway objects created in the class libraries. Real-time code is not compelled to use standard class libraries, but those class libraries are a major attraction of Java and the effort involved in recoding them all to real-time standards would be staggering.

Scoped memory isn't as simple as immortal memory, but it goes a long way toward addressing the problems with immortal memory. In simple applications, scoped memory works like a stack for objects. When the thread enters a memory scope, it starts allocating objects from that scope. It continues allocating objects there until it enters a nested scope or exits from the scope. After the thread exits the scope, it can no longer access objects allocated there and the JVM is free to recover the memory used there.

If a thread enters a scope before calling a method in a standard class library and leaves the scope shortly after returning, all objects allocated by the method will be contained in the scope and freed when the thread leaves the scope.[2] Programmers can safely use convenience objects by enclosing the object creation and use in a scope. The mechanism (called a closure) for using scopes is a little ungainly, but an RTSJ programmer uses closures so much that they soon feel natural.

Performance is the most important cost of immortal and scoped memory. The RTSJ has access rules for no-heap, real-time threads and rules that govern the storage of references to objects in heap and scoped memory. These rules must be enforced by the class verifier or the execution engine. Unfortunately, it seems likely that the execution of the bytecodes that store references will have to do some part of that work. That necessity will hurt the JVM's performance.

---

2. Using standard libraries in scoped memory is not always as simple as it sounds. The most likely problem is that the library method will get a runtime exception when it tries to access heap memory.

Memory Access

Special types of memory, I/O devices that can be accessed with load and store operations, and communication with other tasks through shared memory are important issues for embedded systems. It takes a bit of a stretch to call these real-time issues, but the RTSJ makes that stretch.

Special types of memory are closely related to performance (slow memory, cached memory, high-speed nonsnooped access to sharable memory, etc.) Whereas performance is not a real-time issue in the strictest sense, predictable performance *is* a real-time issue and some memory attributes like cacheable, sharable, and pageable have a large impact on the predictability of code that uses the memory.

The RTSJ "raw" memory access classes give something like "peek and poke" access to memory. They run through the JVM's security and protection mechanisms, so this introduction of pointer-like objects does not compromise the integrity of the Java platform, but it does give enough direct access to memory to support device drivers written in Java and Java programs that share memory with other tasks.

The raw memory classes do nothing to improve the real-time performance of the Java platform. They are there because some of the most enthusiastic early supporters of a real-time Java specification wanted to use Java to write device drivers. It was a painless addition to the specification and it greatly increases the usefulness of Java for the embedded real-time community.

Implementation

An implementation of the RTSJ must include the `javax.realtime` packages. It will almost certainly include a special JVM, and it might include a compiler that can help find memory reference errors.

Any compiler can make classes that use the RTSJ, and special classes on an ordinary Java platform can pretend to conform to the RTSJ. Those were important design goals. We wanted RTSJ users to be able to do a lot of development on standard IDEs.

Class libraries can implement the RTSJ APIs and provide some of the RTSJ functions, but they cannot provide all the services. A true RTJS implementation includes enhancements to the JVM. There are no new bytecodes, but it would be difficult or impossible to enforce memory access rules without enhancing the implementation of the bytecodes that handle references. Asynchronous transfer of control also seems to require changes to bytecode interpretation, this time to the bytecodes that move between methods. The RTSJ also adds new priorities and far stricter scheduling rules than those of the standard JVM.

A special RTSJ compiler would be useful. A compiler cannot always identify memory reference violations, but it can find enough of them to justify trying. It would be far better to find a reference violation as a compile-time error than as a runtime exception.

RTSJ Hello World

Working with the TimeSys reference implementation of the RTSJ installed on a Linux system in /usr/local/timesys and with the Sun JDK tools, we show here a step-by-step procedure for creating and running a hello world program for real time.

Hello world doesn't have significant timeliness constraints, so Example 8–1 will just run the standard hello world in a real-time thread.

Example 8–1 RT hello world program

```
import javax.realtime.*;

public class Hello1 {
   public static void main(String [] args){
      RealtimeThread rt= new RealtimeThread(){
         public void run() {
            System.out.println("Hello RT world");
         }
      };
      if(!rt.getScheduler().isFeasible())
         System.out.println("Printing hello is not feasible");
      else
         rt.start();
   }
}
```

The program shown in Example 8–1 is a complete program. Since it prints "Hello RT world" from a real-time thread, that part of its execution can take advantage of priority inheritance and strictly defined, fixed-priority, preemptive scheduling. Those scheduling properties do not make much difference to the output of one short string, but they are there.

To test the program:

1. If you are developing from the command line, you might use a command
   like this to compile Hello1:

   ```
   javac -classpath /usr/local/timesys/rtsj-ri/lib/foundation.jar Hello1.java
   ```

2. If the real-time JVM is on your execution path and the classpath is set to
   your real-time Java class libraries, a simple command line will run the program:

   ```
   tjvm Hello1
   ```

   More likely, you'll need a command line like this:

   ```
   tjvm -Djava.class.path=/home/dibble/javaprogs/hello1
   -Xbootclasspath=/usr/local/timesys/rtsj-ri/lib/foundation.jar Hello1
   ```

3. The output will be:

   ```
   Hello RT world!
   ```

Closures

Much of the RTSJ involves changing some part of the JVM's state in a controlled way, then being absolutely sure to restore the previous state in an organized way. Method invocation changes several parts of the JVM's state and then restores them on return. Opening curly braces change the name resolution state, and closing braces restore it. The RTSJ needed to add a new mechanism to the Java language so it could control memory allocation and the propagation of asynchronously interrupted exceptions.

We could have extended the language, but on reflection we did not want to stick our heads into that meat grinder. Instead, we used a programing construct, called a *closure*, well known to Scheme and SmallTalk programmers.

The Language Construct

A closure associates some code with some of the environment in which the closure was created. This sounds like an odd concept. Code is created by the compiler. Right?

The ancestor of a closure is a pointer to a function. In the *lexically scoped* C world, where the way in which variables are resolved in the function does not depend on the environment in which the function pointer is used, the idea of a closure is not compelling. If the language is *dynamically scoped*, it resolves names by looking up its call stack. In a dynamically scoped language, function pointers are tricky. When a pointer to function foo is passed from one function to another, the location of variables visible to foo may change. Sometimes you can do clever things with this behavior, but generally it is uncomfortable for the programmer.

A closure lets a programmer say about a function pointer, "when this function pointer is used, resolve its references as if I were using it." The closure can be passed around. Its behavior will still depend on its internal state and on parameters that are passed to it, but these are relatively easy for a programmer to control.

Java Closures

There was no tidy way to implement a closure in a Java program until Java support for inner classes was added in Java 1.1.

Closure Structure

The structure of a closure in the Java language is shown in Example 9–1.

Example 9–1 Java closure

```
public class ClosureExample1 {
    int remote = 0;
    OtherClass c = new OtherClass();

    public void bar(){
        c.foo(new BazClass() {
            public void doIt(){
                remote += 1;
                local = remote; //  local is in BazClass
            }
        });
    }

    static void main(String args[]){
        (new ClosureExample1()).bar();
    }
}
```

The bar method creates an instance of an anonymous local inner class and passes that object to the foo method. When the foo method uses the object by calling baz.doIt, the doIt method executes in the environment of the bar method where it was created, as shown in Example 9–2.

Example 9–2 Using a closure

```
public class OtherClass{
    public void foo(BazClass baz){
        baz.doIt();
        baz.doIt();
        System.out.println("baz.getState()=" + baz.getState());
    }
}
```

If you create the BazClass definition, shown in Example 9–3,

Example 9–3 BazClass definition

```
public abstract class BazClass {
    int local;
    abstract public void doIt();

    public int getState(){
        return local;
    }
}
```

and run the program, the output will be:

```
baz.getState()=2
```

If you then go back to the ClosureExample object and check, the value of the remote instance variable is indeed 2.

Closures in the RTSJ

Closures are intended to be passed elsewhere for use, but the RTSJ arranges to call them right back so they act very much like a block of code marked off by curly braces.

The RTSJ uses closures to give a block of code an invisible prolog and epilog to provide a storage area for the invisible code. The instance variable storage that comes with the Java closure is a nice extra.

Example 9–4 presents a version of OtherClass with some RTSJ-like infra-structure:

Example 9–4 RTSJ-like use of a closure

```
public class OtherClass2{
    //  Store saved state here.
    public void foo(BazClass baz){
        prolog(baz);
        baz.doIt();
        epilog(baz);
    }
    private void prolog(BazClass baz){
        //  Setup environment for doIt()
    }

    private void epilog(BazClass baz){
        //  Clean up and prepare to return
    }
}
```

Starting at bar in Example 9–1, the easy reading of the code ignores the line starting with c.foo. The bulk of bar executes in a special kind of scope that is crudely labeled by the call to c.foo and the creation of a BazClass object. For most purposes, when the RTSJ uses this type of mechanism, you can just read the code in the inner class as executing inline.

What really happens is that control moves over to OtherClass2, where it calls the prolog method, and then returns to the doIt method back in bar. When that method returns, control passes back to foo and it calls the epilog method. Control then returns to bar and continues without further excitement.

Limitations of Closures

The way RTSJ implements and uses closures in the Java language has several limitations. Some limitations are related to local inner classes; those we have to live with. Some only apply to anonymous local inner classes. Those are a matter of choice. Sometimes anonymous classes are much easier to understand. Other times it is better to use named classes.

Readability

The standard recommendation is not to use anonymous inner classes with more than about six lines of code in them, but the RTSJ-style usage can safely be used for any amount of code. In general use of anonymous inner classes, once they get bigger than about six lines it is too easy to forget that the code is just a class definition and is passed elsewhere for execution. In the case of the RTSJ usage, the code will be executed right where it stands. The code in the inner class executes *almost* as if it were inline.

Local Variables

The illusion of simplicity falls apart when a local inner class tries to access local variables or method parameters from the surrounding method. Those references are only valid for variables and parameters that are declared `final`. This limitation is annoying if you have convinced yourself that the code in the inner class really is executing inline, but it is easy enough to work around:

- Pass values from local variables into the `doIt` method as parameters.

- Make local variables that need to be visible in the inner class `final`.

- Copy local variables into `final` variables.

- Use instance variables.

Modifying local variables is a problem since the only ones the inner class can see are `final`. The infrastructure can be set up so the inner block can pass back a parameter. (Imagine that `doIt` returned a value to `foo`, which passed it back to `bar`.) Other than that, only `static` and instance variables are available for two-way communication.

Constructors

Anonymous inner classes cannot have constructors. (Constructors have the same name as the class. What would the constructor for an anonymous class be named?) The limitation is not as big a problem as you might expect. First, when inner classes are used as closures by the RTSJ, they should not need constructors. If they need nondefault initialization, they can use initializers and initialization blocks. Those mechanisms do not offer a way to pass parameters when the object is constructed, but since it is an inner class, it can reach out and use values from the surrounding scope. That is probably bad style, but putting something that complex in an anonymous class was probably the mistake.

Nesting

No limit is enforced on nesting of inner classes, but at some point they become hard to read. At that point, stop using anonymous classes. Get the code out of line, then proceed as before. Example 9–5 revises the code from Example 9–1 to use a named local inner class.

Example 9–5 Named local inner class

```
public class ClosureExample2 {
    int remote = 0;
    OtherClass c = new OtherClass();

    public void bar(){
        class Bazzer extends BazClass {
            public void doIt(){
                remote += 1;
                local = remote; //  local is in BazClass
            }
        }

        c.foo(new Bazzer());
    }

    static void main(String args[]){
        (new ClosureExample1()).bar();
    }
}
```

It is even better if the class can be made into a simple inner class (nonlocal), as shown in Example 9–6.

Example 9–6 Named inner class

```
public class ClosureExample3 {
    int remote = 0;
    OtherClass c = new OtherClass();

    class Bazzer extends BazClass {
        public void doIt(){
            remote += 1;
            local = remote; //  local is in BazClass
        }
    }

    public void bar(){
        c.foo(new Bazzer());
    }

    static void main(String args[]){
        (new ClosureExample1()).bar();
    }
}
```

High-Resolution Time

As you might expect, time is an important feature of many real-time systems. The RTSJ needed a more powerful notion of time than the `java.util.Date` class provides. The `HighResolutionTime` class and its three subclasses—`AbsoluteTime`, `RelativeTime`, and `RationalTime`—do two things for the RTSJ. They give it a polymorphic representation of time that let the RTSJ APIs (and the programs that use them) use intervals in time, points in time, and an interesting representation of frequency. The RTSJ time classes also give it a representation of time that has nanosecond resolution and millions of years of range.

Resolution

This year (2002), a timer resolution of tenths of microseconds would be sufficient for almost any software purpose. No current processor can execute quickly enough to make a microsecond seem like a long time. But processors are still getting faster, and we hope the RTSJ will have a useful life longer than two or three years. Nanosecond measurement is the next stopping place. It seems likely to remain a useful timer resolution for at least a decade. (That sounds a lot like "640K should be enough for anyone" doesn't it?) Specifying a timer resolution of picoseconds seems absurd.

Given nanosecond resolution, a 32-bit integer was definitely too small. It would only represent an interval of about plus or minus 2 seconds. A 64-bit long integer expands the range to about 292 years. Not bad, but someone launching an interstellar probe might want to handle intervals longer than that.

The final `HighResolutionTime` representation works out to about 84 bits. It has nanosecond resolution, but it is represented in two parts: a 64-bit millisecond value and 32-bits of nanoseconds that are added to the milliseconds. Since there are only a million nanoseconds per millisecond, the high order 12 bits of the nanosecond value are actually milliseconds. They could serve to slightly increase the range of a timer, but not enough to increase the time range by a whole bit. The range is about 292 million years. That should suffice even for an interstellar probe.

The "Clock"

The RTSJ supports the notion of multiple clocks. It is not obvious why a system would want more than one clock. In fact, systems with multiple clocks often go to great pains to get the effect of a single clock. If there are multiple clocksand that fact is visible to software, you have to know which clock is associated with any given time and you have to take great care never to compare times that are associated with different clocks.

> **Pick one good clock and stick with it unless hardware restrictions force you to use multiple clocks.**

Here are some excuses for making multiple clocks visible to the Java runtime:

- Battery-backed clocks that keep calendar time whether the system is on or off are slow to read or write and seldom generate good interrupts for high-resolution time. They are mainly useful for setting higher-performance timers at system initialization. Software may refer to a battery-backed calendar from time to time, but it would be painful to be forced to use that clumsy device for all timing services. We address this potential problem by giving the calendar and the real-time clock separate clock IDs.

- Some timer hardware cannot be reset. Once it is started, it will run until it "goes off." Then it can be set for a new interval. This kind of timer can either generate a steady pulse (putting a steady load on the system), or it can support one timer at a time. This type of timer was popular in the 1980s and lost popularity in the 1990s, but it still appears from time to time. If this type of clock is used in its one timer per clock mode, the supporting software needs to make numerous clocks accessible.

Every RTSJ system has at least one clock. You get a reference to it with the class method:

```
Clock.getRealTimeClock()
```

Any other clocks are system dependent.

HighResolutionTime Base Class

The HighResolutionTime class is abstract. It cannot be instantiated, but it stores the millisecond and nanosecond fields for all the other high-resolution time classes and provides the methods that are common to all its subclasses. The methods for HighResolutionTime (and therefore all its subclasses) are listed below:

```
AbsoluteTime absolute(Clock clock)

AbsoluteTime absolute(Clock clock, AbsoluteTime dest)

int compareTo(HighResolutionTime time)

int compareTo(java.lang.Object object)

boolean equals(java.lang.Object object)

boolean equals(HighResolutionTime object)

long getMilliseconds()

int getNanoseconds()

int hashCode()

RelativeTime relative(Clock clock)

RelativeTime relative(Clock clock, RelativeTime time)

void set(HighResolutionTime time)

void set(long millis)

void set(long millis, int nanos)

static void waitForObject(java.lang.Object target,
            HighResolutionTime time) throws
            InterruptedException
```

Some of these methods—compareTo(Object), equals(Object), and hashCode—are required for any well-behaved object. The other methods apply more or less reasonably to all the subclasses of HighResolutionTime.

Neither `HighResolutionTime`, nor any of the derived classes specified in the RTSJ perform any synchronization. If these objects are subject to change and shared among multiple threads, the application must provide its own synchronization.

Absolute Time

The string 2:55:05.000 AM on the 5th of July 2010 represents an absolute time.

Absolute times could be specified relative to any fixed starting time, but for practical (RTSJ and `java.util.Date`) purposes absolute times are specified as an offset from 00:00:00.000 GMT on the 1st of January, 1970.

`AbsoluteTime` adds the following methods to `HighResolutionTime`—

```
AbsoluteTime add(long millis, int nanos)

AbsoluteTime add(long millis, int nanos, AbsoluteTime
            destination)

AbsoluteTime add(RelativeTime time)

AbsoluteTime add(RelativeTime time, AbsoluteTime destination)

java.util.Date getDate()

void set(java.util.Date date)

RelativeTime subtract(AbsoluteTime time)

RelativeTime subtract(AbsoluteTime time, RelativeTime
            destination)

AbsoluteTime subtract(RelativeTime time)

AbsoluteTime subtract(RelativeTime time, AbsoluteTime
            destination)

java.lang.String toString()
```

—that is, the methods enable addition, subtraction, conversion between high-resolution time and `Date` formats, and conversion to a printable format.

The `AbsoluteTime` class offers a service that is common throughout the RTSJ. The methods that return an object reference can allocate that object, or they can use an object that is passed to them. The most interesting case for these methods is that of passing a reference to the `AbsoluteTime` object itself as the destination parameter, for example,

```
newTime = newTime.add(100, 950, newTime);
```

adds 0.100000950 seconds to `newTime` without creating a new object.

The methods allow you to add an interval to the absolute time or subtract an interval from it. Technically, methods that subtract relative times from absolute times are not necessary—subtraction is just adding a negative—but since it isn't convenient to negate a `RelativeTime` object, the `AbsoluteTime` class provides both addition and subtraction of `RelativeTime`. Because integers are easy to negate, the class does not provide subtraction for milliseconds and nanoseconds.

You cannot add two absolute times together, (It makes no sense to add 4 July 1999 to 15 December 2021.) but you can subtract them. That gives you the time interval between the two points in time, a `RelativeTime`.

The `getDate` and `setDate` methods convert back and forth between this highly precise representation of time and the somewhat looser representation in `java.util.Date`.

The `toString` method returns the ASCII representation of the time in a form that matches the format returned by java.util.Date.toString with the sub-second time attached as a postfix.

Relative Time

Relative time is always a duration. It can be positive, negative, or zero.

`RelativeTime` adds the following methods to `HighResolutionTime`:

```
RelativeTime add(long millis, int nanos)

RelativeTime add(long millis, int nanos, RelativeTime
            destination)

RelativeTime add(RelativeTime time)

RelativeTime add(RelativeTime time, RelativeTime destination)

void addInterarrivalTo(AbsoluteTime destination)

RelativeTime getInterarrivalTime()

RelativeTime getInterarrivalTime(RelativeTime destination)

RelativeTime subtract(RelativeTime time)

RelativeTime subtract(RelativeTime time, RelativeTime
            destination)

java.lang.String toString()
```

The function of the arithmetic operations is clear, but the methods that deal in interarrival time introduce a new concept. Interarrival time is basically another word for period. For the base `RelativeTime` class, interarrival time is exactly equal to the interval specified by the time. These methods are here not because they are particularly useful for the `RelativeTime` class, but because they make it compatible with the `RationalTime` class that extends `RelativeTime`.

Rational Time

The RationalTime class extends the RelativeTime class by adding a frequency. It represents *frequency* occurrences of something per interval. Only the methods from RelativeTime dealing with interarrival times need to be overridden. The following methods are added:

```
int getFrequency()

void setFrequency(int frequency)
```

More important, the addInterarrivalTo and getInterarrivalTime methods reveal their purpose in this class. In RelativeTime they were just place-holders so methods that want to deal in interarrival times can easily use either RationalTime or RelativeTime. Here, interarrival time is roughly the interval represented by the millisecond and nanosecond values divided by the frequency.

This class is provided for those applications that care more about the number of times an event occurs in an interval of time than about the period of the event. If you want a time that will make an event fire every 50th of a second, you use a RelativeTime object and set it to 20 milliseconds. If you want to be certain that an event fires 50 times in every second but you mind very much if the interval between events varies a bit, use a RationalTime object with the interval set to 1 second and the frequency set to 50.

The difference is in what you want the system to concentrate on. If you fix the period by using RelativeTime, the system will make its best effort to follow the specified period accurately, but if it runs a microsecond long 30 times in a row and the 20-millisecond period will only deliver 49 events in a particular second, that is not a problem. A RationalTime specification would not worry about letting some intervals be a bit long or short, but would make every effort not to let a second go by without exactly 50 events.

It does not do to think too hard about RationalTime. If you think of it as a commitment to maintain the frequency over every interval, it becomes a tight control on the period *and* a commitment to deliver the frequency. This is not the idea. RationalTime with an interval of 1 second and a frequency of 50 is not instructions to deliver 50 events between 0 seconds and 1 second, and between 0.0001 and 1.0001 seconds and between 0.0002 and 1.0002 seconds, etc. It applies only between the start time and integer multiples of the interval after that.

Rational time addresses the problem of periods that cannot be accurately represented because they are an irrational number in binary. The nanosecond precision of high-resolution time would seem to make concern with rounding to the nearest nanosecond rather fanatical, but realize that the implementation may not be using a clock anywhere close to that precision. If the actual clock rounds to the nearest tenth of a millisecond, rounding could cause real trouble.

The discussion up to here would lead you to think that the time interval for `RationalTime` is fixed at one second. It is not. The interval has the full range and precision of `RelativeTime`. One could adjust the `RationalTime` that specified 50 events per second to call for 50 events in 0.990 seconds. The interval can also get very long. Imagine calling for a device to charge its batteries twice a week, or instructing an interstellar probe to check for nearby stars five times every million years.

Chapter 11

Async Events

▼ BINDING A HAPPENING TO AN EVENT

▼ BASIC ASYNC EVENT OPERATION

▼ ASYNC EVENTS WITHOUT HAPPENINGS

▼ IMPLEMENTATION DISCUSSION

Some of the first people to see drafts of the RTSJ immediately saw that async event handlers were the tool they had been waiting for. They pictured systems with a handful of real-time threads, and hundreds or even tens of thousands of async event handlers.

Much of the processing in a real-time system is triggered by internal and external events: a packet arrives, the temperature reaches a significant value, the dog scratches at the door, an alarm rings, a car pulls out into traffic, someone presses a button, the JVM runs out of memory, a thread misses its deadline, and so forth. These events do not occur on schedule, but the software needs to respond to them.

The first problem is nomenclature. Most embedded real-time literature uses the term *event* to refer to the asynchronously occurring ... mmm ... event. Event is also used to refer to the software mechanism for handling asynchronous events. Java APIs like AWT include events as a fundamental software component. The

123

RTSJ needed to support events, and the event support already in Java technology was not quite right, so we needed a new mechanism and a new name.

The RTSJ refers to external events as *happenings*. (That has a lovely 60s beads-and-flowers ring to it.) The software to handle happenings is contained in the classes `AsyncEventHandler` and `BoundAsyncEventHandler`, known as AEH and bound AEH.

Binding a Happening to an Event

The RTSJ specifies a three-layer mechanism for binding an external happening to an asynchronous event handler:

- **Interface layer** — A platform-specific mechanism informs the Java runtime of an external happening. On UNIX-like operating systems, this would probably be a signal intercept handler. On JVMs that run without the help of an operating system, happenings are probably hardware interrupts and the glue is an interrupt service routine.

  Each happening is given a name. The way names are chosen and assigned is not specified in the RTSJ. Perhaps they are automatically generated, perhaps the names are a permanent part of the Java runtime, or perhaps they are specified in the Java resources.

- **Async event layer** — Objects from the `AsyncEvent` class bind to external happenings with the `bindTo` method:

  ```
  aEvent.bindTo("signal 5");
  ```

  This tells the interface layer to direct happenings with the specified name to this `AsyncEvent` object.

  The logic of the `AsyncEvent` object is fixed. The interface layer calls its fire method when the happening occurs, and the `AsyncEvent` starts all the AEHs and bound AEHs that have been associated with it.

- **Async event handler layer** — `AsyncEventHandler` objects connect themselves to one or more `AsyncEvent` objects with the `addHandler` or `setHandler` methods. When the event is fired, it starts all the handlers attached to it.

An AEH can connect to more than one async event, but that is not wise. A multiply connected handler cannot tell why it is running.

The async event causes the run method in the AEH to execute. The run method calls the handleAsyncEvent method once for every time the event was fired. The content of the handleAsyncEvent method is the code that the developer thinks of as the actual async event handler.

Basic Async Event Operation

An async event has three major method groups:

- **Bind event to trigger.** This group (of one) handles the connection between the async event and the trigger for the event.

- **Bind event to handlers.** Most of AsyncEvent's public methods manage the set of event handlers associated with the event.

- **Fire the event.** This increments the fire count for each async event handler associated with the async event. Any of the handlers not already active are started.

The fire count is an async event handler's hedge against overload problems. An async event handler has five phases:

1. The Java runtime starts the schedulable object the handler will run in.
2. The async event handler sets up to handle an event.
3. The async event handler handles the event.
4. The async event handler does cleanup processing.
5. The Java runtime stops the schedulable object and puts it away.

The RTSJ hints that a quality implementation will minimize the cost of Steps 1 and 5, but that cost may still be comparatively large, especially if the actual activity in Step 3 is something as simple as incrementing a counter.

The infrastructure in the async event handler class checks the handler's fire count. If it is greater than zero, the infrastructure just increments it each time the async event is fired. If it is zero, the infrastructure increments the fire count and starts the event handler running. This avoids Steps 1 and 5 when the event handler is being heavily used.

Example 11–1 demonstrates async event handling for a happening (a UNIX signal). It also demonstrates an aggressive approach to the use of the fire count. Instead of relying on the AsyncEventHandler infrastructure to manage the fireCount, the handleAsyncEvent method in Example 11–1 manages the counter itself.

Example 11–1 Async event handler for a signal

```java
import javax.realtime.*;

class SigHandler extends AsyncEventHandler{
  public void handleAsyncEvent(){
    int pending;
    while((pending = getAndDecrementPendingFireCount()) >= 1)
      if(pending > 1)
        System.out.println("Signal. " + pending + " pending");
      else
        System.out.println("Signal");
  }
}
```

SigHandler is a subclass of AsyncEventHandler with a handleAsyncEvent method. The method handles events by looping once for every pending fire. The programmer could have used the getAndClearPendingFireCount method to make any number of pending fires go away: for example, if whatever the programmer was doing to handle one signal was sufficient to handle any number of waiting signals, or if just knowing how many there were was enough to handle them. Perhaps like this:

```java
count = getAndClearPendingFireCount();
System.out.println(count);
```

The code that demonstrates signal events is unexpectedly complicated. Signals are happenings. In the implementation they may be fired by a no-heap async event handler, so the async event and the async event handler must be created in non-heap memory, as shown in Example 11–2.

Example 11–2 Set up and fire a signal AEH

```java
import javax.realtime.*;

public class SigEvt extends RealtimeThread {
  public void run(){
    MemoryArea immortal = ImmortalMemory.instance();
    AsyncEventHandler handler = null;
    AsyncEvent event = null;
    try{
      handler = (AsyncEventHandler)
        immortal.newInstance(SigHandler.class);
      event = (AsyncEvent)
        immortal.newInstance(AsyncEvent.class);
```

Example 11–2 Set up and fire a signal AEH (Continued)

```
} catch (InstantiationException e){
    e.printStackTrace();
    } catch (IllegalAccessException e){
    e.printStackTrace();
    }

event.addHandler(handler);
event.bindTo("25");// Signal number 25

// Pretend to signal
event.fire();event.fire();event.fire();
try {
    Thread.sleep(1000); //Let the AEH run
} catch(Exception e){}
event.removeHandler(handler);
System.exit(0);
}
public static void main(String [] args){
    SigEvt rt = new SigEvt();
    rt.start();
    try {
        rt.join();
    } catch (InterruptedException e){}
    System.exit(0);
}
}
```

Stepping through Example 11–2, which creates the AEH in Example 11–1 and demonstrates its use, we see the following:

1. The example creates an instance of SigHandler,

2. creates an async event,

3. adds the handler created in Step 1 to the new async event,

4. connects the event to signal 25 by using bindTo("25"). (The reference implementation identifies signals this way.)

5. Now the event would fire automatically every time the Java runtime thought it received a signal 25 that was directed at this async event, but instead of sending a real signal, the example simulates three signals by firing the event three times.

6. The thread sleeps to let the async event handler run.

7.   Since the async event handler has the scheduling parameters of the thread that created it, it will not preempt the main thread, and it doesn't run until the main thread sleeps. Then the handler has three pending fires to handle.

Async Events without Happenings

Although the original motivation for async events was external happenings, it is also a useful tool for things that happen entirely within the Java environment. Such happenings are no problem. Anything that can call the `fire` method on an async event can cause its handlers to run. Firing an async event just releases a group of threadlike entities that registered for that event.

Time Triggering

Many real-time systems are full of the software equivalent of alarm clocks and timers. The RTSJ addresses these needs with the combination of async events and the `Timer` class. The RTSJ provides two types of timers: `OneShotTimer` and `PeriodicTimer`.

A `OneShotTimer` will execute its `handleAsyncEvent` method once at the specified time (or immediately if the specified time is in the past). A `PeriodicTimer` will execute its `handleAsyncEvent` method repeatedly at the specified interval.

Periodic Timers.   An AEH triggered by a periodic timer is roughly equivalent to a periodic thread (see "Periodic Threads without Handlers" in Chapter 12) and even more roughly equivalent to:

```
while(true){
  do something
  sleep until absolute time start of next period
}
```

> ### Periodic execution versus Thread.sleep
>
> Periodic execution will cycle once per period. A loop that uses sleep to execute once per period will cycle too slowly since every iteration of the loop uses sleep time plus the time it takes to execute the code in the loop. This can be nearly corrected by use of a high-resolution timer to compute the execution time of the code in the loop, but that is a lot of trouble. The loop will still drift by the interval between reading the high-resolution timer and starting to sleep, and it can be way off if the code in the loop is preempted.
>
> You will seldom see real-time code use a loop with a sleep in it to drive periodic execution.

The handler runs once every time the timer fires. It will fire at the specified pace until the timer is disabled (by the `disable` method.) The pace can be modified while the timer is running with the `setInterval` method.)

Example 11–3 creates an async event handler that just prints "tick" to its output. The code first attaches that handler to a timer that ticks every 1.5 seconds (1500 milliseconds) and then starts the timer. The main thread sleeps for a while. If it didn't, the application would exit immediately and the async event would never run.

Example 11–3 Periodic timer-triggered async event handler

```
import javax.realtime.*;

public class PTimer {
  public static void main(String [] args){
    AsyncEventHandler handler = new AsyncEventHandler() {
      public void handleAsyncEvent(){
        System.out.println("tick");
      }
    };

    PeriodicTimer timer = new PeriodicTimer(
      null,// Start now
      new RelativeTime(1500, 0), // Tick every 1.5 seconds
      handler);

    timer.start();
    try {
      Thread.sleep(20000);   // Run for 20 seconds
    } catch(Exception e){}
    timer.removeHandler(handler);
    System.exit(0);
  }
}
```

If you run this example, it will print "tick" every 1.5 seconds for 20 seconds, then exit.

One-Shot Timers. Time-outs are one of the main purposes of one-shot timers. This timer can take many forms, including the following:

• **Watchdog timer** — The event handler for a watchdog timer usually initiates massive error recovery—like resetting the computer. While the system is running correctly, it calls the `reschedule` method on the watchdog timer from time to time, rescheduling the timer for a future time. If enough time passes without someone rescheduling the watchdog timer, the watchdog's event handler runs and drastic recovery takes place.

The watchdog is set (as shown in Example 11–4) and reset to an interval that is much longer than the longest time the system should spend between calls to `reschedule`.

Example 11–4 Watchdog timer setup

```
import javax.realtime.*;

public class Dog {
   static final int TIMEOUT=2000;// 2 seconds
   public static void main(String [] args){
      double d;
      long n;
      AsyncEventHandler handler = new AsyncEventHandler() {
         public void handleAsyncEvent(){
            System.err.println("Emergency reset!!!");
            System.exit(1);
         }
      };
      RelativeTime timeout = new RelativeTime(TIMEOUT, 0);

      OneShotTimer dog = new OneShotTimer(
         timeout, // Watchdog interval
         handler);
```

If the watchdog timer ever goes off, it means that the system has jammed somewhere and needs a kick. The code in Example 11–5 uses a random amount of time that has a small chance of being greater than the watchdog interval, then resets the watchdog, and does it again. If you let it run long enough, the watchdog will eventually trip.

- **Time-out** — It takes a long time to start the motor on a floppy disk drive and close the heads on the disk. The drive would keep the motor running and the heads loaded all the time, except that the motor and the disk would both wear out too soon. Instead, there is a time-out in the system. After the drive sits idle for a while (maybe a minute), a one-shot timer fires and the drive is put to sleep. Every time the software accesses the floppy, it reschedules the time-out counter so it can be used continuously for days without ever shutting down, but will turn the motor off a minute after it goes idle. Programmatically, this is like a watchdog, except that the action when the timer fires is to adjust some hardware, not to restart the system.

Example 11–5 Watchdog timer use

```
dog.start();
while(true){
  d = java.lang.Math.random();
  n = (long)(d * TIMEOUT + 400);
  System.out.println("Running t=" + n);
  try {
    Thread.sleep(n);
  } catch(Exception e){}
  dog.reschedule(timeout);
}
```

Other time-outs start a computation: ten seconds after the car is fully inside the garage start closing the garage door, turn on the inside light, and turn off the outside light. That could be expressed as three async event handlers attached to a one-shot timer.

Some time-outs stop a computation. Real-time software can often afford to spend some preset interval at some activity. A one-shot timer can be used to stop the computation after it has run for the allowable interval. Example 11–6 illustrates this.

The async event handler is constructed as usual, but this one just writes a volatile instance variable. The handler is attached to a one-shot timer that will go off ten seconds after it is started.

After it starts the timer, the program loops. It will loop until it sees stopLooping equal to true.

When the one-shot goes off, stopLooping is set to true, and the main thread will complete the loop iteration it is in, then gracefully exit.

If the loop were more complicated, and there was a requirement to respond to the timer quickly, polling a stop flag would not be as elegant as it looks here. The timed code would be full of checks. It would look ugly and degrade per-

---

Volatile

The one-shot timer example works fine on my system whether stopLooping is volatile or not. If your compiler has a better optimizer than mine, it will require volatile.

Volatile makes the compiler recheck the value of stopLoop each time it uses it. A really good optimizer would probably change the while statement into while(true).

Example 11–6 One-shot timer triggered async event handler

```
import javax.realtime.*;

public class OSTimer {
  static boolean stopLooping = false;
  public static void main(String [] args){
    AsyncEventHandler handler = new AsyncEventHandler() {
      public void handleAsyncEvent(){
        stopLooping = true;
      }
    };

    OneShotTimer timer = new OneShotTimer(
      new RelativeTime(10000, 0), //Fire in 10 seconds
      handler);

    timer.start();
    while(!stopLooping){
      System.out.println("Running");
      try {
        Thread.sleep(1000);
      } catch(Exception e){}
    }
    System.exit(0);
  }
}
```

formance. The asynchronously interrupted exception (see Chapter 17) was designed for those situations. That mechanism lets the async event handler attached to the timer throw an exception into the thread.

Enable/Disable. Disabling a timer is like putting your hand on an old-fashioned alarm clock's bell to muffle its sound. A disabled timer is still ticking. If you reenable the timer before it goes off, it will behave exactly as if you had never disabled it. If it goes off while it is disabled, that event is silently lost. If a periodic timer is disabled through the end of one or more periods, the events for all the disabled periods are lost, but the clock is still running and it will fire on schedule on the next period.

If you do not want the services of a timer for a while, you have two alternatives:

1. Set a variable, visible to the timer's handlers, that tells them to count periods but otherwise ignore events. When you want the timer to work again, reset the variable. The system has to be designed for this since the code that wants

to ignore the timer has to know how to communicate with the timer's async event handlers.

2. Disable the timer when you want it quiet, and enable it when you want it to work again.

The functional difference between these two methods is that the first method counts timer events so it can handle them when it is enabled whereas the second one completely ignores the passage of time when it is disabled.

Fault Triggering

Java programmers normally pass faults to other scopes in the following ways:

- Throwing an exception

- Returning an error code

- Calling an error-handling method in some object they know of. (Probably the object was passed to them as a parameter.)

Async event handlers offer an interesting new alternative. The programmer can fire an async event. This has two novel characteristics:

1. The fault handling code runs asynchronously with the code that reports the fault.

2. Anyone, even code executing on other threads (subject to security constraints), can register an AEH with the async event. This gives fault handling a dynamic character.

The RTSJ uses async event handlers to inform threads when the scheduler has determined that they have missed a deadline or used more processor time than they expected.

Another application of a fault-triggered async event might be to log minor problems. The application would fire async events at each minor problem. If the system wanted to know about those faults, it would attach AEHs to those async events that would log them. If it wasn't interested, it would leave the async events empty.

The handler could be low priority. It would log events only when there were no other real-time activities, but it would not miss faults because of the event counting aspect of async events.

Let us look at Example 11–7, an example of fault-triggered async event handlers.

Example 11–7 Fault-triggered async event handlers

```java
public void run() {
  AsyncEventHandler handler = new AsyncEventHandler() {
    public void handleAsyncEvent(){
      System.err.println("Run method: notified");
    }
  };
  AsyncEvent event = new AsyncEvent();
  RealtimeThread thisThread =
      RealtimeThread.currentRealtimeThread();

  handler.setSchedulingParameters((SchedulingParameters)
      (new PriorityParameters(maxPriority-3)));

  event.addHandler(handler);
  process1(event);
  event.removeHandler(handler);
}

private void process1(AsyncEvent notify){
  AsyncEventHandler p2Handler = new AsyncEventHandler() {
    public void handleAsyncEvent(){
      System.err.println("process1 method: notified");
    }
  };
  p2Handler.setSchedulingParameters((SchedulingParameters)
    (new PriorityParameters(maxPriority-4)));
  notify.addHandler(p2Handler);
  process2(notify);
  notify.removeHandler(p2Handler);
}

private void process2(AsyncEvent notify){
  //... something bad happened
  //fire the notification async event.
  {
    notify.fire();
    return;
  }
}
```

Example 11–7 shows some unspecified fault occurring in process2. The code responds by firing the async event it was passed, and then it returns. (It happens to return; for other faults, the code might continue execution after reporting the problem.)

Every method that touched the async event had the opportunity to add one or more async event handlers for the fault. They could also set the priority of the handler they added to reflect the urgency of that routine. In the example, each routine removes its handler when it is no longer on the call stack, but that is not necessary. Since the handlers execute in their own context, they can attach handlers to the event and leave them there if they like.

When `process2` fires the event, its handlers execute in priority order, first the handler from the `run` method, then the handler from the `process1` method.

Software Event Triggering

Faults are not the only kind of software event that might be a good trigger for an asynchronous event. For example, an asynchronous event handler can be one of the following:

1. An easy substitute for real-time threads. Since AEHs do not have thread objects permanently associated with them, they do not have the memory leak potential of real-time thread objects.

2. A distribution facility for occurrences that are not faults but still might be of broad interest. For instance, a system might use async events to spread the word each time a cache is cleared or when the class loader brings in a new class.

3. A general notification mechanism. Asynchronous event handlers might be a good general-purpose replacement for AWT events, and they can serve as AWT-like events that can be used outside the AWT environment.

Implementation Discussion

The RTSJ wants asynchronous event handlers to behave like threads, but it wants them tuned for a different performance profile.

A thread is designed to execute for a long time, and it is expected to wait for resources, sleep, change its priority, and generally take full advantage of the available support services. A production system might see dozens, or even a few hundred active threads. (Very large systems may see thousands of active threads.) There is nothing wrong with creating threads to execute a few lines of code, but it may not be a good performance choice.

An asynchronous event handler is designed to execute a few lines of code, then exit. It is not expected to wait, block, sleep, or change its scheduling parameters. Even a small system should expect to see thousands of asynchronous event handlers in a dormant state and a fraction of that number active.

A simple system (like the RTSJ reference implementation) might just create a thread for an async event handler each time it is fired. That works perfectly but it has poor performance. The system would gain a big performance improvement if it created a thread for each async event handler. That also works perfectly, but each thread uses a few kilobytes.

There are lots of clever ways to make the kind of ultralight threads that are a good fit for async events. The following sample gives you an idea of the kind of support async events might have. Let me reemphasize: This is not a description of an actual implementation. It's only the most obvious way to implement async events without just creating threads for them.

The RTSJ runtime maintains a pool of real-time threads. It makes certain that there is at least one real-time thread in the pool for each priority that has an async event. That is, when you create an async event and give it priority 22, the RTSJ runtime will add a priority 22 thread to the pool if one is not there already.

The threads in the async event pool are basically part of the scheduler. In normal operation they are either waiting for work or running a list of async events.They understand that each routine they call is a separate `Schedulable` entity, and they do housekeeping between them. Provided that the events do nothing that would cause a scheduling point (like sleeping or overrunning a cost estimate), running the events at any given priority in sequence has the same effect as placing each event in a separate thread, but they all share the same thread overhead.

If any async event causes a scheduling point—changes its priority, sleeps, tries to acquire a lock that is not free, does blocking I/O, etc.—the RTSJ runtime will create a new thread and transfer all the async events left unexecuted on the blocked thread to the new thread.

The above design has little overhead per async event. The fixed memory cost for async event handlers that are not in use is only the memory required to describe the events and form them into a doubly linked list. The time to switch between async events is even less than context switching time. The tradeoff is that the first time an async event causes a scheduling point, it incurs the thread creation overhead that it has avoided. This mechanism runs simple async events beautifully, but it surprises async events that are not simple by taking much longer than usual the first time the async event does something "interesting."

Chapter 12

Real-Time Threads

▼ CREATION

▼ SCHEDULING

▼ PERIODIC THREADS WITHOUT HANDLERS

▼ PERIODIC THREADS WITH HANDLERS

▼ PERIODIC THREADS WITH HANDLERS

▼ INTERACTIONS WITH NORMAL THREADS

▼ CHANGING THE SCHEDULER

The work of real-time Java takes place in real-time threads and in asynchronous event handlers (which are a lot like real-time threads.) The `javax.realtime.RealtimeThread` class extends `java.lang.thread` so real-time threads can be used wherever a thread is required, but many of the features of the RTSJ are only available from real-time threads:

• Extended priorities
• Scoped memory
• Service for asynchronously interrupted exceptions
• Periodic scheduling
• Any nonpriority scheduling supplied by the platform

Other features of the RTSJ will probably appear in ordinary threads, but the specification does not require them there:

• Strict priority scheduling
• Priority inheritance protocol for mutual exclusion locks

Wait-free queues (see Chapter 20) will definitely be available everywhere. That mechanism was included in the RTSJ precisely to support convenient communication between code with different timeliness constraints, and conventional threads are the extreme case of code that is not concerned with timeliness.

Creation

Example 12–1 may be the simplest possible complete program that executes something in a RealtimeThread.

Example 12–1 Creating a Basic RealtimeThread

```
import javax.realtime.*;

public class Hello1 {
  public static void main(String [] args){
    RealtimeThread rt= new RealtimeThread(){
      public void run() {
        System.out.println("Hello RT world");
      }
    };
    rt.start();
  }
}
```

This example creates and starts a default RealtimeThread object that should be sufficient for most purposes unless a nonpriority scheduler is active.

Since this RealtimeThread is started by an ordinary thread, it is a special case. It cannot inherit RTSJ attributes from its parent. So, since nothing is specified in its constructor, the new thread gets default values. The most interesting default value is NORM_PRIORITY. This is a priority value one-third of the way up from the bottom of the range from the minimum real-time priority to the maximum real-time priority. The only specified use of NORM_PRIORITY is as the default priority for a RealtimeThread started by a non-real-time thread.

If the new thread was started by a real-time thread, it would use a copy of its parent's scheduling parameters. In particular, it would inherit its parent's priority. It is significant that the new thread gets a *copy* of the scheduling parameters. It does not just use the same scheduling parameters.

RealtimeThread objects are not placed in a special memory area unless the application specifically allocates them there. They can be created in heap memory or in scoped memory. The significance of this property will become clearer in Chapter 13 when we discuss the NoheapRealtimeThread class, but the crux is that it is easy to create thread objects that other threads cannot even reference. The solution to this problem is to create all thread objects in immortal memory, but that constitutes a serious memory leak unless the set of threads is static.

It is even possible to create a thread object that the thread itself cannot use. This misdeed shows up quickly in testing, but it is annoying nevertheless.

The parameter defaults for `RealtimeThread` (and other classes that implement `Schedulable`) are as follows:

• Inherit values from the parent thread.

• If the parent thread does not have a value for the parameter, the default value is the responsibility of the scheduler that will manage the object.

The parameterless `RealtimeThread` constructor called from an ordinary thread and operating under the default priority scheduler creates a thread with the values shown in Table 12–1.

Table 12–1 Default state when a real-time thread is created by an ordinary thread

Field	Default
memoryArea	Memory will be allocated from the heap.
memoryParameters	Memory allocation is not budgeted or restricted.
processingGroupParameters	The thread is not a member of a processing group.
releaseParameters	There are no release parameters. The thread is not periodic and admission control cannot evaluate feasibility if this thread is eligible for scheduling.
scheduler	The thread is schedulable by the default scheduler.
schedulingParameters	NORM_PRIORITY.
logic	The run method in the object.

There are two sets of rules when a real-time thread creates a `RealtimeThread`.

1. If the constructor does not include a parameter for the value, it is inherited from the current thread, as detailed in Table 12–2.

2. If the constructor passes a null value for the parameter, the current thread is ignored and the value is assigned by the scheduler that will handle the new thread. For null parameter values, the defaults are as listed in Table 12–1.

Table 12–2 Default state when a real-time thread is created by a RealtimeThread

Field	Default
`memoryArea`	The memory area that contains the thread object
`memoryParameters`	A copy of the memory parameters in effect when the thread was constructed
`processingGroupParameters`	The processing group in effect when the thread was created
`releaseParameters`	The release parameters in effect when the thread was created
`scheduler`	The scheduler in effect when the thread was created
`schedulingParameters`	A copy of the scheduling parameters in effect when the thread was constructed
`logic`	The `run` method in the object

The most elaborate constructor for a `RealtimeThread` object has six parameters:

```
public RealtimeThread(SchedulingParameters scheduling,
            ReleaseParameters release,
            MemoryParameters memory,
            MemoryArea area,
            ProcessingGroupParameters group,
            java.lang.Runnable logic)
```

- **Scheduling parameters** — For the default priority scheduler, this parameter refers to an object that has the priority with which the new process should start.

- **Release parameters** — For the priority scheduler, release parameters come into play when the thread uses the `waitForNextPeriod` method and when admission control is desired. Using release parameters, the real-time tasks can be characterized as follows:

  - *periodic* – The task uses release parameters of type `PeriodicParameters`. The parameter must have a period and a start time. If its deadline is not equal to its period, it can specify a separate deadline interval. If feasibility analysis is going to be useful, the release parameters must include a cost, that is, the maximum time the task will require in any period.

    If the scheduler notices that a task has not completed its computation by its deadline, it will call the asynchronous event handler (see Chapter 11) designated as the task's `missHandler`.

Cost is platform specific. The application may include code to estimate costs with some startup benchmarks, or determining costs can be a manual operation. This is an important instance of WOCRAC (Write Once Carefully, Run Anywhere Conditionally.)

Overrun is not the same thing as a miss. A thread can overrun its cost estimate in a period and still meet its deadline by using surplus processor resources. Overruns are not failures, but they are a sign of impending trouble. If a thread has set an `overRunHandler`, it will be notified each time it overruns its cost estimate.

If neither a miss handler nor an overrun handler is specified, the scheduler reports these failures through `waitForNextPeriod`. The next call to `waitForNextPeriod` after the deadline miss or overrun will immediately return `false`. If the thread is so late that it passes more than one of its deadlines, `waitForNextPeriod` will immediately return `false`, once for each missed deadline.

- *aperiodic* – Aperiodic tasks have no preset period, but they do have predictable deadlines and costs. Aperiodic tasks are released by some event, are perhaps released by another task, or may be released by an event external to the JVM. Keystrokes would be an example. They appear to the computer to occur at random intervals, but the designer can estimate the cost of servicing each keystroke and set a deadline for completing the service.

Aperiodic release parameters have no required fields, but if there is no deadline, the scheduler will use a value approximately equal to infinite time; if a cost is not provided, the scheduler will assume that it needs no time to complete its computation.

Since there is no limit on how frequently aperiodic tasks can run, there is no limit on their CPU consumption. When an aperiodic task enters the schedule, feasibility analysis becomes less meaningful. Aperiodic tasks can be brought under control by being put into processing groups with aggregate limits, or by being classified as sporadic instead of aperiodic

- *sporadic* – Sporadic tasks (or thread groups) are like aperiodic tasks with a limited frequency. The scheduler can assume that the sporadic task will run with a period equal to its minimum interarrival time and can do meaningful feasibility analysis based on that assumption.

It can also refuse to run the sporadic task more often than indicated by the minimum interarrival time.

> ### Aperiodic threads
>
> Aperiodic and sporadic scheduling doesn't make sense for threads. The thread can have aperiodic or sporadic release parameters, but there is no way for the scheduler and thread to communicate about scheduling events. The waitForNextPeriod method does not make sense here.
>
> The nonperiodic release parameters are intended for async event handlers (see Chapter 11). The AEH system includes suitable APIs for asynchronous and sporadic events.

- **Memory parameters** — Memory parameters set various limits on the thread's use of the memory allocator. They can restrict the thread's use of scoped memory. They can also, separately, limit the thread's use of immortal memory. (If the thread's default memory allocation area is the immortal pool, the effective limit is the minimum of the two limits.)

  Systems with garbage collectors that pace themselves by (for example) running a little each time a thread uses new can regulate the pace of garbage to a thread's requirements if the thread uses memory parameters with a positive allocation rate value. The allocation rate is a hint to the garbage collector, but it is also significant to the scheduler. The scheduler may control the execution rate of a thread such that it does not allocate memory faster than specified in its allocation rate field.

- **Memory area** — Real-time threads allocate their memory from the system heap by default, but they can be directed to use another memory pool. The options are heap, immortal, or scoped (see Chapter 13).

  The memory area is an important RTSJ concept. You'll read a lot more about it in subsequent chapters, but for now we'll ignore it and concentrate on threads that allocate from the heap.

- **Processing group** — Processing groups are intended to bring aperiodic activities under control. Processing groups have all the attributes of periodic release parameters. The scheduler can use any of several mechanisms to schedule the group (see "Aperiodic Servers" in Chapter 6.) The result is that the resource consumption of all activities in the thread group cannot total more than the budget of the processing group in any processing group period.

- **Logic** — The `logic` field refers to an instance of a class that implements the `Runnable` interface. This class creates the thread object with the runnable class preattached. If no logic parameter is specified, the thread defaults to a run method that does nothing. As with ordinary threads, the `RealtimeThread` can be subclassed to override the default run method.

Example 12–2 shows how a real-time thread might be built and started with a constructor that specifies everything but a processing group.

Example 12–2 Building and starting a real-time thread

```
import javax.realtime.*;

public class FullConstr {
  public static void main(String [] args){
    SchedulingParameters scheduling =
      new PriorityParameters(PriorityScheduler.MIN_PRIORITY+20);
    ReleaseParameters release =
      new AperiodicParameters(null, null, null, null);
    MemoryParameters memory =
      new MemoryParameters(MemoryParameters.NO_MAX, // Heap
        0);                        //Immortal memory
    MemoryArea area = HeapMemory.instance();
    ProcessingGroupParameters group =null;
    Runnable logic = new MyThread();

    RealtimeThread rt= new RealtimeThread(scheduling,
        release,
        memory,
        area, group,
        logic);
    rt.start();
    try {
      rt.join();
    } catch(Exception e){};
  }
}
```

Scheduling

The RTSJ permits other schedulers, but it requires a fixed-priority preemptive scheduler with at least 28 distinct priorities. (See Chapter 5 for explanations of these terms and most other scheduling terminology in this chapter.)

In addition to at least 28 real-time priorities, 10 non-real-time priorities are maintained for compatibility with applications written for platforms that do not implement the RTSJ. The RTSJ does not call for improvements in the behavior of the non-real-time priorities, but it does insist that the scheduler treat them all as lower priorities than the lowest real-time priority.

The scheduler has many features that real-time programmers like:

- There are at least 28 priorities. Sometimes, real-time systems want more than 28 priorities, but they seldom suffer serious performance degradation until they are forced to get by with fewer than about 32. Furthermore, the RTSJ requires at least 28, but uses a full 32-bit integer to represent priorities. If the scheduler can support four billion priorities, the RTSJ permits it.

- Tasks at higher priorities will always run in preference to tasks with lower priorities.

- Tasks with higher priorities will preempt lower-priority tasks. The maximum delay between the time a higher-priority task becomes ready to run and the time it gets control is a characteristic of the JVM, the processor, and the supporting operating system. It does not depend on cooperation from the lower-priority task.

- Locks applied to real-time threads always use a priority inversion avoidance mechanism.

Inversion Handling

Every implementation of the RTSJ must support priority inheritance protocol (see "Priority Inversion" in Chapter 5) for all `synchronized` objects. Priority ceiling emulation protocol is described by the standard but is not required.

Technically, the operation of the synchronized primitive must ensure "that there is no unbounded priority inversion." Then it requires that the implementation include priority inheritance and, moreover, that priority inheritance be the default monitor control mechanism.

If the implementation supports only priority inheritance protocol, priority inversion avoidance is just part of the background. Programmers have no control over its operation.

If the implementation also provides priority ceiling emulation or some other priority boosting mechanism, the RTSJ offers interfaces that can change the default mechanism for all real-time threads, as shown in Example 12–3.

It can also change the mechanism or alter its parameters for synchronization on a particular object, as shown in Example 12–4.

Setting a single global priority ceiling is fundamentally different from setting separate ceilings for each lock. The single global ceiling must be set at a priority at least as high as any thread that will ever try to synchronize on an object. To be safe, the priority for a global ceiling should be the highest available priority, and no thread should ever set its priority that high. This strategy makes analysis rela-

Example 12–3 Changing the default priority boosting protocol

```
import javax.realtime.*;

public class ToPcep {
  public static void main(String [] args){
    PriorityCeilingEmulation pce =
            new PriorityCeilingEmulation(27);
    //      Change default control for all sync locks
    MonitorControl.setMonitorControl(pce);
  }
}
```

Example 12–4 Changing the priority boosting protocol for an object

```
import javax.realtime.*;

public class ToPcep2 {
  public synchronized int foo(){
    return 1;
  }
  public static void main(String [] args){
    ToPcep2 obj = new ToPcep2();
    PriorityCeilingEmulation pce =
            new PriorityCeilingEmulation(27);
    //      Set PCEP for just one object
    MonitorControl.setMonitorControl(obj, pce);
    System.out.println(obj.foo());
  }
}
```

tively easy since any thread that holds a lock will run without preemption until it releases the lock. The analyst does not need to consider the possibility that a higher-priority thread might preempt a thread that is holding a lock. The disadvantage of the global ceiling is that high-priority threads cannot preempt a thread that is holding a lock even if the high-priority thread has no interest in the lock and needs to run.

A global priority ceiling may be appropriate for an application that uses synchronization sparingly, but not for a typical multithreaded application for the Java platform. Since multithreaded Java programs tend to synchronize liberally, a global ceiling will cause threads to run at the maximum priority a large part of the time. That effectively reduces the RTSJ to a single priority.

Priority ceiling emulation protocol is more appropriate for individual objects. There you can choose a priority that seizes the entire system or a priority that takes into account the priorities of the threads that are known to compete for that particular object.

> **Priority ceiling emulation is dangerous as a global default protocol. Use it with care.**

Fixed Priority

The RTSJ default fixed-priority scheduler has limited ability to reorder the priorities of threads. It can make temporary adjustments to avoid priority inversion, but it cannot otherwise alter thread priorities. Threads can, however, alter their own priorities, and subject to the JVM's security mechanisms, threads can alter the priority of other threads.

> **Adjusting thread priorities is not a debugging technique! Bugs that disappear when priorities are adjusted are not really gone.**

The priority of a thread is controlled by the `PriorityParameters` object associated with the thread. That gives two ways to alter a thread's priority:

1.   Change the value of the priority in its `PriorityParameters` object, as shown in Example 12–5.

Example 12–5 Changing thread priority by modifying the priority object

```
public class RunMe implements Runnable {
  public void run() {
    RealtimeThread me = RealtimeThread.currentRealtimeThread();
    int initialPriority;
    PriorityParameters pp;

    pp = (PriorityParameters)me.getSchedulingParameters();
    initialPriority =pp.getPriority();
    System.out.println("Initial priority=" + initialPriority);
    pp.setPriority(initialPriority+1);
    System.out.println("New priority=" + pp.getPriority());
```

2. Replace its `PriorityParameters` object with a different one, as shown in Example 12–6

Example 12–6 Changing thread priority with object replacement

```
pp = new PriorityParameters(initialPriority + 2);
me.setSchedulingParameters((SchedulingParameters)pp);
System.out.println("New priority=" +
  pp.getPriority());
```

Either technique achieves the same result, but they are not interchangeable.

The `RealtimeThread` object keeps references to the objects that control its behavior, not copies of those objects. If the programmer chooses to reuse a `PriorityParameters` object for multiple threads, changing the priority in that object will alter the priority of all the threads that use that object. This may be an advantage if it is done intentionally, but it can give rise to interesting bugs.

Replacing a thread's `PriorityParameters` object will not have unexpected side effects on the priorities of other threads, but it involves allocating an object. If the reference conditions for the thread are such that its parameters must be allocated in immortal memory, the `PriorityParameters` objects must be managed carefully to prevent memory leaks (see Chapter 16).

Feasibility

Feasibility analysis is an optional feature for RTSJ schedulers. Threads can ask to be admitted to the feasible set by using

```
public boolean addIfFeasible()
```

which asks the scheduler to admit this thread if it has enough resources to satisfy the resource requirements in the thread's scheduling parameters, release parameters, memory parameters, and processing group parameters. If the scheduler cannot spare the resources, it returns `false` and does not admit the thread.

```
public boolean addToFeasibility()
```

forces the scheduler to admit the thread even if it cannot spare the resources. The call will return `false` if admitting the thread caused the scheduler to become over-extended.

Feasibility analysis is really nothing more than budgeting. Since the scheduler cannot "unadmit" a thread, it just keeps track of uncommitted resources and rejects any thread that causes it to overflow.

A scheduler that implements feasibility analysis but not cost enforcement is slightly useful, but what you really want from a scheduler with feasibility analysis is admission control and a guarantee. The guarantee says that once a thread has been admitted, the scheduler guarantees it the resources it asked for. The scheduler can only do that if it can enforce limits:

- **Admission control** — The scheduler will only run entities that have passed admission control. In most cases, this requirement is impossible to meet perfectly since the system has "nonschedulable entities" that must be executed: page fault handlers, interrupt service routines, and the like. A practical system allocates a liberal allowance for nonschedulable entities and limits admitted entities to the remaining resources.

- **Enforcement** — The scheduler must not permit entities to use more resources than they requested when they were admitted. There are options that will let the scheduler tell a thread when it exceeds a limit, but even if the scheduler does not tell the thread, the scheduler must not permit anything to use resources faster than it is supposed to. Otherwise, other threads would miss their deadlines.

Periodic Threads without Handlers

Although the default scheduler is fixed-priority preemptive, the RTSJ includes periodic scheduling services in the default priority scheduler (see Chapter 7). Several features of the priority scheduler support periodic scheduling, as listed in Table 12–3.

Table 12–3 Optional features of periodic scheduling

Feature	Description
Feasibility analysis	The implementation may implement feasibility analysis algorithms to support the feasibility methods of the `PriorityScheduler` class: `addToFeasibility`, `changeIfFeasible`, `isFeasible`, and `removeFromFeasibility`. If feasibility analysis is not implemented, all loads are treated as feasible.
Deadline aware	The scheduler may notice when threads miss their deadlines. If the scheduler is not able to offer this service, deadlines are not enforced.
Miss handler	When a thread misses its deadline, an asynchronous event handler may be invoked.
Overrun handler	If the JVM is tracking the amount of time a thread uses per period, it may invoke an asynchronous event handler when threads use more processor time than they reserved. This function is not required for a minimal RTSJ implementation.

Table 12–3 Optional features of periodic scheduling (Continued)

ImportanceParameters	Support for importance is another optional feature of implementations of the RTSJ. ImportanceParameters can be used as the SchedulingParameters property of a RealtimeThread. When priority is used to reflect period (for periodic scheduling), importance can be used to pass information to the scheduler that will help it choose which deadlines to miss when it is overloaded and trying to fail gracefully.

Periodic threads have a standard structure. Most of the scheduling characteristics of a periodic thread are passed to the constructor through the release parameter as shown in Example 12–7, or it could be done in the RealtimeThread itself, as shown in Example 12–9.

Example 12–7 Setting up a simple periodic thread

```
import javax.realtime.*;

public class Periodic1 {
  public static void main(String [] args){
    SchedulingParameters scheduling =
      new PriorityParameters(PriorityScheduler.MIN_PRIORITY+10);
    ReleaseParameters release =
      new PeriodicParameters(
        new RelativeTime(),//Start at .start()
        new RelativeTime(1000, 0), // 1 second period
        null,  //cost
        new RelativeTime(500,0),// deadline=period/2
        null,  // no overrun handler
        null); // no miss handler

    RealtimeThread rt= new MyThread(scheduling,
        release);
    rt.start();
    try {
      rt.join();
    } catch(Exception e){};
  }
}
```

The release parameter specifies the following:

• **start** — When the periodic thread should start execution. This can be either an absolute time like 2:30 AM January 1, 2004, or a relative time like 200 milliseconds after I invoke the start method on the thread.

The example shows the simplest form of relative time. The empty constructor is shorthand for *immediately*.

- **period** — The period has to be a relative time since it is the time between iterations of the loop. It is the time from start to start (see Figure 12–1), not from end to start (as shown in Figure 12–2).

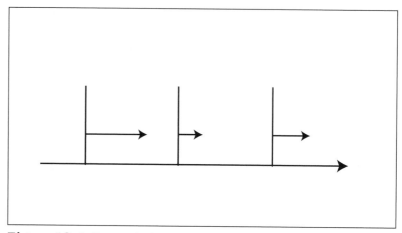

Figure 12–1 True periodic thread

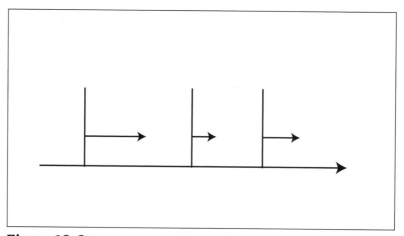

Figure 12–2 Inaccurate periodic thread

- **cost** — The example shows a null cost. This causes the cost value to go to the default. The default value is the deadline value. This is the maximum possible cost for the thread since any higher cost would necessarily miss deadlines. If the deadline is equal to the period, the default cost means that this thread uses 100 percent of available CPU time.

- **deadline** — In Example 12–7 the deadline is set to a tenth of the period. That means that the thread should cycle once per second, but needs to finish its computation within the first tenth of the second. The period is the default value for the deadline.

- **overrunHandler** — This could specify an asynchronous event handler that would be invoked when the thread used more processor time than the specified cost, but the example supplies a null.

- **missHandler** —This could specify an asynchronous event handler to be invoked if the thread misses its deadline. The example only supplies null, so the platform has nothing to call.

The periodic thread (in Example 12–8) shows the structure of any simple periodic thread that does not use miss or overrun handlers. Control enters the thread at the start time specified in its release parameters and executes its first iteration. It runs until it gets to the waitForNextPeriod call, then stops until it is time to compute for the next period.

As long as everything is working correctly, control just runs round the inner do-while loop, but the example is rigged with a steadily expanding load so it will eventually miss its deadline or, perhaps, overrun its cost. At that point, since no handlers are associated with this thread, waitForNextPeriod will return false immediately—without waiting for the start of the next period. If the thread's timing is seriously off, the thread may execute so long that it misses a deadline and the deadlines for subsequent periods. In this case, waitForNextPeriod may return immediately several times in succession. The thread can respond to a false return from waitForNextPeriod in several ways:

- **Good citizen** — If the thread has overrun its time or missed its deadline, it is probably cutting into another thread's time. Without using the miss and overrun handlers there is no easy way to tell what is wrong, but the thread should try to lighten its load a little if it can (as the thread in Example 12–8 does by decreasing bound.) The thread should also invoke waitForNextPeriod until it returns true to make certain that the next iteration will start with a fresh period where it stands a chance of succeeding, and not start partway through one where it will cause ungraceful degradation.

Example 12–8 Body of a simple periodic thread

```java
import javax.realtime.*;

public class MyThread extends RealtimeThread {
  volatile double f;
  public MyThread(SchedulingParameters sched,
      ReleaseParameters release){
    super(sched, release);
  }
  public void run(){
    RealtimeThread me = currentRealtimeThread();
    int bound;

    bound = 0;
    while(true){
      do {
        for(f=0.0; f < bound; f += 1.0);// Use some time
        bound += 10000;// Use more next time
        System.out.println("Ding! " + bound);
      } while(me.waitForNextPeriod());
      // Recover from miss or overrun
      System.out.println("Scheduling error");
        bound -= 15000;
      while(!me.waitForNextPeriod())//Eat errors
        System.out.print(".");
      System.out.println();
    }
  }
}
```

- **Desperate outlaw** — If the deadline is equal to the period, a periodic thread can consider ignoring the return from waitForNextPeriod.

  The thread will then start computing for the next iteration immediately. The thread missed one deadline and is already starting late for the next deadline. This sounds like a way to push the system from missing one deadline to total collapse, but if those deadlines are important, maybe it's a good strategy.

  This only makes even marginal sense for a thread where the deadline equals the period. If the deadline is less than the period, the thread that misses its deadline may be released for what it thinks is its next period before the next period starts. Consider the thread with a period of one second and a deadline of a tenth of a second. If it completes its computation two-tenths of a second after the start of a period, it is very late, but if it then starts on the next computation, it will be starting eight-tenths of a second early.

  Perhaps the desperate thread might try raising its priority when it detects a miss.

Feasibility and cost

The minimum implementation of the RTSJ can ignore cost and implement feasibility analysis by accepting any load as feasible. Programs designed for this class of Java platform are unlikely to migrate smoothly to a platform that implements overrun detection and feasibility analysis.

Consider, for instance, the examples of periodic threads without miss and overrun handlers. Those threads are barely adequate for the base RTSJ implantation because waitForNextPeriod returning false signifies a deadline miss. If it could also signify a cost overrun, The desperate citizen strategy is seriously flawed, and the good citizen strategy should include raising the cost estimate.

Feasibility Analysis

The class in Example 12–9 demonstrates two techniques. It is a periodic thread that sets its own release parameters, thus converting itself from an ordinary priority-scheduled thread to a periodic thread. Compare this with the way the thread in Example 12–7 is configured by its constructor. Example 12–9 also demonstrates the easiest way to cooperate with feasibility analysis. It creates the new ReleaseParameters object for itself, gets a reference to the Scheduler object, and invokes setReleaseParametersIfFeasible method on its thread object. This method atomically checks to see whether the new scheduling attributes are feasible and updates them if they are.

Example 12–9 Thread that configures its own periodic behavior

```
import javax.realtime.*;

public class MyThread2 extends RealtimeThread {
  volatile double f;
  public MyThread2(SchedulingParameters sched){
    super(sched);
  }

  private ReleaseParameters mkRelease(){
      return new PeriodicParameters(
        new RelativeTime(),//Start at .start()
        new RelativeTime(1000, 0), // 1 second period
        null,  //cost
        new RelativeTime(100,0),// deadline=period/10
        null,  // no overrun handler
        null); // no miss handler
  }

  public void run(){
```

Example 12–9 Thread that configures its own periodic behavior (Continued)

```
ReleaseParameters release = mkRelease();
RealtimeThread me = currentRealtimeThread();
Scheduler scheduler = getScheduler();
SchedulingParameters sched = getSchedulingParameters();
System.out.println(sched);

if(me.setReleaseParametersIfFeasible(release)){
  int bound = 0;
  int limit = 50;

  while(true){
    do {
      for(f=0.0; f < bound; f += 1.0);// Use some time
      bound += 10000;// Use more next time
      System.out.println("Ding! " + bound);
      if(--limit <= 0) return;
    } while(waitForNextPeriod());
    //Recover from miss or overrun
    System.out.println("Scheduling error");
      bound -= 15000;
    while(!waitForNextPeriod())//Eat errors
      System.out.print(".");
    System.out.println();
  }
} else
  System.out.println("Load is not feasible");

}
}
```

The `RealtimeThread` class provides two sets of methods to change scheduling parameters. One set of methods sets a parameter or set of parameters if the result is feasible; the other set alters the parameters without considering admission control. Table 12–4 compares the two sets.

The multiple-parameter `setIfFeasible` methods atomically set several parameters that need admission control. This avoids race conditions in which a thread might get different sets of resources depending on execution sequences.

There are other ways to update a thread's scheduling attributes, but they are not safe:

• If a thread tries to add itself to feasibility with new properties, it may be represented twice. That would be disastrous.

Table 12–4 Thread methods that change scheduling parameters

Respects Admission Control	Ignores Admission Control
`addIfFeasible`	`addToFeasibility`
`setIfFeasible` with several different collections of parameters	
`setMemoryParametersIfFeasible`	`setMemoryParameters`
`setProcessingGroupParametersIf Feasible`	`setProcessingGroupParameters`
`setReleaseParametersIfFeasible`	`setReleaseParameters`
`setSchedulingParametersIfFeasible`	`setSchedulingParameters`

- Remove the thread from the feasible set with `removeFromFeasibility`, and add it back in with its new attributes with `addIfFeasible`. If the thread is successfully admitted, all is well. If the thread is not admitted, it might be possible to get back into the feasible set with the original scheduling attributes, but some other thread might have grabbed the resources. This mechanism is acceptable if going back to the original attributes would not have been acceptable in any case.

> Use changeIfFeasible() to update scheduling parameters, release parameters, and memory parameters.

Periodic Threads with Handlers

Periodic threads without async event handlers for overruns and missed deadlines are operating with incomplete information or control. Without handlers, the RTSJ runtime just returns `false` from `waitForNextPeriod` and makes the thread ready to schedule again. With async event handlers, the scheduler starts the appropriate event handler and does not run the periodic thread again until it is instructed to do so, as shown in Example 12–10.

Example 12–11 is a simple example of an overrun handler. It is invoked when the scheduler detects that a thread has overrun the time it reserved. This handler is totally permissive about the overrun. It does not try to figure out why the thread used too much processor time. It just increases the thread's allowance and starts the thread running again.

Example 12–10 Starting a periodic thread with handlers

```
SchedulingParameters scheduling =
  new PriorityParameters(PriorityScheduler.MIN_PRIORITY+10);
ReleaseParameters release =
  new PeriodicParameters(
    new RelativeTime(),//Start at .start()
    new RelativeTime(1000, 0), // 1 second period
    null, // cost
    new RelativeTime(500,0),// deadline=period/2
    new OverrunHandler(),
    new MissHandler());

rt= new MyThread3(scheduling, release);
rt.start();
try {
  rt.join();
} catch(Exception e){};
```

Example 12–11 An adaptive overrun handler

```
public class OverrunHandler extends AsyncEventHandler{
  public void handleAsyncEvent(){
    System.out.println("Overrun");
    ReleaseParameters rp = rt.getReleaseParameters();
    RelativeTime cost = rp.getCost();
    rp.setCost(cost.add(1,0,cost));
    //  Mess with feasibility?
    rt.schedulePeriodic();
  }
}
```

The last statement in the handler, rt.schedulePeriodic, is the most important statement in the handler. Before the scheduler calls an overrun handler, it effectively calls deschedulePeriodic. It cannot return from waitForNextPeriod again until someone calls its schedulePeriodic method. That statement causes the scheduler to allow the thread to be scheduled at its next period.

This is just the skeleton of an adaptive overrun handler. A "real" one might do the following:

* Try to find what problem made the thread overrun its time reservation.

* Limit the amount it raises a thread's cost before it tries some other approach.

- Handle the case in which feasibility analysis rejects an increased cost for the thread.

Example 12–11 operates on the assumption that the periodic thread is fine. The scheduler should reserve it some more time and let it continue to run.

There are three other general approaches:

1. The load on the periodic thread is too heavy. The overrun handler should arrange to decrease the amount of work it has to do per period, then set it running again without changing its cost.

2. There was some transient problem. The overrun handler should ignore the problem and try to get the thread running again in time to meet its deadline.

3. The thread is in trouble. It may have a bug in it, and in any case there are other important things that need to be done. The overrun handler termi-nates the ailing thread (see Example 12–12 and Example 12–13). This proce-dure uses a mechanism called the asynchronously interrupted exception, which is covered in Chapter 17.

Example 12–12 Sudden death overrun handler

```
/**Define the AEH for overruns */
public static class OverrunHandler extends
    AsyncEventHandler {
  RealtimeThread th;

  public void setThread(RealtimeThread th){
    this.th = th;
  }

  OverrunHandler(){
    super(
      new PriorityParameters(
        PriorityScheduler.MIN_PRIORITY+11),
      null, null, null, null, null);
  }

  public void handleAsyncEvent(){
    System.out.println(
      "Zapping thread that's over budget");
    th.interrupt();//Throw an AIE into the thread
  }
}
```

Example 12-13 Periodic thread that interacts with the sudden death handler

```java
/**Define a RT thread that stops quickly in case
   of an AIE.
 */
public static class PeriodicThread
        extends RealtimeThread {
  volatile double f;
  public PeriodicThread(SchedulingParameters sched,
      ReleaseParameters release){
    super(sched, release);
  }

  public void run() {
    try {
      doWork();//call an interruptible method
    } catch (AsynchronouslyInterruptedException e){
      System.out.println("Thread dying");
      e.happened(true);//This isn't required
            //this time but it's a good habbit
    }
  }

  private void doWork() throws
      AsynchronouslyInterruptedException {
    int bound=0;

    while(true){
      do {
        // Use some time
        for(f=0.0; f < bound; f += 1.0);
        bound += 100000;// Use more next time
        System.out.println("Ding! " + bound);
      } while(waitForNextPeriod());
      //Recover from miss
      System.out.println("Scheduling error");
      bound -= 150000;//Lighten load
      while(!waitForNextPeriod())//Eat errors
        System.out.print(".");
      System.out.println();
    }
  }
}
  try {
    rt.join();//Wait for the thread to end
  } catch(Exception e){};
}
}
```

The scheduler can detect an overrun without waiting for the thread to call a scheduler function. If the scheduler has overrun detection and enforcement, it is likely to preempt the thread in the middle of some computation loop, make it nonschedulable for the rest of the period, and start the overrun handler. Unless the overrun handler sends the thread an asynchronously interrupted exception, the thread will resume execution in its next period when its CPU budget is replenished as if it had just been preempted by a higher-priority thread.

A deadline miss is similar to an overrun, and the supporting mechanism is identical. When the scheduler detects that the thread has missed its deadline, it makes the thread nonschedulable and fires its miss handler. The miss handler should take measures to deal with the missed deadline. If it wants the thread to resume execution, it should call the thread's schedulePeriodic method.

The most important consideration for a miss handler is the deadline that was missed:

- For the hardest class of real-time system, the deadline is absolute. There is no way to recover from missing the deadline and no point in trying to do better next time. Missing the deadline was a catastrophe and that is all! Since "the world has ended," there is little point in even building a miss handler for this class of system. For super-hard real-time systems like these, there is little reason to even build a miss handler.

- For many systems missing a deadline is bad, but not such a disaster that it is not worth trying to recover from and maybe prevent a recurrence.

Handlers may lead to ungraceful degradation

Miss and overrun handlers have a cost. They execute for some interval at a time when the system is already under stress. A well-designed overrun or miss handler will complete as quickly as possible. If it has more than a little work to do, it should try to divide the work into a small part that runs in the handler and a larger part that runs in another lower-priority handler or under the supervision of a server.

Missed deadline recoveries are completely application specific, but they fall into the broad classes: junk it, fix it, or apologize. A miss handler might relock database records for which the locks have expired. It might cause an assembly line to discard a part that was damaged because of the missed deadline. It might invoke missing packet routines for streaming media. It might dump some material out of a chemical reactor and start a new flow of ingredients to correct the balance of reagents. It might just display an apologetic message for the operator or log the failure.

After the miss handler worries about the missed deadline, it should concern itself with the thread. First, it might see whether any thread suffered an overrun during this period. If one did, the thread with the overrun is a good place to start looking for a way to prevent the deadline from being missed again.

Finally, the miss handler should decide on the disposition of the thread. It can choose among several strategies:

1. Get the thread executing again as soon as possible by calling `schedulePeriodic` and returning from the miss handler. This may be a good strategy for systems in which the consequences of seriously missing a deadline are worse than the consequences of barely missing it. The problem with this strategy is that the scheduler did not count on any thread continuing to execute after its deadline. The time used to complete this computation may cause the system to miss other deadlines.

2. Send the thread an asynchronously interrupted exception that causes it to abort the current computation, then use `schedulePeriodic` to reschedule it for the next period. This is a good strategy for systems in which a late result is worthless. By aborting the computation that is now too late, the miss handler minimizes the system degradation caused by the miss.

3. If the deadline is not equal to the period, get it out of the way of other threads during the time it would normally be waiting, set a field that is visible to the thread to tell it that it missed a deadline, and then let it resume where it left off.

    ```
    Increment a field to tell the thread it missed a deadline.
    Reduce thread priority.
    SchedulePeriodic for the thread.
    Sleep until the next period start.
    Restore thread priority.
    ```

    If the missed deadline count is greater than 0, the thread needs to decrement it and skip `waitForNextPeriod`.

    This approach will let the thread complete the computation for the missed deadline as the first part of its computation for the next period. This strategy makes no special effort to reduce the computations involved in completion of the late work, and it adds load to the next period. The additional load may cause the thread that misses one deadline to miss many deadlines in sequence as work keeps being deferred from one period to another. This is a strategy for deadlines that are more like recommendations. Its great advantage is that it largely prevents problems with one thread from impacting the performance of other threads.

The passive approach to miss handling uses a deadline miss handler that deals with the consequences of the miss, then just releases the periodic thread, as shown in Example 12–14. It does not do anything to prevent the thread from missing again.

Example 12–14 Passive miss handler

```
import javax.realtime.*;

/**Demonstrate a sudden-death overrun handler */
public class PassiveMissHdlr {
  /**Define the passive AEH for Misses */
  public static class MissHdlr extends
      AsyncEventHandler {
    RealtimeThread th;

    public void setThread(RealtimeThread th){
      this.th = th;
    }

    MissHdlr(){
      super(
        new PriorityParameters(
          PriorityScheduler.MIN_PRIORITY+11),
        null, null, null, null, null);
    }

    public void handleAsyncEvent(){
      //First interact with whatever is bothered
      //by us missing the deadline,

      //then deal with the thread that missed
      System.out.println("Recovering from a miss");
      th.schedulePeriodic();//Let the thread continue
    }
  }

  /**Define a simple periodic RT thread */
  public static class PeriodicThread extends RealtimeThread {
    volatile double f;
    public PeriodicThread(SchedulingParameters sched,
        ReleaseParameters release){
      super(sched, release);
    }
```

Example 12–14 Passive miss handler (Continued)

```java
  public void run() {
    int bound = 0;

    for(int ctr = 0; ctr < 25; ++ctr){
      do {
        for(f=0.0; f < bound; f += 1.0);// Use some time
        bound += 100000; // Use more next time
        System.out.println("Ding! " + bound);
      } while(waitForNextPeriod());
      //Recover from miss
      System.out.println("Scheduling error");
        bound -= 150000;
      while(!waitForNextPeriod())//Eat errors
        System.out.print(".");
      System.out.println();
    }
  }
}

  public static void main(String [] args){
    //Build parameters for construction
    //of RT thread
    MissHdlr missHdlr = new MissHdlr();
    ReleaseParameters release =
      new PeriodicParameters(
        new RelativeTime(),//Start at .start()
        new RelativeTime(1000, 0), // 1 second period
        null,  //cost
        new RelativeTime(500,0),// deadline=period/2
        null,  // no overrun handler
        missHdlr);// miss handler
    SchedulingParameters scheduling =
      new PriorityParameters(
        PriorityScheduler.MIN_PRIORITY+10);

    RealtimeThread rt= new PeriodicThread(scheduling,
        release);
    //Give the miss handler a reference to
    //the thread it is managing.
    missHdlr.setThread(rt);

    rt.start();//Start the periodic thread
```

An aggressive miss handler needs to have a reference to the thread it is managing so it can call schedulePeriodic on the thread, and it needs a reference for an AIE that it can fire at the thread. Example 12–15 requires the application to pass those values to the AIE after the periodic thread is started.

Example 12–15 Event handler for aggressive miss handling

```
/**Define the AEH for overruns */
public static class MissHdlr extends
    AsyncEventHandler {
  AsynchronouslyInterruptedException aie;
  RealtimeThread rtt;

  public void setAIE(
      AsynchronouslyInterruptedException aie){
    this.aie = aie;
  }

  public void setThread(RealtimeThread rtt){
    this.rtt = rtt;
  }

  MissHdlr(){
    super(
      new PriorityParameters(
        PriorityScheduler.MIN_PRIORITY+11),
      null, null, null, null, null);
  }

  public void handleAsyncEvent(){
    //First manage the consequences of missing
    //the deadline
    //...

    System.out.println("Zapping missed computation");
    //Let the target thread go in case it is
    //stuck in waitForNextPeriod()
    rtt.schedulePeriodic();
    if(!aie.fire())//Throw an AIE into the thread
      System.out.println("Fire returned false");
  }
}
```

The constructor for the miss handler gives this event handler higher priority than the thread it is controlling. (Yes, it would be better code if it didn't hard-code the literal value of the priority as it does.)

The `handleAsyncEvent` method is the active part of the AEH. It contains a comment to represent the code that would try to ameliorate the damage caused by the missed deadline, then it makes the target thread schedulable in case the scheduler has already stopped it, and fires an async interrupt at it.

Except for a little setup work, the body of this periodic thread is enclosed in a `doInterruptible` closure.

The thread in Example 12–16 finds its miss handler (in its release parameters) and passes a reference to itself and its AIE to the miss handler. The miss handler will use those values to shake this thread loose from the scheduler and throw an exception that will cause the `Interruptible` object to return immediately.

Example 12–16 is the aggressive approach to a missed deadline. "Stop doing the thing that missed its deadline."

The bulk of the periodic thread activity is in the `Interruptible` class shown in Example 12–17.

Example 12–16 Periodic thread for aggressive miss handling

```
public static class PeriodicThread
    extends RealtimeThread {
  volatile MissHdlr missHdlr;

  /** Constructor */
  public PeriodicThread(SchedulingParameters sched,
      ReleaseParameters release){
    super(sched, release);
    missHdlr = (MissHdlr)release.
        getDeadlineMissHandler();
  }

  /**Run method for the PeriodicThread */
  public void run() {
    AsynchronouslyInterruptedException aie =
      new AsynchronouslyInterruptedException();

    //Tell the miss handler about our AIE

    aie.doInterruptible(new MyInterruptible());
  }
}
```

Example 12-17 Interruptible class for aggressive miss handling

```
/**This class is the executable body of the periodic
   thread phrased as an Interruptible so it can be
   used with doInterruptible.
*/
public static class MyInterruptible
     implements Interruptible {
   public void run(
       AsynchronouslyInterruptedException  e)
     throws
       AsynchronouslyInterruptedException {
     int bound=0;
     double f;
     int ct = 0;
     RealtimeThread rtt =
       RealtimeThread.currentRealtimeThread();

     while(true){
       do {
         if(++ct > 20) return;
         for(f=0.0; f < bound; f += 1.0);
         bound += 100000;
         System.out.println("Ding! " + bound);
         try{
           Thread.sleep(1);
         } catch(Exception ie){
         }
       } while(rtt.waitForNextPeriod());
       //Recover from overrun
       //Miss never gets here because
       //it causes an AIE
       System.out.println("Overrun");
       bound -= 150000;
       while(!rtt.waitForNextPeriod())
         //Eat errors
         System.out.print(".");
       System.out.println();
     }
   }

   public void interruptAction(
       AsynchronouslyInterruptedException e){
     //Recover from missing the deadline
     System.out.println("Recovering.");
   }
}
```

It is the normal form for a periodic thread except for these two caveats:

- The main loop does not expect to handle deadline misses.
- The class has an `interruptAction` method that can share the job of recovering from the deadline miss with the miss handler

Interactions with Normal Threads

The `RealtimeThread` class is designed to work with threads from the `Thread` class, but the accommodation is somewhat one-sided. Ordinary threads can run without modification in a system containing real-time threads. Real-time threads that interact with ordinary threads will suffer performance problems unless they take special care to decouple themselves from the performance of non-real-time threads.

Ordinary threads have a far more limited range of priorities than do real-time threads, but the RTSJ requires priority boosting to operate on them. This means that an ordinary thread may find itself with a priority that is not conformant with the JLS. That should not ordinarily be a problem, but it is a small deviation from the RTSJ's intention to have no impact on ordinary threads.

Real-time threads do everything ordinary threads do, and they provide good real-time behavior. New code for a real-time system should be written to use real-time threads even if the task has no real-time requirements. That way, if they interact with a real-time thread, they will be well behaved in the real-time sense.

Four strategies can migrate a system with a large bulk of legacy Java code to a Java platform that implements the RTSJ:

1. Ignore the real-time facilities. Some of the strengths of the real-time environment may leak through even though the RTSJ does not require any change in the behavior of ordinary threads.

2. Use real-time threads for tasks with real-time requirements. Don't change the legacy code at all. The new real-time code must identify every place it might be blocked by a non-real-time thread. At these points it must consider the possible effect of boosting a non-real-time thread into the real-time range.

3. Use real-time threads for tasks with real-time requirements, and don't change the legacy code. Identify and avoid every place a real-time thread might be blocked by a non-real-time thread. This strategy is a prescription for two systems in one Java runtime. The real-time and non-real-time subsystems do not touch except for minor preemption delays and other overheads in the Java runtime and the supporting operating system.

4. Convert all the legacy threads to real-time threads. If the legacy code was portable across the range of non-real-time Java runtimes, it should run in real-time threads. Even though the legacy code will never intentionally use any of the features of the real-time threads, they and all the other threads in the system will get the performance and scheduling guarantees of real-time threads.

Nonblocking message queues (see Chapter 20) are designed for communication between different levels of real-time support: between real-time and non-real-time threads and between no-heap real-time threads (see Chapter 14) and anything else. They support limited interaction between threads without risking blocking or invoking a priority inversion avoidance protocol.

Changing the Scheduler

Today (2002) priority schedulers are the norm for real-time systems. A periodic scheduler with a notion of deadlines and feasibility might be tacked on the side, but even that much diversion from straight priority scheduling would be unusual. The scheduler situation is actually even less real-time than that. The RTSJ has taken criticism because its fairly strict definition of a fixed-priority preemptive scheduler is challenging for some "real-time operating systems," and very challenging for some operating systems that usually do not make claims about real-time performance.

Given a goal of being implementable under every operating system or kernel that makes a reasonable claim of supporting real-time computing, the RTSJ requires as much as it can: a fixed-priority preemptive scheduler with 28 priorities (plus the 10 loosely defined priorities of the regular Java specification) and a periodic scheduling system that can be superimposed on that priority scheduler. If the RTSJ required a deadline scheduler, its implementation would require kernel work on any of the popular real-time platforms (such as VxWorks, OS-9, QNX, Neutrino, LynxOS, PSOS, and Linux). Instead, the RTSJ has scheduler APIs that are designed to accommodate dynamic priority scheduling algorithms. It even makes an effort to anticipate scheduling paradigms that are unlike anything known today. The goal was to let OS/JVM vendors build new schedulers and make them accessible through the RTSJ APIs.

Unfortunately, the RTSJ does not attempt to expose the interfaces that would let a programmer create a new scheduler. That is a job for someone with access to the internals of the JVM and the supporting system software.

The JVM always starts with the default fixed-priority preemptive scheduler active, but any thread (subject to Java security restrictions) can change the scheduler.

A special scheduler might be on the default class path, or you might know the full path and class name for the scheduler, but the general way to find a new scheduler is through the system properties, as shown in Example 12–18.

Example 12–18 Finding a scheduler through system properties

```
public static Scheduler findScheduler(String policy){
    String key = "javax.realtime.scheduler." + policy;
    String className = System.getProperty(key);

    if(className == null)
        // No system property for this scheduling policy
        return null;

    Class schedClass;
    try {
        schedClass = Class.forName(className);
        if(schedClass == null)
            // The scheduler class was not found
            return null;
        else {
            // Get a reference for the scheduler's
            // instance() method. (with no parameters)
            Method instance =
                schedClass.getMethod("instance", null);
            return (Scheduler)instance.invoke(null, null);
        }
}
```

The instance method in Scheduler is static, so it doesn't need an object parameter, and it takes no args, so the parameters for instance.invoke are null, null.

The instance method in Scheduler will return a reference to a singleton instance of that class.

The try clause around the code that (a) finds the Scheduler class, (b) finds the instance method in it, and (c) invokes the instance method can throw a large collection of exceptions. Most of them are various ways of saying that the class isn't there, you cannot see it, or it is not the sort of class you expected. For all of those, return null.

The security exception is probably interesting to the caller, so the catch clause rethrows that.

```
    } catch (ClassNotFoundException nF){
        // Thrown by forName()
        return null;
```

```
      } catch (NoSuchMethodException nS) {
          //   Thrown by getMethod.
          //   This is a sign of a mal-formed Scheduler class
          return null;
      } catch (SecurityException security) {
          //   This is a runtime exception.
          //   It is thrown by the security manager, perhaps
          //   when it checked for our authority to load a
          //   class.
          throw security;
      } catch (IllegalAccessException access){
          //   Thrown by forName method if the scheduler
          //   class is not public, or by invoke() if the
          //   method is inaccessible (which it should be.)
          return null;
      } catch (IllegalArgumentException arg) {
          //   Since we don't pass arguments, and the
          //   instance() method does not expect arguments
          //   we should never get here.
          return null;
      } catch (InvocationTargetException target) {
          //   Some exception was thrown by instance().
          //   That exception is wrapped by target.
          //   instance() doesn't throw any checked exceptions
          //   so we should never get here.
          return null;
      }
  }
}
```

After finding a scheduling class, we need to tell a thread to place itself under the supervision of that scheduler, as in Example 12–19.

If you happen to have a scheduler with the policy name LLaxity installed in your system, the code snippet in Example 12–19 does the following:

1. Uses the findScheduler method from Example 12–18 to find the class, loads it, and gets a reference to the singleton instance of the least laxity scheduler.

2. If the code found a least-laxity scheduler, it creates a thread with periodic parameters (which least laxity schedulers can use).

3. Uses the setScheduler method on the real-time thread to change its scheduler from the system default to least laxity.

4. Starts the thread.

The above protocol changes the scheduler for a thread, and the static setDefaultScheduler method can change the default scheduler for all real-time threads created after the default is changed.

Example 12–19 Changing the scheduler for a thread

```
Scheduler scheduler = FindScheduler.findScheduler("LLaxity");
if(scheduler == null){
  System.out.println("No least laxity scheduler was found");
} else {
  RealtimeThread rtt = new RealtimeThread(
    null,        //Default sceduling Parameters
    new PeriodicParameters(
      null,        // Begin running at start()
      new RelativeTime(250, 0),//Period is 1/4 sec
      new RelativeTime(25, 0), //Cost is 1/40 sec
      new RelativeTime(200, 0),//Deadline is 1/5 sec
      null,          //No overrun handler
      null),         //No miss handler
    null,        //Default memory parameters
    null,        //Default memory area
    null,        //Default processing group
    new Runnable (){//Logic
      public void run() {
        System.out.println("Running least laxity");
      }
    });
  rtt.setScheduler(scheduler);
  rtt.start();
```

There are some unresolved issues about pluggable schedulers, and they will stay unresolved until an actual alternative scheduler is available.

The new scheduler must document how it will interact with other schedulers. It might be able to coexist with the standard priority scheduler or with other schedulers, or it might be disrupted by any threads that are not under its control. An alternate scheduler might be able to take control of a live thread, or it might insist on becoming the scheduler for a thread before it starts.

The alternate scheduler might be as simple as a scheduler that subclasses the standard priority scheduler and adds feasibility analysis to a scheduler that provides promiscuous feasibility analysis.

The final example in this chapter is a simple version of the preceding scheduler. It is a class that extends the trivial admission control in the reference implementation's scheduler to add very simple feasibility analysis. To keep the example simple, the scheduler in Example 12–20 naively assumes that the caller would never try to add a thread or async event handler more than once to feasibility analysis, would never change the attributes of a schedulable that was not already added, or would never remove a schedulable from feasibility analysis if it was not there.

It is easy to write new `Scheduler` classes to provide different admission control policies, but remember that the scheduler does much more than admission control. It has hidden functions, many of them probably implemented as part of the JVM or the underlying operating system. Example 12–20 avoids *real* scheduling by just extending an existing scheduler.

The synchronization of the methods in the class that manipulates the utilization is important. It keeps changes to the utilization instance variable atomic. It also locks the instance for the duration of the `changeIfFeasable` method. This prevents race conditions on manipulation of utilization.

Example 12–20 Alternate scheduler class

```
import javax.realtime.*;
/**
 * Extend an RTSJ default priority scheduler with
 * admission control/feasibility services.
 */
public class FPriorityScheduler extends PriorityScheduler{

    private double utilization = 0;
    private final static String policy =
     "PriortySchedulerWithFeasibility";
    private static FPriorityScheduler me = null;

   /**The only constructor for this class is private.
    * To get an instance of FPriorityScheduler use the
    * instance method
    */
    private FPriorityScheduler(){
        super.instance();
    }


   /**
    * Add a schedulable (thread or AEH) to the feasible set.
    *
    * Warning, this method will happily add the same thread to the
    * feasible set many times.
    *
    * Note, this class only tracks the total CPU consumption
    * of all registered schedulable entities.
    *
```

Example 12–20   Alternate scheduler class (Continued)

```
 * @param s The schedulable (rt thread or AEH) to add to
     * the feasible set.
     */
    protected synchronized void addToFeasibility(Schedulable s){
        if(!check(s))
            return;
        PeriodicParameters param = (PeriodicParameters)
                s.getReleaseParameters();
        RelativeTime cost = param.getCost();
        if (cost == null)
            cost = param.getDeadline();
        utilization += calcUtilization(cost, param.getPeriod());
    }

  /** Calculate the CPU utilization given cost and period.
   * @param costthe cost of a schedulable
   *   @param period the period of the schedulable
   *   @return the CPU utilization for this schedulable
   */
   private double calcUtilization(RelativeTime cost,
                              RelativeTime period){
        double costMicros = (cost.getMilliseconds() * 1000.0) +
                        (cost.getNanoseconds() / 1000.0);
        double periodMicros = (period.getMilliseconds() * 1000.0) +
                        (period.getNanoseconds() / 1000.0);
        return costMicros / periodMicros;
    }

  /** Check a Schedulable's eligibility for admission control
   * @param sThe Schedulable to test
   *   @returnTrue if the schedulable is eligible
   */
   private boolean check(Schedulable s){
        if(s.getReleaseParameters() instanceof
PeriodicParameters){
            PeriodicParameters param = (PeriodicParameters)
                    s.getReleaseParameters();
            if(!positive(param.getPeriod())) throw new
                IllegalArgumentException("period <= 0");
            if( param.getCost() == null &&
            param.getDeadline() == null)
          return false;
            return true;
        } else
            return false;
    }
```

Example 12–20 Alternate scheduler class (Continued)

```java
/**
    * Return the name of the policy this scheduler implements.
    *
    * @return The name of this policy
    *         "Priority Scheduler with Feasibility"
    */

   public java.lang.String getPolicyName(){
       return policy;
   }
   /**
    * Return a reference to the singleton instance of this class.
    * If the class has not yet been instanciated, construct it.
    *
    * @return A reference to an instance of class
    *         FPriorityScheduler
    */

   public static PriorityScheduler instance() {
       if(me == null)
           me = new FPriorityScheduler();
       return me;
   }
   /**
    * Return true if the set of schedulables that have been through
    * addToFeasible, but not removeFromFeasible do not use more
    * than 100% of CPU time
    *
    * @return True if the load is feasible, false otherwise
    */

   public boolean isFeasible(){
       return utilization <= 1.0;
   }

   /**
    * Change the scheduling attributes of the specified
    * schedulable.
    *
    *
    * WARNING: This method assumes that the schedulable entity is
    * already feasible
    *
    * @param schedulable A reference to a rt thread or AEH that
    *         should be changed
```

Example 12–20 Alternate scheduler class (Continued)

```
 * @param release The release parameters that should be
 *         tested for feasibility
 * @param memory The memory parameters that should be
 *         tested for feasibility
 * @return true if the change is feasible, false otherwise
 */
public synchronized boolean changeIfFeasible(
                Schedulable schedulable,
                ReleaseParameters release,
                MemoryParameters memory){
    RelativeTime cost;
    double oldUtil;
    double newUtil;
    if(!check(schedulable)) //  Check schedulable's attributes
        return false;   //  Don't add ill-formed schedulables
    if(release instanceof PeriodicParameters){
        PeriodicParameters param = (PeriodicParameters)
                schedulable.getReleaseParameters();
        cost = param.getCost();
        if (cost == null)
            cost = param.getDeadline();
        oldUtil = calcUtilization(cost, param.getPeriod());
        param = (PeriodicParameters)release;
        if(!positive(param.getPeriod())) throw new
            IllegalArgumentException("period <= 0");

        cost = param.getCost();
        if(cost == null)
            cost = param.getDeadline();
        newUtil = calcUtilization(cost, param.getPeriod());
        if(utilization + newUtil - oldUtil <= 1.0){
            utilization += (newUtil - oldUtil);
            return true;
        } else
            return false;
    } else { // Not PeriodicParameters
        throw new
            IllegalArgumentException(
                    "release must be periodic");
    }
}
```

Example 12-20 Alternate scheduler class (Continued)

```
/**
 * Remove the specified schedulable entity from
 * feasibility analysis.
 *
 * WARNING: This method does not check that the schedulable is
 * current in the feasible set.
 *
 * @param s A reference to a schedulable entity
 */
protected synchronized void removeFromFeasibility(
   Schedulable s){
     if(!check(s))
        return;
     PeriodicParameters param = (PeriodicParameters)
           s.getReleaseParameters();
     RelativeTime cost = param.getCost();
     if (cost == null)
        cost = param.getDeadline();
     utilization -= calcUtilization(cost, param.getPeriod());
}

/** Test for relative time greater than 0
 *@param t RelativeTime value
 *@return true iff time > 0
 */

private boolean positive(RelativeTime t){
   if(t.getMilliseconds() == 0)
     return t.getNanoseconds() > 0;
   else
     return t.getMilliseconds() > 0;
}

/** main method to test this class */
static public void main(String [] args){
   //**start**
   RealtimeThread rtt = new RealtimeThread(
     null,       //Default scheduling Parameters
     new PeriodicParameters(
        null,       // Begin running at start()
        new RelativeTime(250, 0),//Period is 1/4 sec
        new RelativeTime(25, 0), //Cost is 1/40 sec
        new RelativeTime(200, 0),//Deadline is 1/5 sec
        null,            //No overrun handler
        null),           //No miss handler
```

Example 12–20 Alternate scheduler class (Continued)

```
      null,       //Default memory parameters
      null,       //Default memory area
      null,       //Default processing group
      new Runnable (){//Logic
        public void run() {
          System.out.println("Running " +
            RealtimeThread.currentRealtimeThread().
              getScheduler().getPolicyName());
        }
      });
    rtt.setScheduler(FPriorityScheduler.instance());
    rtt.start();
    try{
      rtt.join();
    } catch(Exception e) {}
  }
}
```

Chapter 13

Non-Heap Memory

Garbage collection is terrible for real-time systems. Most garbage collectors cause the system to stop and collect garbage at hard-to-predict intervals. Others have other bad habits. Someone may come up with a completely satisfactory technique for real-time garbage collection, but the Real Time Java Expert Group went with the conservative engineering approach and did not call for magical real-time garbage collection. Instead, the RTSJ depends on two observations: code that does not create garbage will not cause "demand" garbage collection, and code that does not reference objects in the heap can preempt the garbage collector with no regard for normal garbage collector preemption issues.

Allocation of objects that are not garbage collected is the topic of this chapter. Threads that permit instant preemption of the garbage collector because they avoid objects that are subject to garbage collection are covered in Chapter 14.

The Advantage of Non-Heap Memory

No competent JVM would let background garbage collection interrupt an application thread. Only demand garbage collection, which takes place when new cannot find enough memory, might run while application threads are ready to run.

A Java application will avoid garbage collection delays in its real-time section if background garbage collection is disabled and if the application is structured to complete all object creation from the heap before it starts running real-time code. That goes a long way toward giving the application real-time performance, and it can be done on any JVM, but it is awkward. The Java language is not designed to work well without creating objects. The RTSJ's non-heap memory classes can be a little tricky to use, but they let programmers control garbage collection delays by allocating objects without using the heap.

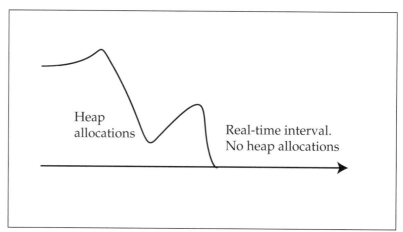

Heap allocations

Real-time interval.
No heap allocations

Figure 13–1 Execution with a real-time phase

The Allocation Regimes

The RTSJ defines two new types of memory that are free from garbage collection:

- Immortal memory—Contains objects that will never be garbage collected or defragmented (or freed.) The RTSJ platform uses immortal memory for various objects, and immortal memory is also shared among all threads. The only disadvantage of immortal memory is that objects in it are immortal. It should be used only for objects that actually are immortal—that will remain in use until the JVM terminates.

- Scoped memory—Has a defined lifetime. Objects allocated from a memory scope will stay allocated until the scope is no longer active. At that time, all the objects in the scope can be freed.

And the RTSJ continues support for the normal types of Java memory:

- Heap memory — Garbage-collected at essentially unpredictable intervals. The runtime environment guarantees that heap memory will never free an object until it can no longer be reached. The heap may also be compacted from time to time. This process moves objects around to coalesce free memory.

- Local variables — Allocated when control enters a method and freed when control leaves the method. The Java programming language does not allow objects to be stored in this type of memory.

During intervals when a thread allocates only from immortal and scoped memory, it will not cause demand garbage collection. This greatly reduces the impact of garbage collection on that thread, as outlined below:

- The thread may be delayed while demand garbage collection caused by a lower-priority thread is preempted. The worst-case value for this preemption delay is available from the garbage collector:

  ```
  RealtimeSystem.currentGC().getPreemptionLatency()
  ```

- If the thread waits for a lock held by a thread that is currently executing demand garbage collection, the normal priority boosting algorithm will operate, but nevertheless the garbage collection will complete before the lock is released.

- Any higher-priority thread that is executing demand garbage collection or that is blocked by a thread executing demand garbage collection will affect the execution of lower-priority threads.

- If the threads are under the control of a dynamic priority scheduler, interactions between threads will be documented for that particular scheduler, but the impact of garbage collection on a thread that does not allocate from the heap will be limited.

Combining the disciplined scheduling of real-time threads with non-heap allocation domains gives sufficiently deterministic execution to meet the needs of many real-time applications.

Rules

The JVM has to enforce certain rules to keep the new types of memory from breaking the garbage collector's commitment not to leave bad pointers. The underlying rule is that a reference variable cannot contain a reference to an object that can be freed before the reference variable. This rule is enforced by the JVM. Table 13–1 summarizes the assignment rules.

Table 13–1 Assignment rules

	Reference to Heap	Reference to Immortal	Reference to Scoped
Heap	Yes	Yes	No
Immortal	Yes	Yes	No
Scoped	Yes	Yes	"Available" scopes
Local variable	Yes	Yes	"Available" scopes

If it must, the JVM can enforce the assignment rules when it executes the byte-code instructions that store object references, but since that enforcement slows execution of the JVM, a quality implementation, when it loads a class, will make every effort to verify that each operation which stores a reference abides by the assignment rules; or perhaps a trusted compiler could verify the correctness of many assignments. If the Java runtime catches an assignment that violates a rule in Table 13–1, it throws an `IllegalAssignmentError`.

Table 13–1 shows that the RTSJ permits references to objects in heap or immortal memory to be stored in any class of memory. The garbage collector ensures that objects in the heap always survive at least as long as references to those objects. Since objects in immortal memory last as long as the application, no reference to an object in immortal memory will ever become invalid.

References to scoped memory are not always permitted. Objects in immortal memory or the heap can *never* point to objects in a scope. Objects in a scope are freed when the scope is no longer active. If an object in the heap or in immortal memory contained a reference to an object in a scope, that reference would become invalid and one of the Java environment's basic guarantees would be violated.

A scope can always contain objects with references that refer to other objects in that scope. The lifetime of those objects is the same, so references between them are always safe. Objects in scopes can also contain references to other scopes that the JVM knows will have a lifetime at least as long as the reference. This is discussed in more depth in "Mechanisms for Allocating from Scoped Memory" on page 184.

References to objects are a primitive data type in the Java language and can be stored in local variables. Local variables can hold references to objects in a scope that the JVM knows will live longer than the references.

> **Assignment rules cannot be fully enforced by the compiler. Some violations must be detected at runtime.**

Mechanisms for Allocating Immortal Memory

The RTSJ supports five mechanisms for allocating objects in immortal memory:

- **implicit.** The Java runtime environment may determine that an object must be unexceptionally referenceable from anywhere. It turns out that only immortal memory meets that requirement. A high-quality implementation of the RTSJ may employ a "trick"—like memory objects that are supervised by a special reference-counting garbage collector—to handle some of these objects, but they must behave as if they were immortal.

- **newInstance.** Any thread can get a reference to the immortal memory object and use its `newInstance` methods to allocate memory. This is a good technique for code that wants to allocate just one immortal object. It may be the best technique for all immortal allocation since it is a bit long-winded and makes it perfectly clear that a particular allocation is from immortal memory

  In Example 13–1, immortal memory's `newInstance` method is used to create an exception object in immortal memory.

Example 13–1 Creating an immortal object using newInstance

```
try{
   e = (IllegalArgumentException)
     ImmortalMemory.instance().newInstance(
       IllegalArgumentException.class);
} catch (IllegalAccessException access) {
   System.out.println(access);
} catch (InstantiationException instant){
   System.out.println(instant);
}
```

The form of `newInstance` method in Example 13–1 is used with no-arg constructors for the objects it creates. For objects that can be created and then configured, this limitation is at worst an inconvenience. Another form of `newInstance` uses reflection and can use constructors that have arguments, as coded in Example 13–2.

Example 13–2 Creating an object by using newInstance and reflection

```
try{
  Class [] paramTypes = new Class[1];
  paramTypes[0] = Class.forName("java.lang.String");
  Class cType = Class.forName("java.lang.Integer");
  Constructor constructor = cType.getConstructor(paramTypes);
  Object [] params = new Object[1];
  params[0] = new String("314159");
  n = (Integer)ImmortalMemory.instance().newInstance(
    constructor, params);

} catch (IllegalAccessException access) {
  System.out.println(access);
} catch (InstantiationException instant){
  System.out.println(instant);
} catch (ClassNotFoundException cnf){
  System.out.println(cnf);
} catch (NoSuchMethodException nsm) {
  System.out.println(nsm);
}
```

- **newArray.** This method allocates an array of objects, as shown in Example 13–3. It accepts the type of object that will populate the array, but it does not allocate the members.

Example 13–3 Creating an array of objects with newArray

```
try{
  aeh =  (AsyncEventHandler [])
    ImmortalMemory.instance().newArray(
      AsyncEventHandler.class, 10);
} catch (IllegalAccessException access) {
  System.out.println(access);
} catch (InstantiationException instant){
  System.out.println(instant);
}
```

- **enter.** The enter method of the immortal memory object lets a thread temporarily make immortal memory the default for all its allocation, as shown in Example 13–4.

The new exception created in the run method and assigned to e is immortal.

Example 13–4 Creating an immortal object with enter

```
ImmortalMemory.instance().enter(
  new Runnable() {
    public void run(){
      //In this scope immortal is the default for
      //memory allocation
      o = new Object();//This Object is immortal
    }
  }
);
```

Specifying a new default memory allocation area is one of the primary uses of the *closure* concept introduced in Chapter 9. You can see how a new kind of bracketing would have been a nice way to define a section of code that should use immortal memory, but the closure is almost as easy to read and it did not require language changes.

- **New thread.** A real-time thread's initial default memory allocation area can be specified when the thread is constructed. If `ImmortalMemory.instance` is used as the area parameter to the `RealtimeThread` or `NoHeapRealtimeThread` class (see Example 13–5), that thread will make all allocations from immortal memory unless the thread uses `newInstance` or `enter` to allocate memory from a different area.

Example 13–5 Creating a thread that will default to immortal memory

```
Runnable logic = new Runnable(){
  Object  o;
  public void run() {
    o = new Object();
  }
};

RealtimeThread rt= new RealtimeThread(null, null, null,
    // This starts the thread in immortal
    ImmortalMemory.instance(),
    null, logic);
rt.start();
```

- **executeInArea.** This method is called like `enter` and works similarly, but it has a different interaction with the way other memory scopes can be entered. (See "Using executeInArea" on page 202.)

In most cases, objects in immortal memory should be allocated when an application is initialized. If an application creates objects in immortal memory as it runs, it is difficult to know in advance just how much immortal memory will be required to run the application. The likely consequence is that the application will run out of immortal memory and die.

Ideally, the design of an application should include a list of the objects that must reside in immortal memory. These can be created when an application is initializing itself, and programmers can subsequently forget that there is any way to create immortal objects. Unfortunately, immortal objects are extremely convenient. It is most likely that developers will frequently discover "one more" object that should be in immortal memory. When possible, these new additions to immortal memory should be added to the set that is created at initialization time, not allocated as they are needed.

Mechanisms for Allocating from Scoped Memory

Scoped memory might be called "temporary immortal" memory. It is never garbage collected, but it has a limited lifetime—as long as any thread has access to it. The four types of scoped memory are summarized in Table 13–2:

Table 13–2 Types of scoped memory

Allocation Time	Name
Linear	LTMemory
Linear	LTPhysicalMemory
Variable	VTMemory
Variable	VTPhysicalMemory

Chapter 18 shows how memory can be allocated from particular areas of physical memory. Physical memory is mentioned in Table 13–2, but for the purposes of this chapter, it is equivalent to its nonphysical analog.

Allocation Time

Since objects in scoped memory are all freed together, the algorithm for allocation can be simple.

Algorithm 13–1 is a constant time algorithm, and a fast one. It is approximately the algorithm you will usually find supporting the LTMemory class. The class is called LTMemory (representing linear time allocation memory) instead of CTMemory (for constant time allocation memory) because after the memory for an object is allocated, the JVM is required to initialize the object. At a minimum, the object is initialized to constant values, so the total time to allocate the object is the constant time to get the memory plus an amount of time that depends on the size of the object (or is *linear* in the size of the object) to initialize it. Thus, it is called linear time memory. Since the worst-case time to create an object cannot be faster than some constant times the size of the object, the constant time memory allocation algorithm in Algorithm 13–1 could be replaced with anything up to an algorithm that takes time proportional to the size of the object being allocated.

Algorithm 13–1. Constant-time allocation pseudocode

```
static long * nextPtr;
static long * endPtr;

long * ctAllocate(const int longs){
  nextPtr += longs;
  if(nextPtr > endPtr)
    return null; // Out of memory
  else
    return nextPtr;
}
```

If an implementer can think of some clever way to use the extra time, the RTSJ permits such use.

> A possible class of advanced memory allocation algorithm for LTMemory would let the memory area span several extents. That would make the area easier to allocate in a system with fragmented memory and expanding the memory area if it overflowed would also be easier. In the worst case, the memory allocator would have to attempt allocation from each extent. That would make allocation time depend on the number of extents.
>
> The allocation algorithm could afford to check a number of extents—a fixed multiple of the number of bytes it was asked to allocate—before the cost of finding memory would dominate the cost of initializing memory.

The time it takes to create an object in LTMemory is easily predictable (and will always be nearly the same unless the implementation gets very fancy), and although a new from LTMemory will fail if that memory area is exhausted, allocation from LTMemory will *never* provoke garbage collection. These properties make LTMemory an attractive place to allocate new objects when predictable performance is an issue.

VTMemory is permitted to take any amount of time. This allows the RTSJ implementation to use any algorithm to manage the free memory. The implementation might choose to use this freedom to support VTMemory with a C `malloc` function. The `malloc` function usually takes time proportional to the amount of memory managed by `malloc` or (if `malloc` uses a buddy allocator) to the log of that size. The supporting code for this type of VTMemory implementation would allocate memory for each new object by using `malloc` and would maintain a linked list of the objects in a memory. When the scoped memory area became inactive, the code supporting VTMemory would walk the linked list, using the C `free` function to return each block of memory to the free pool.

It might be possible to implement a garbage collection service in VTMemory areas that would take advantage of the assignment rules to run faster than standard garbage collectors. Nothing in the RTSJ would prevent an implementation from doing that, provided that garbage collection delays were only visible during allocation of new objects from the scope.

The RTSJ does not specify any advantages that VTMemory has over LTMemory, so a designer cannot assume that VTMemory will be anything more than a wrapper that gives LTMemory a different name. Still, when an application does not need the strong object-creation performance guarantee of LTMemory, it can use VTMemory and give the implementation a chance to use memory more efficiently, or it can do whatever the RTSJ implementation chose to do with the additional freedom granted by VTMemory.

Creating Scoped Memory

Before a scoped memory can be used, it must be created.

```
LTMemory mem = new LTMemory(1024*16, 1024*16);
```
creates a 16-kilobyte memory area object named `mem`.

You can create scoped memory any time with a normal `new` statement. The memory area object is a normal object, but the allocatable memory associated with the object is allocated in a special area (perhaps directly allocated by the JVM with `malloc`), so the memory used for the scope does not carry implicit reference restrictions.

Where scoped memory is allocated and when it is freed

The RTSJ requires that the memory represented by a scoped memory area "not exist on the Java heap, and is not subject to garbage collection."

The scoped memory area object itself is a normal object. It can be stored in heap, immortal, or scoped memory.

The integrity of the Java environment requires that the memory represented by the scoped memory cannot be freed until it contains no accessible objects and the corresponding memory area object is eligible to be freed.

The constructor for scoped memory passes the initial size and maximum size of the area. In the standard Java environment, the size of objects is not specified and cannot even be determined without violating the spirit of the language. The RTSJ lets you determine the size of an object fairly easily (with `memoryConsumed`), but it does not specify the size of objects, so the size required for a given set of objects cannot be calculated in advance. Constant values for the initial and maximum size will work, but they have to be tested on each new Java platform. Alternatively, the `SizeEstimator` class can be used as a portable way to size a memory area to fit a particular mix of objects, as shown in Example 13–6.

Example 13–6 Using SizeEstimator to set the size of a memory area

```
SizeEstimator sizeEst = new SizeEstimator();

//Reserve space for four realtime thread objects
sizeEst.reserve(RealtimeThread.class, 4);
//and space for an Integer
sizeEst.reserve(Integer.class, 1);
//and a RawMemoryAccess object
sizeEst.reserve(RawMemoryAccess.class, 1);
LTMemory mem = new LTMemory(sizeEst, sizeEst);
System.out.println("Memory in scope " + mem.memoryRemaining());
//Add another rt thread
sizeEst.reserve(RealtimeThread.class, 1);
mem = new LTMemory(sizeEst, sizeEst);
//And see how much more memory it wants
System.out.println("Memory in scope " + mem.memoryRemaining());
```

A scoped memory area need not *be* contiguous, but the memory allocated for its initial size must *behave* contiguous. If you can ever fit a set of objects into a scoped memory area, those objects will always fit. An interesting test object for this rule is an object that completely fills the memory scope when it is contiguous. If you can fit a 16-kilobyte object in a 16-kilobyte scoped memory area, the area is contiguous enough for practical purposes.

The `maximumSize` property of `LTMemory` and `VTMemory` is for optimists. If an implementation of the RTSJ succeeds in creating a memory scope, it cannot fail to provide the initial size of the memory scope for subsequent uses of the scope. It is not obliged to do anything particular about memory beyond the initial size. It need not allocate memory beyond the initial allowance, and if it does honor requests beyond the initial memory, it need not use contiguous memory. It can also take unoccupied memory beyond the initial size away from a memory area. That means that a memory scope might successfully expand to 100 kilobytes, then fail to hold 50 kilobytes when it becomes inactive and is reused milliseconds later.

Testing MemoryArea size

A typical requirement would direct that a memory scope be able to hold a certain mix of objects with a specified safety margin. A configuration section of the application is required to find the required size. It would create a MemoryArea that is clearly oversized and allocate the mix of objects into it, then use the memoryConsumed method to find the exact amount of memory used for those objects.

The above method is not portable, since objects could use different amounts of memory in different execution environments. The application could benchmark memory requirements at runtime, but it is easier and automatically portable to use SizeEstimator. The SizeEstimator class does not guarantee a tight fit. Since it does not know the order of allocation, it has to assume worst-case padding for allocation and other variables. Still, it is a portable way to estimate memory requirements and far better than testing a guess on a few machines and shipping the application.

Variable-sized memory scopes could be used in situations in which the application can benefit from extra memory in a scope but can easily tolerate OutOfMemoryError.

Allocation Mechanisms

There is an important distinction between allocating a scoped memory object and allocating an object *from* a scoped memory object. The scoped memory object is an object of some class derived from ScopedMemory. One or more pointers to memory are hidden somewhere in the invisible implementation part of the object. This hidden memory is the memory associated with the object. It can be used to store objects that are allocated in that scoped memory.

The RTSJ supports four mechanisms for allocating objects in scoped memory:

- **newInstance** — The newInstance and newArray methods from MemoryArea allocate objects from some memory area other than the current scope. You can allocate from any memory area you can access, but you cannot store the object reference that is returned from newInstance except in fields that meet the restrictions in Table 13–1. Heap and immortal memory cannot hold references to objects in scoped memory. Scoped memory can hold references to scoped memory, but only to objects in scopes with longer lifetimes.

  You can use newInstance or newArray to create an object in the heap, in immortal memory, or in a surrounding scope. You can store a reference to that object in the current scoped memory area. References to heap or immortal objects can also be stored in outer scopes. References to scoped memory objects can be stored in any scope from the current scope to the one that contains the object.

- **enter** — When a thread calls a memory area's `enter` method, the default allocation context for that thread switches to that memory area; it changes back when control returns from the `enter` method.

Example 13–7 shows a way to use scoped memory that looks too elegant to be wrong. It works, but it looks like the new `Runnable` will be creating an object in `mem`. It will not. The `Runnable` is constructed before `enter` moves the allocation context into `mem`. This code snippet will create a new `Runnable` object every time around the loop, and the new objects will not be automatically freed each time around the loop. This is a subtle memory leak.

Example 13–7 Do not use this pattern; use enter in a loop

```
mem = new LTMemory(8*1024, 8*1024);

for(int i = 0; i < this.args.length; ++i){
   final int j = i;
   //The Runnable allocated in the next
   //line does not come from mem.  One is
   //allocated every time around the loop
   //and there is nothing here to free them.
   mem.enter(new Runnable() {
      public void run() {
         Integer n = Integer.valueOf(args[j]);
         intArgs[j] = n.intValue();
      }
   });
   System.out.println(intArgs[i]);
}
```

Example 13–8 demonstrates a better way to use scoped memory in a loop. It shows a simple application of a nested scope. Each time around the `for` loop, control calls `mem`.'s enter method. New objects allocated in the `run` method come from `mem`. Each time control returns from `enter`, the implementation can free any objects allocated in `mem`. This loop can run forever without using up heap memory (and forcing garbage collection).

Example 13–8 is not as easy to read as Example 13–7, but it creates only one `Runnable` to use in the loop.

Example 13–8 A better pattern for using enter in a loop

```
class Action implements Runnable{
   int j;
   public void run() {
      Integer n = Integer.valueOf(args[j]);
      intArgs[j] = n.intValue();
   }
}
mem = new LTMemory(8*1024, 8*1024);
Action  action = new Action();

for(int i = 0; i < this.args.length; ++i){
   action.j = i;
   mem.enter(action);
   System.out.println(intArgs[i]);
}
```

Example 13–9 is almost the same as Example 13–8, but it associates the
Runnable with the memory when it constructs the memory area.

Example 13–9 Another good pattern for using enter in a loop

```
class Action implements Runnable{
   int j;
   public void run() {
      Integer n = Integer.valueOf(args[j]);
      intArgs[j] = n.intValue();
   }
}
//Give  mem a Runnable when we create it.
Action action = new Action();
mem = new LTMemory(8*1024, 8*1024, action);

for(int i = 0; i < this.args.length; ++i){
   action.j = i;
   mem.enter();
   System.out.println(intArgs[i]);
}
```

- **New thread** — Passing a scoped memory area to a new thread will let that
  new thread start operation with the memory scope as its default memory
  area. This is critical for the no-heap real-time threads that are discussed in

Chapter 14 since those threads are not allowed to touch heap memory under any circumstances. Example 13–10 creates an LTMemory area with an initial and maximum size of 16K.

Example 13–10 Shared memory scope

```
LTMemory mem = new LTMemory(1024*16, 1024*16);
System.out.println("Memory used in fresh area = " +
  mem.memoryConsumed());

RealtimeThread
  rt= new RealtimeThread(null, null, null,
    mem, //The new thread will use LT Memory
    null,
    new MyThread());
System.out.println("Mem used after new thread = " +
  mem.memoryConsumed());
rt.start();
```

The code in Example 13–10 prints the amount of consumed memory—0. It then creates a new real-time thread that will use the LTMemory area and again checks the memory consumed—0. Then it starts the new thread. The new thread creates an array of 100 Integer objects.

```
public void run() {
   System.out.println("Running in a scope!");
   Integer [] x = new Integer[100];// Use a lot of memory
}
```

After the new thread exits, we find that 444 bytes have been used in the LTMemory scope. The reference implementation is so coded that the scope is not cleared until it is about to be reused, so it continues to show 444 bytes used until the scope is passed to another real-time thread or until the thread calls the scope's enter method.

- **executeInArea** — The executeInArea method is called like enter and works similarly, but it has a different interaction with the way other memory scopes can be entered. (See "Using executeInArea" on page 202.)

Finalizers

Finalizers for objects allocated in a memory scope run when those objects are freed. That can happen any time between the moment the memory scope becomes inactive (the reference count for the scope goes to zero) and the moment the scope is reentered or passed to another thread.

If the memory scope is not reused, the finalizers for objects in the scope will run no later than the time at which the memory area itself is freed, as follows:

- If the scope object is immortal, that is no sooner than the end of the application.
- If the scope object is in a scope, the timing is dictated by the lifetime of the enclosing scope.
- If the scope object is on the heap, the finalizers will run no later than the time the scope object is garbage collected.

The finalizer for an object will run in the memory area in which the object was created.

Using Nested Scoped Memory

A scoped memory area is activated for allocation by its enter method and becomes inactive when the enter method returns. When it is used this way, the scoped memory is a *nested* scope.

Assignment rules (see Table 13–1) are governed by what behaves like a stack of nested memory areas.

You can nest memory areas any way you like provided that they follow the *single parent rule*. The scope's enter method throws a ScopedCycleException if it is called on a memory area that any thread has already entered from a different scope.

In its full complexity, supporting the single parent rule and the assignment rules require two types of data structures: a directed acyclic graph (DAG) shared by the all threads and a tree per thread.

The Scope Stack (Tree)

When a real-time thread is created, the constructor initializes its scope stack, as follows:

- If the thread is constructed in scoped memory, its initial scope stack will contain a copy of the parent thread's scope stack at the time the child thread was constructed.
- If the thread is constructed in heap memory, its scope stack will initially contain only heap memory.
- If the thread is constructed in immortal memory, its scope stack will initially contain only immortal memory.

If the thread's initial memory area (as specified in its constructor) is not already the current scope on the child's scope stack, the thread constructor will add it to the scope stack, following the same rules as it would if the child thread had entered the memory area.

This gives each real-time thread a scope stack that the implementation uses to enforce the assignment rules. The implementation can access the scope stack with a collection of static methods on `RealTimeThread`:

- `getMemoryAreaStackDepth` — Returns the size of the current thread's scope stack.

- `getOuterMemoryArea(int index)` — Treats the scope stack like an array. The stack grows in the direction of higher indexes, so scope stack entries remain at fixed indexes as the stack grows and shrinks.

- `getCurrentMemoryArea` — This returns the memory area that is the current allocation context. It works the same as
`getOuterMemoryArea(getMemoryAreaStackDepth() -1)`

- `getInitialMemoryAreaIndex` — A thread's initial memory index is the marker between scopes that the thread has pushed on the stack with `enter` and scopes that it inherited from its parent. This method returns the index of the current thread's stack's initial memory area in its scope stack.

One static method in `MemoryArea` also affects a thread's scope stack. The scope stack is actually a scope tree because of the `executeInArea` method on the `MemoryArea` class. The stack turns into a tree if the code executed by `executeInArea` calls `enter` on a memory area other than the one from which the thread originally entered. (See "Using executeInArea" on page 202.)

The DAG

The single-parent rule prevents reference cycles between memory areas, and it prevents stale references in memory areas.

The single-parent rule

Background

Every scoped memory area that can be found on any thread's scope stack is also represented in the scoped memory DAG.

The root of the scoped memory DAG is called the primordial scope. It represents heap and immortal memory. (And is the only node in the DAG that does not represent scoped memory.)

A scoped memory area's parent is either the next scoped memory up a thread's scope stack or the primordial node if there is no scoped memory above it on the scope stack.

The rule

Every scoped memory node in the scoped memory DAG has one parent.

The primordial node has no parent.

Many less restrictive rules were proposed—insisting that the graph be a DAG was one proposal—but they all permitted situations that could leave a memory area containing stale references to objects in another area that had been freed.

DAG fragment

Scope stack fragments for two threads

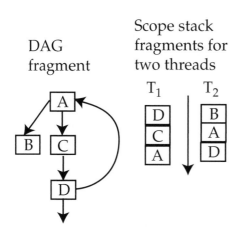

Simple Cycles. The assignment rules become ambiguous if the scoped memory graph contains cycles. Imposing rules on the scope stack does not help; it only makes the problem require more than one thread.

The illustration shows fragments of the two scope stacks and a scoped memory graph. T_1 entered memory area D, then C, then A. Thread T_2 entered B, then A, then D. The resulting graph is shown. Note that there is a cycle in the scoped memory graph even though no cycle is visible in either thread's scope stack.

Graph fragment

Scope stack fragments for two threads

The problem is that the assignment rules for thread T_1 will let it store references to memory area A in area D. If both threads now leave two scopes, objects in memory area A can be freed even though memory area D still contains references to those objects. This would violate "referential integrity." That must not be permitted.

DAG Is Not Enough. Forbidding cycles in the scoped memory graph (thus, a DAG) would seem to be enough to prevent bad references, but it is not. Pratik Solanki (part of the TimeSys reference implementation team) invented Pratik's problem, a way that two threads could cooperate to generate a reference problem even if the reference graph were required to be a DAG.

This scoped memory graph contains no cycles, but it still generates a problem with referential integrity.

Let thread T_1 create X in memory area C and save a reference to it in memory area A. This is legal. Now let T_1 leave scopes A and C. The implementation is permitted to free objects in C since the memory area is not currently in use. (It must free the objects before C is reused, so if you want to make certain that there is trouble, have thread T_1 reenter C.) Now thread T_2 is using memory area A, which contains an invalid reference to X.

DAG fragment

Scope stack fragments for two threads

But the reference to X is unreachable

No it's not. Scoped memory areas have a device called a portal that lets any thread that has access to the scope also have access to selected objects allocated in the scope. Thread T_1 could have made X accessible through the portal.

The Single-Parent Rule Is Enough.   The single-parent rule is much more restrictive than the requirement that the graph be a DAG. In fact, a graph that obeys the single-parent rule is a tree with each scoped memory area represented at most once in the tree. It forces every thread that uses a memory area to give it exactly the same scoped memory parentage as any other thread. This may be more restrictive than necessary, but it certainly rules out any reference problems caused by threads that use memory areas in different reference environments.

Heap and Immortal Are Wild Cards.   Except for the primordial scope, heap and immortal memory are not represented in the scoped memory graph. That means that entry to heap or immortal memory is invisible to the single-parent rule.

1.   A thread can always enter heap or immortal memory.

2.   A thread can enter any scope from heap or immortal memory that it could have entered from the last scoped memory up the stack.

3. If there is no scoped memory on a thread's scope stack, that thread can enter any scoped memory area that does not have a parent (is not in use) or can enter any scope whose parent is the primordial scope.

Practical Use of Nested Scopes

Example 13–11 shows a program that uses a memory scope to prevent buildup of temporary objects involved in converting strings into integers.

Example 13–11 Using a nested scope

```
String [] args;
int [] intArgs;
LTMemory mem;
LTMemory mem2;

public Nest1(String [] args){
  this.args = args;
  intArgs = new int[args.length];
}

class Action implements Runnable {
  int i;
  public void run() {
    // ... compute some
    //Now nest deeper
    mem2.enter(new Runnable() {
      final int j = i;
      public void run() {
        Integer n = Integer.valueOf(args[j]);
        intArgs[j] = n.intValue();
      }
    });
  }
}

public void run(){
  mem = new LTMemory(8*1024, 8*1024);
  mem2 = new LTMemory(8*1024, 8*1024);
  Action action = new Action();

  for(int i = 0; i < this.args.length; ++i){
    action.i = i;
    mem.enter(action);
    System.out.println(intArgs[i]);
  }
}
```

Every time around the `for` loop, the program enters scoped memory area
`mem`; then (just to make the example interesting), inside the logic argument for the
`enter` in the `for` loop, it enters scope `mem2`. While it is using scope `mem2`, the program creates an `Integer` object and uses it to convert a string into an `int`. Then
the program returns from the `run` method and leaves the `mem2` scope, which permits the Java runtime to free the `Integer` object it left in `mem2`. Then the program
leaves scope `mem` … thereby giving the runtime permission to free the `Runnable`
for the nested `enter`.

By creating the temporary object in a memory scope, the code in Example 13–
11 does not create waste objects that the garbage collector will need to find and
free. The nested scope mechanism lets the code dispose of the temporary `Integer`
objects immediately after creating them.

Walkthrough.   Nested scopes are not as straightforward as they sound. The reference rules in Table 13–1 will make programming tedious unless you stay alert to
where each object is stored. Let's start after the `for` loop in Example 13–11.

1.   The `action.i = i` statement copies `i` into an instance variable where the
`run` method in action can easily reach it.

2.   Now we reach the `enter` method. It saves the old memory scope, makes the
new scope current, then calls the `run` method of action. Now the memory
area is `mem`, and control moves up to the `run` method in the `Action` class.

3.   The `run` method starts with some lines of comments, then enters another
scope, but the parameter for `enter` has to be evaluated before control enters
the nested scope; in this case, evaluating the argument means creating an
object. The `Runnable` object is created, and any initializers execute in the current allocation context (which is the heap). This `Runnable` does not have any
obvious instance variables, but it is going to reference the final variable `j`
from the surrounding scope. The machinery of the Java compiler causes the
inner class to generate a separate class and gives the inner class access to
`final` variables by copying the ones it uses into invisible instance variables
in the inner class. Code in the `run` method seems to reference the local `j`
from the surrounding scope, but it is really referencing an instance variable
copy of `j` that is part of the object and therefore allocated in `mem`, the allocation scope of the `new` that constructs the `Runnable`.

4.   The `enter` method executes. It saves the current scope (`mem`), and makes the
`mem2` scope current, then it calls the `run` method.

5.   The innermost code creates an `Integer` object in the `mem2` memory area, uses
that `Integer` object to compute the integer value of a string, then assigns the
primitive `int` value of that integer to an instance variable in the outer scope,
a heap variable.

This example relies on a trick. An int value is not an object. It and the other primitive values are not in any memory scope. If the example had tried to store a reference to n, the Integer object created in the inner scope, instead of storing the primitive value returned by n.intValue, then the assignment would have caused an IllegalAssignmentError.

Every Nested Scope Involves Two Memory Areas

Step 3 above shows that nested scopes cannot easily treat the closure mechanism as a simple inner class. The assignment rules say that a field in an outer scope cannot contain a reference to an object from an inner scope. That means that Example 13–12 will generate an IllegalAssignmentError when it attempts to save the new Integer object reference into n.

Example 13–12 Illegal assignment

```
mem1.enter(new Runnable() {
   Integer n;
   public void run(){
     n = new Integer(1);
   }
});
```

The IllegalAssignmentError tar pit only applies to *storing* references. A nested scope can load references to objects in any scope it can reach.

It is possible for nested scopes to save into their instance variables. Programmers have to realize that although their intuition suggests that the current object should be in the current scope, the object is in the surrounding scope. Any objects they want to store in an instance variable should be created in the outer scope.

Example 13–13 demonstrates two techniques. It stores an object reference in an instance variable without causing an exception, and it demonstrates a good way for the run method in a nested scope to return data to surrounding scopes.

Return values from nested scopes use an instance variable in the nested scope.

The example enters a nested scope that allocates a StringBuffer object containing the string Hello World and leaves that object in an instance variable named s. When it returns, the surrounding scope looks into scope4, the object that hosted the nested scope, recovers s, and prints it.

Example 13–13 Successfully storing into an instance variable

```
//Named inner class
class XScope4 implements Runnable {
  StringBuffer s;
  public void run(){
    int currentIdx = RealtimeThread.
                      getMemoryAreaStackDepth() - 1;
    int idx = currentIdx - 1;
    MemoryArea outerScope =
      (MemoryArea)RealtimeThread.
              getOuterMemoryArea(idx);
    try {
      //Allocate an object in the next scope out
      //and store the reference in that scope
      s = (StringBuffer)outerScope.
          newInstance(StringBuffer.class);
    } catch (InstantiationException instance){
    } catch (IllegalAccessException access) {
    }
    s.append("Hello World");
  }
};

mem2.enter(new Runnable() {
  public void run(){
    XScope4 scope4 = new XScope4();
    mem1.enter(scope4);
    System.out.println(scope4.s.toString());
  }
});
```

The code is different from previous examples of nested scopes in two ways. First, it uses a named class for the inner scope and stores a reference to the inner scope object in a local variable. That lets the nested object remain accessible long enough for the calling scope to recover s from it. Second, it uses newInstance to create the string buffer in a nondefault memory area: specifically, the allocation context of the surrounding scope.

Pitfalls

A few tricky aspects of using scoped memory deserve special emphasis.

Illegal Nesting.   Example 13–14 tries to nest a use of scoped memory area mem inside itself. It doesn't do so directly. There's a layer of heap memory between the

two layers of mem, but the mem scope is still reentered. This violates the single-parent rule. The RTSJ runtime catches this error and throws
`java.lang.ScopedCycleException: Entering this memory area causes a cycle on the memory area stack.`

Example 13–14 Illegal use of nested scopes

```
mem = new LTMemory(8*1024, 8*1024);
final int j = i;
mem.enter(new Runnable() {
  public void run() {
     // ... compute some
     HeapMemory.instance().enter(new Runnable() {
       public void run(){
          //Now we're back on the heap
          //Now try to nest again
          mem.enter(new Runnable() {
            //This is illegal
            //The mem memory memory's parent is already
            //primordial, we cannot enter it with
            //a scoped memory area on the stack...
            //even mem :-)
            public void run() {
               Integer n = Integer.valueOf(args[j]);
               intArgs[j] = n.intValue();
            }
          });
        }
     });
   }
});
System.out.println(intArgs[i]);
```

The `HeapMemory` memory area nested between the first entry into the mem scope and the attempt to enter it again serves a useful purpose. If it is not there, you do not see the `ScopedCycleException`; instead, you see a `ThrowBoundaryError`.

Throw Boundary.   Without the heap memory interposed between the scoped memory and the attempt to enter a scoped memory area, the throw boundary error would have happened because a scoped cycle exception is thrown when the thread tries to enter mem for the second time. Since memory is being allocated from the mem scope, the exception is allocated there. There is no catch clause for the exception in the enter's run method, so the JVM tries to propagate it out to the surrounding scope. By the assignment rules in Table 13–1, a reference to an object (like the exception) in an inner scope (like mem) cannot be assigned to a field in an outer scope. If the catch clause attempted to store a reference to an exception allocated in an inner scope into a variable in an outer scope, it would cause an IllegalAssignmentError. Instead of attempting to propagate the exception into code that cannot catch it, the RTSJ runtime replaces the exception that is about to become inaccessible with a ThrowBoundaryError that is allocated from the scope that is about to catch the exception.

A try/catch block inside the run method is the easiest way to determine the cause of the exception that turned into a throw boundary error. In the run method, you can diagnose the exception before it becomes inaccessible.

Static Almost Equals Immortal. The RTSJ specifies that class objects[1] and class variables must behave like immortal memory. (They must be unexceptionally referenceable from every execution context.) Assume that the implementation uses immortal memory unless you know otherwise and do not intend to run your code on a machine that does use immortal memory for this purpose. The actual implementation may choose to use real immortal memory to store this class-related information, or it may do something clever. The probable immortality of class objects has two important consequences:

1. Classes consume immortal memory. Complex classes with the corresponding large class objects use a relatively large amount of memory. The JVM is allowed to free memory associated with a class. The requirement from *The Java Language Specification*, Second Edition, is "A class or interface may be unloaded if and only if its defining class loader may be reclaimed by the garbage collector…" A class loader can be reclaimed, even in a system that contains immortal memory, but not if any object in immortal memory was loaded by it.

2. The assignment rules for immortal memory apply to class fields. Class fields cannot refer to scoped memory.

> **Class (static) variables can never refer to objects in scoped memory.**

---

1. A class object is the object that contains information about the properties of a class. The JVM generates one for each class it loads.

Using executeInArea

There are two ways to move the current execution context in the scope stack without otherwise changing the stack: the two newInstance methods—the newArray method and the executeInArea method.

When an application uses one of the newInstance family on memory area mem, the implementation moves the current allocation context up the scope stack until it finds mem, allocates the object there, runs the constructor starting in that context, and then repositions the current allocation to its location before creating the new object.

The executeInArea method is a relatively elegant tool for running arbitrary code at some location up the scope stack. Very likely the implementation will use executeInArea as the supporting mechanism for the newInstance methods:

```
public void executeInArea(Runnable logic)

public synchronized Object newInstance(
        java.lang.Class type)

public synchronized Object newInstance(
        java.lang.reflect.Constructor constructor,
        java.lang.Object [] params)

public synchronized Object newArray(
        java.lang.Class type,
        int number)
```

In summary, if the memory area is a scoped memory on the current thread's scope stack, executeInArea behaves as if it had moved the allocation context up the scope stack to that memory area before running the logic. If the memory area is heap or immortal, executeInArea executes the logic with an empty scope stack and the memory area as the current allocation context. If the memory area is a scope that is not on the scope stack, executeInArea throws an InaccessibleAreaException.

These methods have an interesting effect on the scope stack—they can make it into a tree. When the current location of the stack is moved up and the code enters a memory area from that point, it creates a branch in the "stack," as shown in Figure 13–2.

Heap and immortal memory could appear many times in a scope stack, and consequently the semantics of executeInArea cannot be simply extended to

Figure 13–2 executeInArea creating a scope tree

Action	Picture
Initial state	

```
Heap
  a
  b
  c    current
```

a.executeInArea(logic1)

```
Heap
  a    current
  b
  c
```

d.enter(logic2)

```
Heap
  a
b       d    current
c
```

Return from enter

```
Heap
  a    current
  b
  c
```

Return from executeInArea

```
Heap
  a
  b
  c    current
```

cover heap and immortal memory. Instead, they are overloaded such that calling the method on a scoped memory area moves the current execution context in the scope stack, but calling the method on heap or immortal memory starts a new scope with only the specified memory area in it, as shown in Figure 13–3.

Figure 13–3 executeInArea with immortal memory

Action	Picture
Initial state	

```
┌──────┐
│Heap  │
├──────┤
│  a   │
├──────┤
│  b   │
├──────┤
│  c   │  current
└──────┘
```

```
HeapMemory.instance().executeIn
Area(logic)
```

```
┌──────┐      ┌────────┐
│Heap  │      │immortal│ current
├──────┤      └────────┘
│  a   │
├──────┤
│  b   │
├──────┤
│  c   │
└──────┘
```

```
d.enter()
```

```
┌──────┐      ┌────────┐
│Heap  │      │immortal│
├──────┤      ├────────┤
│  a   │      │   d    │ current
├──────┤      └────────┘
│  b   │
├──────┤
│  c   │
└──────┘
```

```
leave d.enter
```

```
┌──────┐      ┌────────┐
│Heap  │      │immortal│ current
├──────┤      └────────┘
│  a   │
├──────┤
│  b   │
├──────┤
│  c   │
└──────┘
```

Figure 13–3 executeInArea with immortal memory (Continued)

Action	Picture
leave `executeInArea`	

```
┌──────┐
│ Heap │
├──────┤
│  a   │
├──────┤
│  b   │
├──────┤
│  c   │  current
└──────┘
```

The special value of `executeInArea` on heap or immortal memory is that the immortal or heap memory in `executeInArea`'s scope stack is the primordial scope. It lets the application reach scopes that have already been given a parent by another thread.

If thread1 has a scope stack containing (a, b, c) and thread2's scope stack contains (d, e, f), then thread1 cannot enter scope d, e, or f without using `executeInArea` to start a new scope stack in heap or immortal memory and then entering d, e, and f in the same order as thread2.

Using Standard Classes

Nothing prevents an application from using a library class from a non-heap memory allocation context. Nothing guarantees it will work either.

Methods that have no persistent state can be used in scoped memory, but with these caveats:

If a library function creates no objects, it will work perfectly in a scoped memory allocation context, but the scoped memory won't make any difference.

If a library function creates temporary objects and perhaps returns one of them to its caller, it will work perfectly in a scoped memory allocation context, provided that the scope is big enough to hold the objects it creates. This will benefit performance substantially since all the temporary objects created in the library call will be automatically and efficiently freed.

If a method stores a reference to an object it creates in a class variable or a heap object, it will throw an `IllegalAssignmentError`.

If a new release of a library introduces persistent state, code that uses it in a scoped memory allocation context will stop working. Whether a class maintains persistent state is not part of its published "contract."

The careful programmer will probably avoid executing any standard libraries from scoped allocation contexts unless they include RTSJ characteristics in their documentation.

I suppose a careful programmer might catch illegal assignment errors and switch to heap memory if a library throws one. That would not be acceptable if the performance of the code were critical, but it would be a nice way to take advantage of the performance advantages of scoped memory but fail softly if a method uses persistent objects.

Algorithm 13–2. Adaptive use of scoped memory for a library routine

```
if useScope      //   useScope is a persistent variable particular
                 //   to this method call.
     try
           enter scope and call method
     catch IllegalAssignmentError
           useScope = false
if not useScope
     call method
```

Using Shared Scoped Memory

Scopes can be shared among threads either by inheritance or by the same scopes being entered in multiple threads. This engages the reference-counting aspect of scoped memory.

> Objects in a scoped memory are not freed until after the reference count goes to zero.

Objects in scoped memory are not eligible to be freed until the reference count on the scope goes to zero. This sounds simple, but threads are inherently asynchronous. The usage pattern of shared scopes can easily become complicated, and unless you check the reference of memory areas by using the getReferenceCount method on ScopedMemory, the clue that the reference count did not go to zero when you expected is that allocations from the memory area will start throwing OutOfMemoryError.

Remember: Until the reference count goes to zero, all the objects in the scope will remain allocated even if they are unreachable. The system is saved from mysterious failure by the size limit on the memory area. The size limit will cause memory to run out when being allocated from the scope. Memory allocation from other areas is not constrained by the size limit, so the out of memory errors are focused on the code that is exceeding its budget.

The memory leak in a shared scope comes about something like this:

1. Somehow, thread *A* believes that the reference count for memory area *M* has gone to zero and that memory area *M* is now empty. For instance, thread *A* creates threads *B*, *C*, and *D* and starts them all in memory area *M*. Thread *C* enters scoped memory *N* and creates thread *F*, which starts with a scope stack that includes *M* and *N*. When thread *A* sees that *B*, *C*, and *D* have completed, it assumes that the reference count for *M* has gone to zero; but if *F* has not exited, *M* is still active—hidden below *F*'s initial memory area on its scope stack.

2. Since thread *A* believes that memory area *M* is empty, it reuses the memory area for a new batch of threads …

3. Even if thread *F* exits (and decrements the use count of *M*), *M* is now being used by other threads so it has a positive use count and will remain active.

4. Until *M*'s reference count goes to zero, no objects in it can be freed.

The Scope Stack Revisited

The allocation context behaves like a stack. The `enter` method on `MemoryArea` objects pushes and pops the stack. This may not be the way memory scopes are implemented, but it is a useful and accurate model.

Using the convention that the stack grows down, here are the rules for nested memory areas, expressed as if the areas were on a stack:

1. Each thread has a scope stack.

2. The top scope on the stack is the current allocation context. It is returned by `getCurrentMemoryArea` on the `RealtimeThread` class and by `getOutMemoryArea(getMemoryAreaStackDepth() - 1)`.

3. A real-time thread's initial scope stack is constructed when the thread object is allocated and constructed; see Figure 13–4. The scope stack is initialized as follows:

```
if the allocation context is heap
    the new thread's initial stack contains only heap
else if the allocation context is immortal
    the new thread's initial stack contains only immortal
else
    the new thread's initial stack is a copy of the parent's
        scope stack down to and including
        the allocation context
```

```
if the new thread's initial memory area is
         not the current scope
    enter the initial memory area on behalf of the child
```

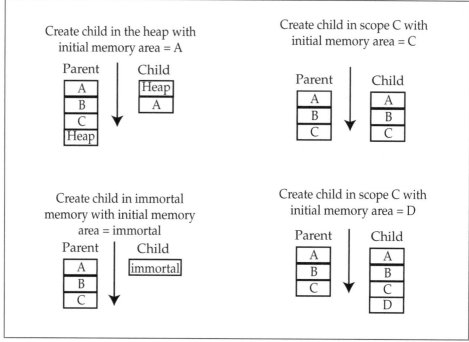

Figure 13–4 Initial scope stack construction

4. A thread can access and create objects in any scope above the current scope in its scope stack.

At every point a scoped memory area's reference count equals the number of threads that have access to that memory area.
The objects in the area can be freed when the reference count goes to zero.

---

5. Accessing and creating objects in a less deeply nested scope than the current scope is problematic since neither the current scope nor current local variables can hold a reference to such objects.

Figure 13–5 shows the evolution of a scope stack as a family of threads uses it. In this example, when threads share common scopes, their stacks are represented in a single tree.

Figure 13–5 Evolution of a scope stack when used by a thread family

Thread	Action	Illustrating Picture (Numbers are reference counts)
rt1	Starts in heap.	Heap rt1 current
rt1	Enters sm1.	Heap / sm1 (1) rt1 current
rt1	Creates and starts rt2. The Runnable and the thread object are in sm1, and the thread's initial memory area is sm2. Rt2 sees one scope stack that includes the scopes visible to rt1 when it created rt2. Rt1 cannot see rt2 scopes that are below the point of rt2's creation in the stack.	Heap / sm1(2) rt1 current / sm2(1) rt2 current
rt1	Returns from sm1. Now rt1's scope stack contains only heap memory, but the sm1 frame is still there because rt2 can see it.	Heap rt1 current / sm1(1) / sm2(1) rt2 current

Real-Time Java Platform Programming

Figure 13–5 Evolution of a scope stack when used by a thread family (Continued)

Thread	Action	Illustrating Picture (Numbers are reference counts)
rt2	Enters heap memory, then enters scope sm5.	Heap — rt1 current sm1(1) sm2(1) Heap sm5(1) — rt2 current
rt1	Enters sm1. Rt1 may be operating under a dangerous assumption. If the programmer is not aware that sm1 is active in other threads, the program may be coded under the assumption that all the objects in sm1 were eligible to be freed when rt1 left that scope. Now the program may be reentering sm1, assuming that all the memory allocated to that scope is available for its use. It isn't. Objects in sm1 have not been freed since the beginning of this example.	Heap sm1(2) — rt1 current sm2(1) Heap sm5(1) — rt2 current

Figure 13–5 Evolution of a scope stack when used by a thread family (Continued)

Thread	Action	Illustrating Picture (Numbers are reference counts)
rt1	Creates and starts rt3. The Runnable and thread object are in sm1, and the thread's initial memory area is sm2.	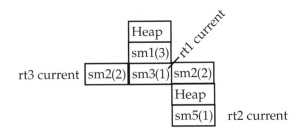
rt1	Enters sm3.	

Figure 13–5 Evolution of a scope stack when used by a thread family (Continued)

Thread	Action	Illustrating Picture (Numbers are reference counts)
	At this point the scope DAG looks like this. 1. sm5 can only be entered by threads in sm2. 2. sm3 can only be entered by threads in sm1. 3. sm2 can only be entered by threads in sm1. 4. sm1 can only be entered by threads created in heap or immortal memory, or in the context of `executeInArea` on heap or immortal memory.	(diagram) Primordial ooze ← sm1(3) ← sm3(1); sm2(2) → sm1(3); sm5(1) → sm2(2) Thread 1 could not simply enter sm5 at this point. That would give sm5 two parents (sm2 and sm3) and would violate the single-parent rule. If thread 1 wanted to enter sm5 without help from thread 2, it would have to leave sm3, then enter sm2, and finally enter sm5. That is an example of the general rule. If a thread wants to enter a thread that is held by another thread, it has to build a scope stack that differs from the other stack only in the way it incorporates heap and immortal memory.
rt2	Leaves sm5. This zeros the reference count for sm5. Objects in sm5 will be freed before that area is reused.	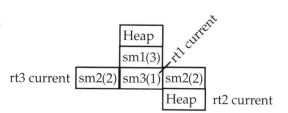

Figure 13–5 Evolution of a scope stack when used by a thread family (Continued)

Thread	Action	Illustrating Picture (Numbers are reference counts)
rt1	Leaves sm3 and sm1, then enters sm5. Notice that the sm1 entry that used to be shared among all three stacks is now only shared between rt2 and rt3. Rt1 has headed off on its own branch of the stack, but all three threads still share the heap stack entry.	rt1 current sm5(1) sm1(2) / Heap / rt3 current sm2(2) sm2(2) / Heap rt2 current
rt3	Starts rt4 with its `Runnable`, thread object, and initial memory area all set to heap. Since rt4 does not have a scoped initial memory area, it starts a new memory stack	rt1 current sm5(1) sm1(2) / Heap / rt3 current sm2(2) sm2(2) / Heap rt2 current / rt4 current Heap
rt1	Exits. The heap stack entry from rt1 stays around because it is also part of the stacks of rt2 and rt3.	Heap / sm1(2) / rt3 current sm2(2) sm2(2) / Heap rt2 current / rt4 current Heap

Scope Portals

A memory scope can be used by many threads. Each can allocate and use its own objects in the scope.

The RTSJ goes to great lengths to let memory scopes be used concurrently by multiple threads. This supports two important uses:

1. Threads can be created in memory scopes. If there were no support for sharing scopes between threads, no thread other than the one that created it would be able to access the thread object allocated by a thread object in a scoped memory. The new thread would not be able to access its own thread object!

2. Shared memory scopes provide an object store through which real-time threads can share data. The lifetime of the data is managed by reference counting the memory scope. The alternatives to scoped memory are heap memory, which brings garbage collection problems with it, and immortal memory, which has no garbage collection issues but cannot contain temporary objects.

Shared scopes would be sufficiently justified by their utility in containing thread objects, but portals are a useful addition. They ease inter-thread communication by letting a scoped memory object carry one object within it bound in a way that makes it available to any thread that has access to the memory scope.

A portal is really nothing more than a standard Object reference that is part of every scoped memory. Subject to the normal assignment rules, an application can point the portal at any object. If the application needs to have a portal that references multiple objects, the portal object can be an array of object references or an object containing references to other objects.

While a scoped memory is in a thread's stack, it is easily available to all that thread's children, and references to objects in the scope can easily be passed to those child threads. Portals have limited use in this context.

If multiple threads start at heap or immortal memory and build similar scope stacks, they cannot pass references to objects in scoped memory from one to another at birth. Heap and immortal memory cannot contain references to objects in scoped memory. The normal ways to pass data to and fro are to store into instance variables or pass data to methods that belong to an object that is used by both threads. But how should a thread get the reference to that shared object? A portal.

Example 13–15 illustrates the use of a portal. The example is one of the few complete applications in this book. It is all here because it demonstrates the use of portals, and it is as careful with memory as a typical RTSJ application needs to be if it chooses to avoid heap memory.

Example 13-15 Portal into a shared scope

```
import javax.realtime.*;
/** Demonstrate the use of a portal shared between a parent thread
  and two children.
*/

public class UsePortal extends RealtimeThread {
  /**The class that will be attached to the
     getPortal method in a VTMemory area.
  */
  public class Port {
    char [] s;
    int counter;
    boolean stopper;
  }

  /**Two RT threads will use this class as
     the logic for a memory area enter method.
     They differ in the characters they
     store into portal.s, and in the period
     they use.
  */
  class ThAction implements Runnable {
    private Port portal;
    private char [] tag;

    /**Constructor for ThAction inner class */
    ThAction(char [] tag){
      int idx = RealtimeThread.currentRealtimeThread().
        getMemoryAreaStackDepth() - 1;
      portal = (Port)((VTMemory)getOuterMemoryArea(idx)).
          getPortal();
      this.tag = tag;
    }

    /**Run method for ThAction. */
    public void run() {
      try {
        synchronized(portal){
          portal.s[0] = tag[0];
          portal.s[1] = tag[1];
          portal.counter++;
        }
      } catch (Throwable e) {
        System.out.println("Throw in thread action" + e);
        e.printStackTrace();
      }
```

Example 13–15 Portal into a shared scope (Continued)

```
    }
  }

/**Class used for the two threads that share the
   shared memory area with the master thread.
*/
public class TH extends RealtimeThread {
  private char [] tag;

  /**Constructor for TH */
  public TH(char tag1, char tag2, long period){
    super(null,
      //Make this a periodic thread
      new PeriodicParameters(null,
        new RelativeTime(period, 0),
        null, null, null, null)
    );
    tag = new char[2];
    tag[0] = tag1;
    tag[1] = tag2;
  }

  /** Run method for TH. */
  public void run(){
    ThAction action =  new ThAction(this.tag);

    VTMemory mem =    new VTMemory(2048, 2048);
    while(!action.portal.stopper){
      mem.enter(action);
      //Wait for next period
      while(!waitForNextPeriod());
    }
  }
}

/**Run method for the UsePortal class */
public void run(){
  (new VTMemory(8*1024, 8*1024)).enter(new Runnable(){
    public void run(){
      final VTMemory outerMem =
        (VTMemory)getCurrentMemoryArea();
      final Port portal = new Port();
      outerMem.setPortal(portal);
      portal.s = new char[2];
      TH  rt1 = new TH('t', '1', 500);
```

Example 13–15 Portal into a shared scope (Continued)

```
            THrt2 = new TH('T', '2', 300);
            rt1.start();
            rt2.start();

            VTMemory mem2 = new VTMemory(2048, 2048,
              new Runnable() {
                public void run() {
                  try{
                    Thread.sleep(400);
                  } catch (InterruptedException e){
                    //Ignore these exceptions
                  }
                  synchronized(portal){
                    String s = new String(portal.s);
                    System.out.println(
                      s + " = " +
                      portal.counter +
                      " outer mem free = " +
                      outerMem.memoryRemaining());
                  }
                }
              });
            for(int i = 0; i < 50; ++i)
              mem2.enter();

            portal.stopper = true;
            try{
              rt1.join();
              rt2.join();
            } catch (InterruptedException e){}
          }
        });
    }

    public static void main(String [] args){
      try {
        UsePortal rt = new UsePortal(); //make a rt thread
        rt.start();
        try {
          rt.join();
        } catch (InterruptedException e){
          //Ignore the exception
        }
        System.exit(0);
```

Example 13–15 Portal into a shared scope (Continued)

```
            } catch (Throwable e){
      System.out.println("Throw in main");
      e.printStackTrace();
    }
  }
}
```

Program Layout.   Reading from the end of the program up:

*   **main** — This executes in the ordinary thread that the JVM uses to start the application. The main method instantiates the object it is in, Portal, and since Portal is a subclass of RealtimeThread, main can just start it to get a RealtimeThread.

*   **run** — Almost every method in this application is named run, but the large block of code above main is the run method that makes Portal act like a thread. It is the run method for the application's main thread.

    The main thread immediately creates a VTMemory area and enters it. Just to show that it can, the method enters the memory area without even giving it a name. Entering a memory area right at the beginning of a thread's run method like this has the same effect as using a scoped memory area as the MemoryArea parameter to the constructor for a RealtimeThread.

    Right after not bothering to save the memory area reference anywhere, the application uses getCurrentMemoryArea to obtain a reference to the memory area. Then the application creates and initializes a portal object in its current memory area. Still in that memory area, the application creates two objects and executes them as RealtimeThreads.

    Now the thread creates a VTMemory object that is bound to a Runnable class from its construction. The Runnable class is created in the current memory area. It sleeps for 400 ms, then prints some fields from the portal object.

    After that, the method enters the just-created memory area 50 times. Since the method bound a Runnable to the memory area when it created the memory area, each enter invokes the run method associated with the memory area.

    We then tell the two threads we just created to stop, and we wait for them to complete. This thread is now finished.

*   **TH** — Further up the program we get to the definition of the TH class. This is another class that extends RealtimeThread. This class has a constructor that stores values in instance variables and makes the thread into a periodic thread.

The run method of TH creates a Runnable object, called action, and another scoped memory area. It loops until the stopper field in the portal object turns false. Each time around the loop, run invokes the action class it just created in the scoped memory class it also just created.

The loop uses waitForNextPeriod to let it the loop execute once per period. (As discussed in Chapter 12.) Each time waitForNextPeriod returns true, the thread completed its computation by its deadline and waitForNextPeriod waited for the next period. If it waitForNextPeriod returns false, the thread missed its deadline and waitForNextPeriod did not block.

- **ThAction** — Near the top of the program is the ThAction class. This is the Runnable that is executed in TH's main loop. It just sets three fields in the portal object and returns.

The constructor for ThAction demonstrates the methods that are used to reach up the stack through nested memory areas. In this case, the method is only a complicated way to get a reference to the current memory area. If we wanted to get at the memory up the stack from the current one (which would be Heap), we could find it at getOuterMemoryArea(idx -1).

The Portal.   The application in Example 13–15 uses three real-time threads. The main thread executes a loop 50 times, once every four-tenths of a second. Each time around, the main thread prints the contents of an array of characters and an integer value that it finds in a shared memory scope. After 50 times through the loop, the main thread sets a boolean value in the shared scope, called stopper, to true.

The two other real-time threads share the memory scope with the main thread. Each of these threads loops with a different period, and each one writes different values into the array of characters. Both of them increment the integer counter in the shared scope. When they see stopper become true, they exit.

No Leaks.   UsePortal has several loops that could leak memory. Its main run method runs in a memory scope and has a loop that creates a string and invokes System.out.println each time around the loop. That would probably use a few hundred bytes each time around the loop. One solution would have been to use SizeEstimator to make the outer memory area big enough for 50 copies of each object created in the loop. It is better to enter a memory area for the body of the loop. That way any memory allocated in the loop is freed. The memory area for the loop only has to be big enough for the objects created in a single pass. You'll find that trick repeated several times throughout the application.

Games with Portals.   A portal is an `Object` reference. In the simple case, all the methods that use the portal need to know the details of the object.

```
public class MyPortal {
   AsyncEvent warning;
   RealtimeThread logger;
   StringBuffer title;
};
```

This is probably the right way to code a portal object in most cases. If threads are sufficiently closely related to share a scoped memory area, they can both depend on a shared object layout.

Some situations, however, require a more flexible portal. Here are some options:

- Use a linked list of hook objects that contain a `nextHook` reference and a generic object reference. This structure can hook anything together, but it doesn't give much clue as to what the objects are.

- Add a name string to the hook:

```
public class Hook {
    Hook nextHook; // For the linked list
    Object payLoad;
    String name;
};
```

- Put the hooks in a tree and make it fast for users to find an object by its name. This generalizes the portal into something that contains an index of objects that any method can use just by knowing the API for the portal object and the name of the object it wants.

Fine Print

The RTSJ refers several times to memory that can be unexceptionally referenced from any scope. Since "any scope" includes no-heap real-time threads (see Chapter 14), "unexceptionally referenceable" means something that acts like immortal memory. The specification does not actually demand immortal memory. That purposeful omission gives implementations the flexibility to do "something clever." For instance, it might be possible to use JVM-supported reference-counted objects.

The important thing from a programmer's point of view is that many implementations are likely to use plain immortal memory for these things. A program might be able to get away with saving a reference to an object in scoped memory in a class variable on some exotic implementation of the RTSJ, but that would be a very nonportable practice. *Not recommended!*

The RTSJ contains another bit of artful flexibility. Objects in immortal memory persist as long as the application that created them. This behavior is intended to be general enough to apply gracefully to machines that execute bytecodes in hardware and may not strictly speaking have a JVM, but it allows some wiggle room for an implementation to free objects in immortal memory from time to time.

The closest I can find to a definition of application in the Java context is this quote from *The Java Virtual Machine Specification*, Second Edition, "Alternatively, the initial class could be provided by the implementation. In this case the initial class might set up a class loader that would in turn load an application, as in the Java 2 SDK, Standard Edition, v1.2." This leaves room for an RTSJ implementation to define a clean point at which immortal memory can be swept clean.

In any case, rules like "Objects created in any immortal area live for the duration of the application" apply to behavior, not implementation. If the implementation can delete objects in immortal memory without an application being able to tell that it happened, the implementer gets extra credit.

Quick Examples

This section presents seven examples of frequently-used scoped memory programming techniques.

newInstance can be used with constructors that have arguments, but the code that demonstrates that procedure is a bit long-winded. See Example 13–2.

Example 13–16 Allocating immortal memory

```
    Object alsoImmortal;

public void run(){
  // Create an immortal object using the simple
  // form of newInstance
  try{
    Object inImmortal = ImmortalMemory.instance().
      newInstance(Object.class);
  } catch (IllegalAccessException access){
    System.out.println(access);
  } catch (InstantiationException instant){
    System.out.println(instant);
  }
```

Example 13–16   Allocating immortal memory (Continued)

```
//Enter immortal, and use it to create an immortal
//object
ImmortalMemory.instance().enter(new Runnable() {
  public void run(){
    QuickImmortal.this.alsoImmortal = new Object();
  }
});

//Create a new thread that will start with its
//memory allocation context == Immortal
RealtimeThread nRtT = new RealtimeThread(null, null, null,
  ImmortalMemory.instance(),
  null,
  new NestedThread());
nRtT.start();
try{nRtT.join();} catch(Exception e){}
```

Example 13–17   Using a simple nested memory scope

```
//There are three forms of enter
//for nested scopes:
//Completely in-line
LTMemory lt = new LTMemory(1024, 2048);
lt.enter(new Runnable() { public void run(){
  System.out.println("Running in scoped memory");
}});

//Preallocated Runnable, but still
//dynamically bound to memory area
Runnable action = new Runnable() { public void run() {
  System.out.println("Running in scoped memory 2");
}};
lt.enter(action);

//Preallocated Runnable bound to memory
//at construction
LTMemory lt2 = new LTMemory(1024, 1024, new Runnable() {
  public void run() {
    System.out.println("Running in scoped memory 3");
  }
});
lt2.enter();
```

Example 13–18 Nesting a Heap memory area

```
HeapMemory.instance().enter(new Runnable(){
  public void run(){
    System.out.println("Running in heap");
  }
});
```

Example 13–19 Nested scope with parameters

```
class ActWithParm implements Runnable {
  public int parameter1;
  public Integer parameter2;
  public void run(){
    System.out.println("Parameter1 is " + parameter1);
    System.out.println("Parameter2 is " + parameter2);
  }
};
ActWithParm act = new ActWithParm();

act.parameter1 = 1414;
act.parameter2 = new Integer(3142);
lt.enter(act);
```

Example 13–20 Nested memory scope with return values

```
class ActWithReturn implements Runnable {
  int rInt;
  Object  rObject;
  public void run(){
    rInt = 707;
    class DynamicParm implements Runnable {
      public void run(){System.out.println("Sneaky");}
    }
    try{
      //We have to allocate the object in the
      //scope of the caller or a scope further
      //out than that.
      //"this" was created by the caller, so
      //it's a scope we can use to pass something
      //back to the caller
      rObject = MemoryArea.getMemoryArea(this).
        newInstance(DynamicParm.class);
```

Example 13–20 Nested memory scope with return values (Continued)

```
        } catch (InstantiationException e){
          System.out.println(e);
        } catch (IllegalAccessException e){
          System.out.println(e);
        }
    }
};
ActWithReturn actR = new ActWithReturn();
//This call returns an int and a Runnable
lt.enter(actR);
System.out.println("Returned " + actR.rInt);
((Runnable)actR.rObject).run();
```

Example 13–21 Thread using a shared scope

```
class ThreadAction implements Runnable {
  public void run(){
    System.out.println("In a thread");
  }
}
RealtimeThread rtt = new RealtimeThread(
  null,//Default scheduling parameters
  null,//Default release parameters
  null,//Default memory parameters
  new VTMemory(2048, 3000),//Initial memory area
  null,//Default group parameters
  new ThreadAction());//Runnable for the thread
rtt.start();
try{rtt.join();} catch(Exception e){}
```

Example 13–22 Thread using a memory area portal

```
class ThreadActionWPortal implements Runnable {
  public void run(){
    System.out.println("In a thread");
    System.out.println("Portal contains: " +
      ((ScopedMemory)getCurrentMemoryArea()).
        getPortal());
  }
}
final VTMemory pMem = new VTMemory(2048, 3000);
pMem.enter(new Runnable() { public void run(){
  pMem.setPortal(new String("This is a portal"));
  RealtimeThread rttp = new RealtimeThread(
    null,//Default scheduling parameters
    null,//Default release parameters
    null,//Default memory parameters
    null, //Initial memory area (pMem)
    null,//Default group parameters
    new ThreadActionWPortal()); //Runnable for the thread
  rttp.start();
  try{rttp.join();} catch(Exception e){}
}});
```

Chapter **14**

Non-Heap Access

▼ INTERACTION WITH SCHEDULER

▼ RULES

▼ SAMPLES

▼ FINAL REMARKS

The RTSJ defines a type of real-time thread that is not allowed to use objects in the heap. It cannot allocate them or touch them in any way. This is certainly an inconvenience, but it lets those threads behave as if there were no garbage collector. Most threads are delayed until the garbage collector gets to a clean point before they are allowed to interrupt it. A NoHeapRealtimeThread can preempt a thread that is in the garbage collector as quickly as it can preempt any other thread.

Some systems will find the strictly enforced ban on access to heap objects a convenient barrier between real-time and non-real-time threads, but for most applications, the discipline is seldom worth the pain.

Interaction with Scheduler

A simple priority scheduler will pay no attention to whether or not a thread can use the heap. The programmer can freely set the priority of a heap-using thread

227

above the priority of a no-heap thread (though this is not recommended practice), and the scheduler will respect the programmer's wishes.

Unless a no-heap thread is delayed by a higher-priority (or otherwise more eligible) thread that is using the heap, the scheduler does not need to include any garbage collection overhead, not even the garbage collector's normal preemption delay, in the overhead for the no-heap thread.

A sophisticated scheduler or a human architect working out a scheduling problem is interested in no-heap nature because it changes the preemption time for that thread, possibly by two or three orders of magnitude.

When a scheduler (human or mechanical) is computing whether a thread can meet its deadline, it has to include overhead. The time it takes to preempt the previous thread is part of that overhead. Most real-time environments keep the preemption time fairly short and predictable, but a Java runtime that includes garbage collection suffers preemption times that lengthen at hard-to-predict intervals

Threads that allocate from the heap need to include a time allowance for garbage collection. This can be such heavy overhead that it basically rules out threads that allocate from the heap for real-time purposes, unless the JVM uses garbage collection hardware or an incremental garbage collector.

Note that a human scheduler can see that a real-time thread is allocating exclusively from scoped or immortal memory, but the scheduler. in the Java run-

---

Real-time performance without RTSJ

Forcing garbage collection to become predictable is one of the two techniques that enabled the Java programming language real-time applications before the RTSJ. Although the specifications did not require it, the System.gc method would force a garbage collection on every JVM I know of. By coding System.gc at every point at which the application knew it would be idle long enough to complete a garbage collection cycle and by sizing the memory and the CPU appropriately, a programmer could ensure that the system never ran the garbage collector at an inconvenient time.

The other technique for making a conventional JVM run real-time code has little to do with the Java language—run critical tasks in native threads. Most of the code in a typical real-time application has timing requirements that are easy to meet in a conventional JVM (though the parts with tough timing requirements may use a large majority of the runtime). Code in the Java language the things that the Java environment can easily handle, and code the rest in C.

time cannot see that.[1] It has to assume that threads which can allocate from the stack will suffer garbage collection delays. The scheduler cannot even bound the number of garbage collections that will occur.

Incremental collectors are much easier to schedule. They do suffer garbage collection delays, and generally they come as slower memory allocation. This is convenient since garbage collection is part of each computation's normal runtime, not a nonschedulable overhead. Still, a warning: incremental collectors depend on an accurate estimate on the rate at which each thread will use memory. Using memory too fast may result in a stop-and-collect collection, or the scheduler may see it as an overrun. In either case, it disrupts the schedule.

Threads that do not allocate from the stack are still subject to garbage collector preemption delays. The worst-case preemption latency is available from the garbage collector:

```
RelativeTime n = RealtimeSystem.currentGC().getPreemptionLatency()
```

Even with a simple mark-and-sweep collector, the preemption latency is much less than the worst-case garbage collection time, but it is still much more than normal thread preemption time.

Table 14–1 shows times for a fictional Java runtime. They illustrate the difference between the delays inherent in dispatching and running threads.

Table 14–1 Example of garbage collection delays

Event	Time (microseconds)
Typical preemption	20
Worst-case preemption without garbage collection	60
Stop-and-collect garbage collection (assuming no finalizers)	800,000
Preempt the garbage collector	900

Rules

No-heap real-time threads must not touch the heap. If they did, they could cause corruption in the JVM. Figure 14–1 shows an example of a destructive interaction between a thread and the garbage collector it preempts.

---

1. It may be too strong a statement to say that the scheduler cannot see that a thread will not allocate from the heap during a particular computation. In many cases, it could see that by inspecting the bytecode. It is doubtful that the scheduler would bother since it could only make this computation when the code path was predictable.

Figure 14–1 Example of an unregulated no-heap thread corrupting the JVM

Thread	GC
	Inspects object A and notes that it contains a reference to object B.
	Inspects the no-heap thread's stack and sees no reference to object C.
Copies a reference to C from object X to the field in A that used to reference B.	
Moves null into the field in X that contained the reference to A.	
	Completes the mark phase. It sees no references to C, so it releases the memory for that object.
Stores into C. Since the memory that contained this object has been returned to the free pool, this store will probably cause some sort of corruption.	

The RTSJ does not permit a no-heap real-time thread to load or store a reference to an object in the heap. It is free to use objects in immortal or scoped memory.

The specification does not insist that each load or store[2] of a reference be checked at runtime, but references must be checked before the load or store completes. That could possibly be done by a trusted compiler or a verifier that runs when the class is loaded, but you can also assume that the check will be done when the bytecodes execute.

There is actually one thing a no-heap thread can do with a reference to a heap object. It can, validly, replace it with a reference to a non-heap object or a null. At worst, such a reference can cause an interrupted garbage collection to treat an object as alive when the last reference to the object was just obliterated by the no-heap thread. The garbage collection of an object is delayed until the next pass of the garbage collector, but with no actual harm done.

A no-heap thread has to be almost impossibly disciplined. Just loading a reference from a class variable will throw a `MemoryAccessError` if some thread stored a reference to a heap object in the variable. This is a serious problem that the RTSJ considers generally unrecoverable; it throws an *error*, not just an exception.

---

2.   An implementation need not check instructions that a store object references since the no-heap thread could not load a reference to an object on the heap into a place from which it could be stored.

Threads need access to their thread object. For a no-heap thread, this means the thread object must be in immortal memory or scoped memory.

Samples

Example 14–1 demonstrates creation of a NoHeapRealtimeThread that is rooted in immortal memory.

It is probably possible to create a NoHeapRealtimeThread in a non-real-time thread, but it will be painful. The NoHeapRealtimeThread object and all the objects it references have to be allocated in non-heap memory. You can allocate in non-heap memory from a regular thread, but NoHeapRealtimeThread has a no-arg constructor, so you need to use the long form of newInstance that uses the reflection classes. The code is much easier to write if you enter the scope you want to use, but you have to be in a real-time thread to use enter.

The NoHeapRealtimeThread object will be constructed in the memory area in which the constructor is called. It will contain lots of references, including a reference to the initial memory area for the thread. If the thread object is immortal,

Example 14–1 No-heap thread in immortal memory

```
/**A little Noheap thread */
public static class NhRTT extends NoHeapRealtimeThread{
  /** Constructor for NhRTT */
  public NhRTT(SchedulingParameters sched,
        MemoryArea mem){
    super(sched, mem);
  }
  public void run(){
    System.out.println("In NOHEAP!");
  }
}

/**Run method for a RealtimeThread */
public void run(){
  ImmortalMemory.instance().enter(new Runnable() {
    public void run(){
      NhRTT nhrtt = new NhRTT(null,
        ImmortalMemory.instance());
      nhrtt.start();
      try{
        nhrtt.join();
      } catch (InterruptedException e){}
  }});
}
```

the initial memory has to be immortal or at least be a scope created in immortal memory.

For purposes of rooting threads, scoped memory can be thought of as temporary immortal memory. The scoped memory will last as long as the thread—probably longer if the scope is used by other threads.

The main differences are these:

- A thread that is rooted in scoped memory will inherit the scope stack from its parent. This gives it easy access to shared scopes.
- Scoped memory is not viral. Scoped memory can contain references to heap (although a no-heap thread could not use those references), immortal, and other scoped memory with a longer lifetime. Immortal memory cannot hold references to scoped objects, and a no-heap thread cannot use references to heap. If you start in immortal memory, it is hard to get out.

Example 14–2 creates the no-heap thread and its initial memory area in the same scope. Since mem1 is the current memory area when the thread is constructed, it would have been the default initial memory area for the new thread. It is specified only for clarity.

Threads can share data if they have a memory area in common. Immortal memory works for everyone. Scoped memory works for threads with a common heritage. Example 14–3 illustrates threads that share data, and Example 14–4 shows how such threads are started.

Example 14–2 No-heap thread in scoped memory

```
private VTMemory mem1; //Memory for NH thread to use

/**Run method for a RealtimeThread */
public void run(){
  //Create the memory area the noheap thread
  //will use
  mem1 = new VTMemory(32*1024, 32*1024);

  mem1.enter(new Runnable() {public void run(){
    NhRTT nhrtt = new NhRTT(null,
      InScope.this.mem1);
    nhrtt.start();
    try{
      nhrtt.join();
    } catch (InterruptedException e){}
  }});
}
```

Example 14–3 Threads that share data

```
/** Something to share */
static class Sharable{
  private int value=0;
  synchronized void modify(int x){value += x;}
  int getValue(){ return value;}
}

/**A little Noheap thread */
static class NhRTT extends NoHeapRealtimeThread{
  Sharable foo;
  int adder;
  /** Constructor for NhRTT */
  public NhRTT(SchedulingParameters sched,
          MemoryArea mem,
          int adder,
          Sharable foo){
    super(sched, mem);
    this.foo = foo;
    this.adder = adder;
  }
  public void run(){
    for(int i = 0; i < 50; ++i){
      foo.modify(adder);
      try{sleep(500);
      } catch(InterruptedException e){}
    }
  }
}
```

Example 14–4 Starting the threads in Example 14–3

```
/**Run method for a RealtimeThread */
public void run(){
  //Create the memory area the noheap thread will use
  VTMemory mem0 = new VTMemory(8*1024, 8*1024);
  final VTMemory mem1 = new VTMemory(8*1024, 8*1024);
  final VTMemory mem2 = new VTMemory(4096, 4096);

  mem0.enter(new Runnable() {public void run(){
    //Make the things the threads will need
    final Sharable foo = new Sharable();
    NhRTT nhrtt1 = new NhRTT(null, mem1, 2, foo);
    NhRTT nhrtt2 = new NhRTT(null, mem1, -1, foo);
```

Example 14–4 Starting the threads in Exampl e14–3 (Continued)

```
//The threads don't need the monitor,
//but this is a good place to make it.
Runnable monitor = new Runnable() {
  public void run(){
    System.out.print(
      foo.getValue() + " ");
    try {
      Thread.currentThread().sleep(100);
    } catch (InterruptedException e){};
  }
};

//Start the threads
nhrtt1.start();
try{//Put a little delay between the threads
  sleep(200);
} catch (InterruptedException e){}
nhrtt2.start();

//Watch them run for a while.
for(int i = 0 ; i < 100; ++i)
  mem2.enter(monitor);

try{
  nhrtt1.join();
  nhrtt2.join();
} catch (InterruptedException e){}
}});
}
```

Final Remarks

A no-heap thread is easy to use if you control object creation, but you can never relax. Any time the thread needs to create an object that it does not want to create forever, you must enter a scoped memory. Any time you want to create an object with a lifetime that is less than the lifetime of the thread but does not fit a scope, you must create a special-purpose allocator for that type of object. (See Chapter 16.)

Even creation of no-heap threads can force the programmer to think too hard. All the initial parameters of the thread have to be accessible in the thread. That means they have to be in immortal memory, in the scope of the thread object, or in a scope outside the scope of the thread object. If the thread object is immortal, everything it references, including all the scope objects it enters, has to be created in immortal memory. (That does not mean you cannot use scoped memory. It does mean that you cannot enter a scoped memory that is created in another scoped memory. That `enter` will throw an error.)

My recommendation: Until you are very comfortable with the memory rules, start with the examples in this chapter, and if the no-heap thread needs to communicate with other threads while it runs, use only the one that uses immortal memory. Even then, try to start the no-heap thread in a scope and share that.

Memory leaks are easier to find in a little scope that is used in a small body of code than when you are allocating from a large immortal memory shared with all application code and the RTSJ implementation.

Notes

1. The RTSJ insists that no-heap threads must be able to access static fields and class objects. That does not mean a no-heap thread can use references stored in static fields. Applications commonly create an object and store a reference to that object in a static variable (consider the normal design pattern for a singleton object.) A no-heap thread is permitted to load only one of those references if the referenced object is not in heap memory.

2. The rules for no-heap threads do not say anything about storing references over heap references. If you want to store into `foo.bar`, you need to be certain that `foo` is not in heap memory, but you do not care what the previous value of `bar` is.

3. No-heap threads should not use thread enumeration. If a no-heap thread tries to enumerate the threads in a group that includes thread objects that are in heap memory, it will get values it cannot use.

    Thread objects in scoped memory already broke thread enumeration. The RTSJ permits thread objects in scoped memory, but only "related" threads would be allowed to see those objects.

Chapter **15**

More Async Events

▼ ASYNC EVENTS AND THE SCHEDULER
▼ THE CREATERELEASEPARAMETERS METHOD
▼ BOUND ASYNC EVENT HANDLERS
▼ ASYNC EVENT HANDLERS AND NON-HEAP MEMORY
▼ NO-HEAP EVENT HANDLERS VS. NO-HEAP THREADS
▼ SCHEDULING
▼ ASYNC EVENT HANDLERS AND THREADS
▼ SPECIAL ASYNC EVENTS

The discussion in Chapter 11 covers the use of basic async event handlers, but there is more. Async event handlers can use scoped memory, and like a `NoHeapRealtimeThread`, an async event handler can rise above the garbage collector.

For most purposes, a no-heap async event handler is a better way to run in no-heap mode than is a no-heap real-time thread.

Async Events and the Scheduler

When an async event is fired, the scheduler should activate all the async event handlers bound to that async event and increment a fire count associated with that handler. Each handler should remain active until its fire count reaches zero. Normally, the handler will just complete its `handleAsyncEvent` method, drop out the end, and become inactive, but if it is fired fast enough, the fire count may

237

become greater than 1. In that case, some of the details of the wrapper for handleAsyncEvent become visible:

```
do {
  handleAsyncEvent();
} while getAndDecrementPendingFireCount() > 1)
```

At first glance, it looks like the test in the while should be for > 0, or maybe even ≥, 0, but the test is after a call to handleAsyncEvent, and getAndDecrementPendingFireCount returns the value of fire count from before the decrement.

The scheduler has to watch all the methods on AEH that alter the value of the fire count.

The createReleaseParameters Method

Release parameters include fields like period, deadline, and cost. In the async event world, period is a characteristic of an async event, cost is related to each event handler, and deadline is shared between the event and the handler. The createReleaseParameters method on the AsyncEvent class is an aid to programmers. It constructs a new ReleaseParameters object (subclass, depending on the characteristics of the async event), fills in the values it knows, and inserts pessimistic values for things it does not know. The application should set values it knows before using this release parameters object for an async event handler.

Bound Async Event Handlers

A bound async event handler is permanently associated with a thread. Depending on the details of the implementation, a bound async event handler might be able to respond more quickly to events. An implementation could implement this so all bound async event handlers were bound to one shared thread, but that would violate the spirit of the specification. The idea is to *reserve* a thread for the AEH. The runtime can prime the thread to execute the AEH with execution poised to enter the AEH's handleAsyncEvent method. When a bound AEH fires, the runtime can handle it relatively quickly and predictably.

A side effect

Async event handlers are schedulable entities. They have (by the spec) all the capabilities of threads, but they do not have all the methods of a thread.

To get at those methods, the async event handler can get the current real-time thread (or no-heap real-time thread...depending on the heap discipline of the async event handler) and invoke its methods. The async event handler must be coded to expect a new thread every time it runs *unless it is a bound async event handler.*

You have to think about the ways async event handlers might be implemented to see the value of a bound async event handler. If the runtime creates a new thread for every async event handler, all async events are bound. But since the system is supposed to expect vast numbers of async event handlers, creating a thread per handler would be wasteful. Telling the runtime to bind an AEH to a thread tells the system that this AEH is important enough to warrant a little extra memory.

From the point of view of resource consumption, a bound async event handler is a thread, but unlike a thread, an AEH can be easily fired. A thread can be event driven and simulate the behavior of a bound async event handler, but programmers are better off using bound async event handlers. The RTSJ implementation has already built the mechanism for attaching them to an async event, and programmers can convert bound async event handlers to unbound ones and back by typing a few characters. Switching between thread and async event handlers is only easy if the thread duplicates the async event handler API.

Async Event Handlers and Non-Heap Memory

An async event handler can perform like a no-heap realtime thread, but the distinction is a constructor parameter, not a whole new class. If an `AsyncEventHandler` is constructed with the no-heap parameter `true`, the Java runtime will execute that AEH with the same reference tests (see "Rules" on page 229) and performance advantages (see "Interaction with Scheduler" on page 227) as a no-heap thread.

An async event handler that is constructed in scoped memory inherits the scope stack of the thread that creates it just as if it were a thread. This becomes important when the AIE needs to communicate with threads. It can always communicate through immortal memory, but if it uses scoped memory, it can share memory areas with its thread ancestors.

No-Heap Event Handlers vs. No-Heap Threads

Async event handlers can do anything a thread can do, but only bound async events have (something like) a thread object of their own.

A no-heap real-time thread can

- be placed in scoped memory and follow complex rules about references,
- run in immortal memory and take pains not to leak memory, or
- run partly in immortal and partly in scoped memory, which is easy if kept simple.

Unlike async event handlers, threads based in immortal memory have to contort themselves to be reusable. There is no way to change the run method on a thread.

Changeable run methods are a core technology for async event handlers. Somewhere under the hood, the system is hooking async event handlers to something like a thread and then hooking on another async event handler when that one handler completes.

Scheduling

Real-time threads and async event handlers are schedulable entities. They are officially equivalent from the point of view of the scheduler, but in fact, they have little overlap.

Threads are good at periodic scheduling. Async events are good at aperiodic scheduling.

The RTSJ has no way for a thread to tell the scheduler that it has finished handling an aperiodic event and is ready for another. There is no waitForNextTrigger.

The waitForTrigger function is part of the basic function of async event handlers, but they have nothing like waitForNextPeriod. PeriodicTimer is a subclass of AsyncEvent, but it does not have easily accessible release parameters. It is not designed for the application to modify its release parameters, and it has little flexibility in how it tells the scheduler it has completed a period.

Minimum Interarrival Time

Strictly aperiodic events are "unanalyzable." If you don't know how often the event handler will run, even one that costs very little could use 100 percent of the processor time. Sporadic events are aperiodic events with a budget.

Sporadic events are characterized by a minimum interarrival time (MIT.) The RTSJ platform does not have to service these events if they drive less than minimum interarrival time after the previous event. This sets a bound on the maximum processor time that can be used by the event handler, and the events become analyzable.

Enforcing minimum interarrival time for sporadic events calls for two decisions:

- *What to do if the event is fired too soon:*

    There are four choices.

    1. Ignore the fire.

2. Ignore the fire and throw an exception at the thread that invoked `fire`. (This is not much use if the event is fired by a happening.)

3. Replace the last fire. Doing so updates the deadline for handling the event to be relative to the new fire. This turns into `ignore` if the last fire has already caused an AEH to run to completion. It is also the same as `ignore` if the system is not enforcing deadlines.

4. Save the fire, but shift its completion deadline so it is one minimum interarrival time after the last fire.

   If the implementation is saving deadlines for MIT violations or if the deadline is greater than the MIT, the system may need to maintain a queue of pending deadlines.

- *What to do if the queue overflows:*

   1. Ignore the overflow and discard the new fire.

   2. Ignore the overflow, discard the new fire, and throw an exception.

   3. Replace the deadline at the tail of the queue with the new deadline.

   4. Lengthen the queue so it can hold the additional deadline. (This option is difficult to implement, probably slow, and may possibly leak immortal memory.)

Selection of the MIT-violation and queue-overflow policies is a graceful degradation question. The application cannot assume that there will be time to handle events that come faster than expected. Sometimes, it is not as difficult as it seems:

- If MIT violations are caused by the equivalent of someone pressing a doorbell button so the bell rings twice in quick succession and you want the deadline for answering the door to be expressed relative to the first ring, choose `ignore`.

- If you want it to be relative to the second ring, choose `replace`.

- If you want to tell the doorbell ringer how you feel about frantic visitors, choose `ignore` and throw an exception.

Async Event Handlers and Threads

An async event handler is not a thread, but it is schedulable. The distinction is confusing, and it may lead to trouble.

A `BoundAsyncEventHandler` is permanently bound to a thread. That thread must always be available to run the bound AEH. That may save time since the platform will not need to do anything to bind the AEH's state to a thread, but it may not do anything. It is an implementation detail.

Special Async Events

The RTSJ defines several internal uses for async events.

1.   If a thread (or AEH) misses its deadline, the scheduler can fire an AIE (Asynchronously Interrupted Exception—covered in Chapter 17).

2.   If a thread (or AEH) overruns its CPU budget, the scheduler can fire an AIE.

3.   The physical memory allocator can use async event handlers to notify callers when memory is inserted and removed.

4.   The `PeriodicTimer` and `OneShotTimer` classes fire async event handlers when they expire.

Chapter 16

Reusing Immortal Memory

▼ USING FIXED-OBJECT ALLOCATORS

▼ RECYCLING RT THREADS

▼ RECYCLING ASYNC EVENT HANDLERS

Prevent immortal memory leaks with this rule:

> **Do not allocate an immortal object from code that is executed more than once in the life of the application.**

And the corollary:

> **Try to create all immortal objects in static initializers.**

These restrictions rule out actual dynamic creation of immortal objects, but they do not prevent dynamic use of immortal objects. This is the motivation for reuse of immortal objects.

Using Fixed-Object Allocators

The fastest class of memory allocation algorithm is the fixed-block allocator. It uses constant time for memory allocation and constant time to return memory to the free pool. Its only problem is that all of its allocations are the same size. If you use a fixed-block allocator in a language like C, you can choose a likely size (say, 50 bytes), create an allocator with a pool of 50-byte blocks, and use those blocks for any structure whose size is not greater than 50 bytes.

The Java programming language does not support the concept of blocks of memory. The Java equivalent of a fixed-block allocator is an allocator that controls a pool of preallocated objects.

Carrier Objects

The free pool for a fixed-block allocator is normally kept in a singly linked list. When memory is returned to the allocator, the allocator redefines the memory as a structure with a link field in it and places that structure at the head of the free list. Java does not let us redefine memory in that way. If the objects in the free list already have a reference field that we can use to string them into a free list, excellent. If they don't, the allocator needs to provide little carrier objects (see the four examples below) to hold the next pointers.

Example 16–1 Fixed-object allocator declarations

```
class FreelistHook {
    FreelistHook next;
    StringBuffer payload;
}


private FreelistHook unusedHooks;
private FreelistHook freeList;
```

Example 16–2 Fixed-object allocator constructors

```
public BufferAllocator(){
    this(50);
}
public BufferAllocator(int num){
    for(int i = 0; i < num; ++i)
        freeHook(new FreelistHook());
    for(int i = 0; i < num; ++i)
        free(new StringBuffer());
}
```

Example 16–3 Hook management

```
private void freeHook(FreelistHook hook){
    hook.next = unusedHooks;
    unusedHooks = hook;
}

private FreelistHook getHook(){
    FreelistHook hook = unusedHooks;
    if(hook != null)
        unusedHooks = hook.next;
    return hook;
}
```

Example 16–4 Fixed-object allocate and free

```
public synchronized void free(StringBuffer node){
    FreelistHook hook = getHook();
    if(hook == null)
        throw new RuntimeException("Too few hooks");
    hook.payload = node;
    hook.next = freeList;
    freeList = hook;
}

public synchronized StringBuffer allocate(){
    FreelistHook hook = freeList;
    freeList = hook.next;
    StringBuffer node = hook.payload;
    freeHook(hook);
    if(node != null)
        node.setLength(0);
    return node;
}
```

Limitations

A fixed-object allocator is nearly useless for immutable objects. The Integer class is a good example of a class that defines an immutable object. Integer objects are assigned a value when they are created, and that value is permanently fixed in the Integer. We could build an allocator for Integer objects with the value 42, but we could not maintain a free list of Integer objects ready to take on a value.

The more an object can be modified after it is constructed, the more easily it can be used with a fixed-object allocator.

Recycling RT Threads

There is no way to give a thread a different `run` method after it has been created. Furthermore, there is no way to restart a terminated thread. In this respect threads are somewhat like the basic `java.lang` immutable objects: `String`, `Integer`, `Float`, etc. A `RealtimeThread` allocator that allows an application to reuse `RealtimeThread` objects in immortal memory needs to contend with those two problems.

The `run` method in a thread or real-time thread is invoked by a wrapper method that is part of the implementation. The wrapper calls the `run` method, and if the `run` method returns, the wrapper exits the thread. It also catches all throwables so they don't attempt to run off the end of the thread's stack.

The `run` method in a thread is fixed when the thread is constructed. There isn't any special trick for changing the `run` method for a real-time thread, but the problem can be solved with an added level of indirection. Instead of letting a programmer determine the `run` method for a thread, define a new class that uses a fixed `run` method which calls an inner `run` method that can be replaced.

The implementation of a reusable real-time thread can be an extension of `RealtimeThread`, or it can be a class that includes a `RealtimeThread` as a member. The latter works better because it lets the recycleable thread be a `Realtime-Thread` while it is in execution (not a subclass of `RealtimeThread`.) It also lets `ReusableThread` use method names that are final (and consequently not overrideable) in `RealtimeThread`. For instance, `join` on a reusable thread should return when the thread finishes executing and is ready to be reused. The `final join` method in `Thread` would never return since the thread itself never terminates.

The unfortunate aspect of not making `ReusableThread` a subclass of `RealtimeThread` is that it cannot be passed to methods that expect a `Thread` or `RealtimeThread`. It does implement `Schedulable`, so it can be used anywhere that requires a `Schedulable` or `Runnable` object.

The crux of a recycleable thread is the fixed master `run` method and a `start` method that releases the client thread (see Example 16–5).

Example 16–5 Master run method for reusable RealtimeThread

```java
private boolean keepAlive = true;
private boolean active = false;
private boolean started = false;
private boolean waitForStart = true;
private Runnable go = null;
private Object lock = new Object();
private int exitCt = 0;

/** This will be the run method for the client thread */
public void run(){
  while(keepAlive){
    //  active is false

    synchronized(lock){
      //  Wait until start() releases us to run
      //  or end() releases us to exit
      try {
        while(waitForStart && keepAlive)
          lock.wait();
        if(!keepAlive)
          break;
      } catch (InterruptedException e){
        continue;
      } finally {
        active = true;
        waitForStart = true;
      }
    } // end sync
    //  active is true
    //  Since start will throw an exception if it is
    //  called while active is true, and it is the only
    //  other method that writes waitForStart,
    //  waitForStart is also true.

    try {
      if(go == null)dummyGo();
      else
        go.run();  // Run the payload in this thread
    } catch(Exception e){
      //   Discard all exceptions
    } catch(Error t){
      keepAlive = false;
      throw t;
    } finally {
```

Example 16–5 Master run method for reusable RealtimeThread (Continued)

```
//  Wake anyone waiting in join
        synchronized(lock){
          active = false;
          exitCt += 1;
          lock.notifyAll();
        }
      }
    }
}

/** Use this method if the logic is still unspecified */
  private void dummyGo(){
    return;
  }
```

With all the synchronization and most of the special cases left out, the master run method is just a while loop like this:

```
while(keepAlive){
  try {
    go.run();
  } catch (Exception e){ // ignore them
  } catch (Error err) { // don't ignore these
  }
}
```

The thread's actual run method is the master run method above. The RealtimeThread class offers no way to replace the run method of a thread. The ReusableThread class doesn't solve this problem direction, but the master run method dispatches control to a second run method, go.run, which can be changed.

The synchronized blocks at the beginning and end of the master run method let it handshake with start, join, and end methods (see Example 16–6).

Example 16–6 Methods that handshake with the master run

```
/** Let the run method return next time through the loop.*/
  public void end(){
    synchronized(lock){
      keepAlive = false;
      lock.notifyAll();
    }
  }
}
```

Example 16–6 Methods that handshake with the master run (Continued)

```
/** wait for the run method to complete a task */
  public void join() throws InterruptedException {
    int lastExitCt = exitCt;
    synchronized(lock){
      if(!keepAlive) return;
      while(exitCt == lastExitCt)
        lock.wait();
    }
}

  /** If the run method is executing a task or about
   *  to execute a task, wait for it to complete.
   */
  public void joinIfRunning() throws InterruptedException {
    int lastExitCt = exitCt;
    if(active || !waitForStart)
      join();
  }

  /** Is the rt thread executing its payload? */
  public boolean isActive(){
    return active;
  }


  public void start(Runnable logic){
    synchronized(lock){
      if(active)
        throw new
          RuntimeException(
            "starting a running thread");
      if(!keepAlive)
        throw new
          RuntimeException(
            "starting a dead thread");
      go = logic;
      if(!started){
        started = true;
        innerThread.start();
      }

      //  Release the RT thread.
      //  It must be waiting or active would not be false
      waitForStart = false;
      lock.notifyAll();
    }
  }
```

In most respects, reusable threads act like ordinary ones. The logic running in the thread does not need to adapt to being in a reusable thread. The code that starts the thread needs to pass a `Runnable` as a parameter of the `start` method, and it needs to take extra care when using `join` since the thread may terminate multiple times.

The `join` method interacts with the `synchronized` block at the end of the master `run` method. The `start` and `end` methods interact with the `syncrhonized` block at the beginning.

The rules for interaction are as follows:

- **start.** This method will throw an exception in either of two situations:

  - If it is called on a `ReusableThread` that is currently running

  - If it is called on a `ReusableThread` that has stopped because its `end` method was called or because its client thread threw an error.

  If `start` does not throw an exception, it will release the client thread to run the payload `Runnable` passed to `start` and return to its caller.

- **join.** This method will throw `InterruptedException` if it returns because it was interrupted. Otherwise, it will wait for a client thread to complete and then unblock its caller.

  The `join` method will wait for the client to complete even if the master `run` method is idle when `join` is invoked. This is usually convenient, but it is a little dangerous.

- **joinIfRunning.** This method is designed for simple start/join sequences.

  ```
  rThread.start(logic);
  rThread.joinIfRunning();
  ```

  The `joinIfRunning` method will not block unless `rThread` is active or about to become active.

- **isActive.** This method simply tests whether the reusable thread is busy.

- **end.** This method will not interrupt the thread while it is running, but it will cause the master `run` method to exit the next time it completes a client. If the reusable thread is not busy, it will terminate immediately.

A set of constructors for recycleable threads mirrors the constructors of `RealtimeThread`. Example 16–7 shows a set of constructors that roughly mirrors the constructors for single-use real-time threads.

Example 16–7 Reusable RealtimeThread constructors

```
import javax.realtime.*;

public class ReusableThread implements Schedulable {
  /** A link field for the free list */
  public ReusableThread next = null;
  /** The hidden client thread. */
  private RealtimeThread innerThread;

  public ReusableThread(){
    create(null, null, null, null, null, go);
  }

  public ReusableThread(SchedulingParameters sched){
    create(sched, null, null, null, null, go);
  }

  public ReusableThread(SchedulingParameters sched,
      ReleaseParameters release){
    create(sched, release, null, null, null, go);
  }

  public ReusableThread(SchedulingParameters sched,
      ReleaseParameters release,
      MemoryParameters memory,
      MemoryArea area,
      ProcessingGroupParameters group,
      Runnable logic){
    create(sched,
        release,
        memory,
        area,
        group,
        logic);
  }

  private void create(SchedulingParameters sched,
      ReleaseParameters release,
      MemoryParameters memory,
      MemoryArea area,
      ProcessingGroupParameters group,
      Runnable logic){
    if(logic != null)
        go = logic;
```

Example 16–7 Reusable RealtimeThread constructors (Continued)

```
innerThread = new RealtimeThread(sched,
       release,
       memory,
       area,
       group, this);
}
```

A large set of methods does nothing but transfer operations on the thread from the recycleable object into the real thread. Example 16–8 contains a few examples of the accessor methods. There are many more, but they all follow this pattern.

Example 16–8 Some accessor methods

```
public boolean addIfFeasible(){
  return innerThread.addIfFeasible();
}

public boolean addToFeasibility(){
  return innerThread.addToFeasibility();
}

public void deschedulePeriodic(){
  innerThread.deschedulePeriodic();
}

public MemoryParameters getMemoryParameters(){
  return innerThread.getMemoryParameters();
}
```

Recycling Async Event Handlers

An async event handler is similar to a thread. Ideally, it will be a lighter-weight construct than a thread, so recycling it should generally be unnecessary unless the system moves through multiple phases each of which uses a separate large collection of async event handlers.

A reusable async event handler is surprisingly different from a reusable thread. The fundamental difference is that the JVM executes the run method of a thread once, but the RTSJ executes the handleAsyncEvent method of an async event handler repeatedly. (Or, if the async event handler was constructed with a logic parameter, it will call the run method of that object repeatedly.) It does not have a join method or a start method and turns out to be a fine candidate for implementation as a subclass of AsyncEventHandler. This is fortunate, since finding a way to make async events work with something other than async event handlers would have been difficult.

The reusable AEH (Example 16–9) consists of a set of constructors that override all AEH constructors that pass logic to the AEH, a fixed `handleAsyncEvent` method, and a new method, `setLogic`, that changes the code that will be executed when the AEH is invoked.

Example 16–9 A reusable async event handler

```
import javax.realtime.*;

public class ReusableAEH extends AsyncEventHandler {

  /** A link used to put this object
      in a free list */
  public ReusableAEH next;
  private Runnable logic;  //  The resettable logic

  public ReusableAEH(){
    super();
  }

  public ReusableAEH(boolean nonHeap){
    super(nonHeap);
  }

  public ReusableAEH(boolean nonHeap, Runnable logic){
    //  Note: Since we override handleAsyncEvent
    //  passing a logic parameter to the constructor
    //  has no effect.
    super(nonHeap);
    setLogic(logic);
  }

  public ReusableAEH(Runnable logic){
    setLogic(logic);
  }
  public ReusableAEH(SchedulingParameters scheduling,
      ReleaseParameters release,
      MemoryParameters memory,
      MemoryArea area,
      ProcessingGroupParameters group,
      boolean nonHeap,
      Runnable logic){
```

Example 16-9 A reusable async event handler (Continued)

```
  super(scheduling, release,
    memory, area, group, nonHeap,
    logic);  // Note: Passing in logic is harmless
  setLogic(logic);
}

// ... and other constructors matching all the
// AEH constructors.

/** Change the logic executed by this AEH */
public void setLogic(Runnable logic){
  this.logic = logic;
}

/** Call the runnable logic */
public void handleAsyncEvent(){
  if(this.logic != null)
    this.logic.run();
}
```

The code in Example 16–10 shows a way to use a reusable async event handler. The code does the following:

- Creates a reusable AEH.

- Creates an async event (a PeriodicTimer) attached to the AEH.

- Uses setLogic to set a Runnable to the AEH.

- Starts the timer.

- And sleeps for a while to show the async event working.

Up to this point, the reusable async event handler has worked like an ordinary one except that the logic was passed to it with setLogic instead of through the constructor.

If we were going to return the reusable AEH to a free list, we would want to detach it from its async events. That would be done with the removeHandler method on each associated async event. In the example, we do not need to completely free the AEH, just change its action, so the example just uses setLogic.

Example 16–10 Using a reusable async event handler

```
//  Make a reusable AEH
ReusableAEH rAEH = new ReusableAEH();

//  Make a source of events and attach
//  it to our reusable AEH
PeriodicTimer timer = new PeriodicTimer(
  null, // start now
  new RelativeTime(1000, 0),// tick once per second
  rAEH);

//  Associate a Runnable with the AEH
rAEH.setLogic(new Runnable() {
  public void run(){
    System.out.println("tick");
  }
});

timer.start();

//  Let the AEH print ticks for a while
try {
  Thread.sleep(10000);
} catch(Exception e){}

//  Attach a new Runnable that prints tocks
rAEH.setLogic(new Runnable() {
  public void run(){
    System.out.println("Tock");
  }
});

//  Now let it print tocks for a while
try {
  Thread.sleep(10000);
} catch(Exception e){}

//  Unhook the AEH from the timer
timer.removeHandler(rAEH);
```

Chapter 17

Asynchronous Transfer of Control

Asynchronous transfer of control (ATC) is a mechanism (broadly similar to `Thread.stop`) that lets one thread throw an exception into another thread. ATC is important for some classes of real-time applications. The RTSJ defines a class, called `AsynchronouslyInterruptedException` (AIE), for asynchronous exceptions, with special rules that make the exceptions safe for use with the Java programming language:

1. The target thread will not service an asynchronously interrupted exception until it reaches a method that explicitly throws `AsynchronouslyInterruptedException`.

2. The AIE will be asserted immediately if the target thread is in a method that throws it; otherwise, the AIE will remain pending until it enters such a method.

3. When control enters a method that throws AIE and an AIE is pending, it is thrown immediately.

4.   The pending AIE remains pending until it is serviced.

5.   An AIE can be thrown at a thread that already has an AIE pending. The new AIE will replace the pending one if it is aimed at a less deeply nested method.

The AIE was invented because some real-time programmers find this type of function crucial. Others find it repulsive. If you are in that class, don't use ATC. The RTSJ does not force you to learn to use ATC in order to use its other features.

AIE is similar to longjmp from a signal handler

The C language allows a program to jump to a saved point somewhere up the stack from the point of the jump. It is a powerful feature that lets a program leap instantly to a fixed location no matter where it has called from that function.

The signal intercept routine is another interesting feature of C in a UNIX-like system. It is a function that the runtime environment calls when a signal is sent to the thread. It works as if something inserted a call to the signal handler function between two instructions in the thread. If the signal handler returns, the interrupted thread resumes where it was interrupted.

Since the signal handler is executed in the context of the interrupted thread, it can longjmp to contexts saved by that thread. This makes it easy to code things like "execute this function for 20 seconds, then jump here," or "do what you like, but if this child process exits unexpectedly, jump here immediately."

C++ added exceptions as one of its extensions to the C language. Exceptions offer all the good points of longjmps, except speed, and have removed most of the problems inherent in long uncontrolled leaps around a program.

Many programmers (justifiably) dislike longjmp and signal intercept routines individually and together.

The RTSJ uses an exception for the abrupt transfer of control and a carefully worked out mechanism for the insertion of exceptions in a running thread. Time will tell whether it is a better mix of power and safety than longjmp from a signal handler.

Below are some problems asynchronous transfer of control was invented to solve:

- A system should run a computation for *n* microseconds. It is the type of computation (maybe calculating pi) that will continue to refine its result as it runs, so it is not an error for it to want to run forever.

- A thread with timing constraints wants to call a blocking service. Perhaps it wants to open a file. It is willing to wait *n* milliseconds for the open method to return, then it has to continue whether the file is open or not.

- A thread has gone out of control. A supervisory thread needs to terminate it.

- A periodic thread with an overrun handler needs to change its logic as soon as an overrun is detected.

Thread Interrupt in Context

Thread interrupt is an old feature of the Java language. Calling a thread's `interrupt` method puts the thread into the interrupted state Blocking services that do not have effects other than blocking (like `sleep`, `join`, `wait`, `waitForAll`, `getNextEvent`, and others), unblock and throw an `InterruptedException` if `interrupt` is called on the blocking thread or if the thread is in interrupt state when the call is made. I/O calls are also supposed to unblock and throw an exception if the thread is interrupted. For I/O operations, the exception is `InterruptedIOException`, which allows the I/O operation to include information about how far the I/O operation got before it was interrupted.

The Java programming language formerly included a `stop` method on the `Thread` class. It would throw a `ThreadDeath` exception into the thread immediately unless the thread was in the middle of acquiring a lock. The `stop` method was deprecated for two reasons:

1. It suggests more than it delivers. The `ThreadDeath` exception is as catchable as any other exception; consequently, the `stop` method cannot stop a malicious thread or even one that accidentally catches and ignores the `ThreadDeath` exception. (It is pretty easy to ignore `ThreadDeath` accidentally—just use `catch(Throwable e)`.)

2. It may cause corruption of objects. `Thread.stop` can interrupt a thread that is holding a lock and maintaining a data structure. It unceremoniously releases the lock even if that leaves the data structure partially updated.

So, Java has already tried a version of ATC and rejected it as a bad idea, but the language still has a mechanism that interrupts many blocking calls and sets a bit in the interrupted thread object that the thread can check. Why does the RTSJ add a new mechanism? Is it really new?

The standard `interrupt` mechanism is insufficient because of the following behaviors:

1. A conforming implementation of the JVM can completely ignore interrupts during I/O operations or other blocking methods. A real-time application needs a stronger assurance than this.

2. The conforming standard JVM can even ignore interrupts during non-I/O blocking operations.

3. The interrupt actually causes an exception (optionally) only when the thread is blocked. At other times the thread must poll for an interrupt.

The worst-case response time for polling depends on the frequency of polling. A thread that needs to respond quickly to being interrupted will be cluttered with `if(!interrupted())` and `while(!interrupted)`. This is hard to read and all the extraneous tests degrade overall performance. It is especially hard to maintain proper polling of the interrupted attribute when the thread moves through methods that are shared among threads with different responsiveness constraints and through standard libraries that may ignore the interrupted state altogether.

4. Interrupts are not tagged. A standard Java platform makes no provisions for a thread that is interrupted while it is already in interrupted state.

The `stop` method on thread objects is insufficient for these reasons:

1. It is deprecated. The RTSJ could have restored the mechanism, but the claims against `ThreadDeath` are valid and important.

2. `ThreadDeath` can be caught inadvertently by `catch(Throwable e)`.

3. `ThreadDeath` can interrupt a thread when it is not prepared to be interrupted. In particular, `ThreadDeath` can interrupt the thread in a synchronized block. This behavior is very difficult to program around.

4. There is no provision for interrupting a thread that has a `ThreadDeath` exception "in flight."

The RTSJ mechanism for asynchronous transfer of control addresses these difficulties, except for termination of malicious threads.

- **Consistent implementation.** The RTSJ requires that every blocking operation be interruptible by an AIE. The specification does not require a particular response time, but the delay cannot be unbounded. I/O operations are required to unblock if they are interrupted.

- **Consistent conversion to an exception.**
  `AsynchronouslyInterruptedException` cannot be ignored without serious effort. An application is unlikely to ignore the exception by mistake.

- **No polling.** Polling for AIE is not required. As with `stop`, calling `interrupt` on a `RealtimeThread` object will throw an exception into the target thread almost immediately.

- **Hard to discard inadvertently.** An AIE can be caught inadvertently, but the platform will raise the exception again if it is not handled according to a particular formula. That is, it can be caught inadvertently, but it will not stay caught.

- **Safe with legacy code.** Only methods that are designed to handle asynchronous exceptions can be interrupted by them. Unless a method signature throws `AsynchronouslyInterruptedException`, it cannot be interrupted asynchronously. Methods that do not throw that exception will run to completion. By doing nothing, an application protects uninterruptible operations.

- **Safe with locks.** Interrupting synchronized code is unwise, and the RTSJ does not do it. Synchronized blocks, even when they appear in methods that throw `AsynchronouslyInterruptedException`, cannot be interrupted. If an algorithm really wants to find out about an AIE in the middle of a synchronized block, it can poll the `isInterrupted` method for it.

- **Provides for reinterrupt.** A `RealtimeThread` can be reinterrupted while an AIE is in flight. Rules in the RTSJ determine whether the new exception will replace the previous one.

Asynchronous Interrupt Firing

The RTSJ provides three ways to raise an AIE. The `interrupt` method on `RealtimeThread` throws a *generic* AIE into the thread, the `fire` method on `AsynchronouslyInterruptedException` causes an AIE that is directed at a particular method, and at an assigned moment a `Timed` object throws an AIE at the `run` method it is given. (A thread can also just `throw` an AIE at itself, but then it isn't actually asynchronous.)

The Timed Class

Real-time applications frequently contain specifications like

> Wait 200 milliseconds for a response, then stop the process and initiate recovery

or

> Spend up to 1022 microseconds refining the computation, take the best result, and pass it to the next step in the computation

or

> The thread should not execute for more than 10 seconds. If it does, warmstart the subsystem by killing threads A, B, and C, cleaning their data structures, and restarting them.

or other instructions that include a time limit. The forms are so common in real-time systems that the RTSJ includes a subclass of `AsynchronouslyInterruptedException` that is specialized for time-based exceptions.

The `Timed` class is a self-firing AIE. It executes the `run` method of its `Interruptible` argument until its alarm goes off and then fires itself at the `run` method.

This is not sophisticated code. If the `Timed` class were not part of the RTSJ, it would definitely be an example in this chapter. Since it will probably be one of the most frequently used applications of ATC, it deserves several pages of careful treatment, but it is also simple. Do not be misled by the numerous pages this chapter spends on obscure topics like seizing an exception intended for another method. Timed is important.

The constructor for a Timed object includes a HighResolutionTime parameter. If the time is an interval, it is measured from some point between the time at which control enters doInterruptible and the time at which it enters the run method. If the time is an absolute time, the timer expires at the designated moment.

Since it would be a shame to construct a Timed object and only get to use it once, the Timed class includes a resetTime method that replaces the time attribute of a Timed object.

Reuse of a Timed object

A Timed object can be constructed once and used many times. If its time-out value does not vary, it can be reused without modification. If the time-out must change, the resetTime method can alter the time-out.

If you do not use the resetTime method, a Timed object that uses a relative time can be used repeatedly so long as the application doesn't want to change the interval. Changing the interval, or reusing the object if it was set with an absolute time, requires the use of resetTime.

It is particularly easy to see the importance of the mechanism for nearly forcing AIEs to have target methods and propagate until they get to those methods.

The basic timed method goes like this:

Example 17–1 Basic timed method

```
Timed timed = new Timed(new RelativeTime(1000,0));
timed.doInterruptible(new Interruptible() {
    public void run(
            AsynchronouslyInterruptedException e)
            throws AsynchronouslyInterruptedException{
        while(true){
            System.out.print(".");
            try {Thread.sleep(10);}catch(Exception ie){}
        }
    }
    public void interruptAction(
            AsynchronouslyInterruptedException e){
    System.out.println("In interruptAction");
    }
});
```

There is not much to say about this example except that the Interruptible object should not assume that it ran for its full allotted time. It can be interrupted by an AIE other than the one that signifies that its time is up—perhaps by another timer in a method somewhere on the call stack or by a non-time-based AIE.

Many of the examples in this book include sleeps that seem unnecessary. They are there because of an artifact of one version of Linux. High (real-time) priorities are only accessible to tasks with root privileges. Without access to higher priorities for event handlers, busy wait loops will lock out an event handler and the examples will run incorrectly.

The sleeps give the event handler a chance to run even if it is forced down to the same priority as the main thread.

If the method in Example 17–1 were called from another timed method, the timers would be kept straight. If the method in the example ran out of time first, it would be interrupted. The outer timed method could find out that this method had been interrupted, but the outer timed method would run normally until it completed or until its time ran out.

If the time for the outer method ran out first, the method in the example would be interrupted but the AIE would continue to propagate from that Timed object until it reached the Timed object that had expired.

This all happens automatically. It only gets nasty if you want to make it work some other way.

The interrupt Method

The interrupt method on RealtimeThread is largely compatible with the same method on regular Thread objects. Like interrupt on an ordinary thread, interrupt on a RealtimeThread sets the interrupted attribute of the thread. If the thread is blocked in an I/O operation and cannot be certain it will unblock in a bounded length of time, the system will break out of the I/O operation and throw an InterruptedException.

In any case, if the thread is not ATC deferred, it is immediately thrown an AsynchronouslyInterruptedException. If it is ATC deferred, the AIE remains pending on the thread until it enters code that is not ATC deferred; then the exception is thrown immediately.

The exception generated by the public interrupt method on RealtimeThread is called a generic AIE. It is not associated with a doInterruptible method. Its target is the thread itself, and it will usually kill the thread.

Calling `interrupt` on a `RealtimeThread` object is an excellent way to terminate that thread. If the target thread is expected to catch the exception and continue
execution, the `fire` method is a better way to trigger the asynchronous exception.

The fire Method

The `fire` method on `AsynchronouslyInterruptedException`, together with the
AIE object's `doInterruptible` method, allows asynchronous interrupts to be
directed at particular methods. Unless the programmer takes extraordinary measures, the AIE will propagate until it reaches the target method, at which point it
can be caught and deactivated.

This targeting of AIEs is included in the RTSJ to let routines with various
requirements for asynchronous interrupts be nested without requiring special
cooperation between the routines. Imagine methods `foo` and `bar`. Each of these
methods was coded with the bulk of their processing enclosed in a `Timed` object
that protects them against using excessive time by firing an AIE targeted at the
`Timed` object after a preset interval.

`Foo` can call `bar` or `bar` can call `foo` without confusion. An AIE directed at
the inner method will interrupt its timed component and be caught there. An AIE
directed at the outer method will interrupt the inner method and be caught there,
but the platform will automatically rethrow the exception until it reaches the
outer method.

Simple use of ATC involves the following steps:

1.   Create an `AsynchronouslyInterruptedException`.

This a blatant example of the thread cooperating with the entity that will
throw an asynchronous exception at it.

The thread should make certain that the exception will be accessible in the
thread that will fire it and the thread that created it. Since the exception will
not propagate up the stack from this point in the target, it does not need to
be accessible there.

```
import javax.realtime.*;

public class One extends RealtimeThread {

    AsynchronouslyInterruptedException aie;

    public void run(){
        One.this.aie =
            new AsynchronouslyInterruptedException();
```

2. **Write interruptible code and call it with `doInterruptible`.**

The `doInterruptible` method uses the closure idea. Code inside `doInterruptible` expects to be interrupted by its own AIE. The exception will propagate to this point and disappear.

The argument to `doInterruptible` is a class that implements the `Interruptible` interface. The interface includes two methods:

- `public void run(`
    `AsynchronouslyInterruptedException ex)`

- `public void interruptAction(`
    `AsynchronouslyInterruptedException ex)`

The `run` method can be written without

`throws AsynchronouslyInterruptedException`

but that would be unusual since that would cause AIEs to remain pending during execution of the `run` method, and the point of the exercise is managing an AIE.

```
One.this.aie.doInterruptible(
      new Interruptible() {
   private volatile int n;
   public void interruptAction(
      AsynchronouslyInterruptedException aie){
    System.out.println("Interrupted at " + n);
   }

   public void run(
         AsynchronouslyInterruptedException aie)
         throws
         AsynchronouslyInterruptedException {
      for(int i = 0; i < 10000000; ++i){
       try{Thread.sleep(1);} catch(Exception e){}
       n += 1;
      }
      System.out.println("Something's wrong.");
   }
});
```

Interruptible methods can be interrupted by any AIE directed at their thread, not just the AIE from which they are called.

3.   Fire the interrupt.

The thread could fire the exception at itself, but that would have to be called
a degenerate case. It is more interesting when another thread or an async
event handler fires the exception.

If no thread is currently using the AIE's doInterruptible method, the
fire method immediately returns false.

```
if(rt1.aie.fire())
    System.out.println("Fire returned true");
else
    System.out.println("Fire returned false");
```

If the AIE is enabled and the target thread is executing a method that throws
AsynchronouslyInterruptedException and it is not in synchronized code,
the AIE will be thrown immediately.

- *If control is in a method that does not throw AIE:*

  The exception will remain pending until control enters a method that
  does throw AIE, then it will be thrown immediately.

- *If the AIE is disabled:*

  The AIE will be flagged so an interrupt will be thrown when the AIE is
  reenabled. The AIE can be successfully fired multiple times while it is disabled. The fire will behave as if the AIE was not masked, and the interrupt will either be dropped or replace the saved interrupt according to the
  same replacement rules that govern interrupts that are fired while one is
  already propagating.

4.   Deal with being interrupted.

The exception will percolate up the call stack until it reaches the run method
called by doInterruptible. If the interruptAction method is empty,
control will quietly jump from the middle of the run method.

The interruptAction method is provided for cases in which the code
needs to know it has been interrupted and take some action: store final
results, log an error, set up for a future run, or whatever.

In Summary

Methods that do not throw AIE and synchronized blocks are ATC deferred. In
these lexical contexts, asynchronous interrupts are made pending. They remain
pending until control enters an area that is not ATC deferred, then they are
propagated.

When an AIE is fired at a thread, when it is thrown, or when it is propagated,
it transfers control to the nearest suitable catch or finally block. The suitable
target will be in an ATC-deferred region.

If the thread is blocked in `wait`, `sleep`, `join`, or in an I/O operation that throws `InterruptedIOException`, the AIE will unblock the thread.

If control leaves an ATC-deferred region because the code throws an exception other than an AIE, the pending AIE will replace the thrown exception. If the thrown exception is an AIE, replacement rules apply.

Replacement Rules

It is possible to call the `fire` method on `AsynchronouslyInterruptedException` object `aie1` while an AIE is already "in flight" on the target thread. If the `doInterruptible` for `aie1` is currently on the call stack, `fire` will return true, and the following actions then occur:

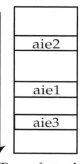

1. If the AIE in flight is `aie2`, which is deeper on the stack than `aie1`, then the new exception will be silently ignored

2. If the AIE in flight targets `aie3`, which is less deeply nested on the call stack, then `aie1` will replace `aie3` and exception processing in the target thread will continue with the new exception.

Rule 2 is the replacement rule. The RTSJ runtime can replace an AIE with another AIE at any time up to the moment when the internals of the target `doInterruptible` (probably a call to happened) recognizes the interrupt. Before that time, the runtime can replace an AIE with another one that is aimed farther up the stack, without disrupting operation.

Top of stack

The RTSJ also specifies replacement when an AIE collides with another exception. The AIE always replaces other exceptions. While a thread is in an ATC-deferred state, it can throw and catch other exceptions, but at the moment when the thread leaves ATC-deferred state, any pending AIE will auto-propagate, for example, if

```
method x()
  calls
  method y throws AIE
    calls
    method z() throws IOException,
```

and the thread receives an AIE while z is executing. Even if z throws `IOException`, reentry into y will cause the AIE to auto-propagate and the AIE will immediately be thrown into method x. It does not matter whether method z returns normally or throws an exception, no code in method y will execute, any exception will be lost, and control will land in a `catch` clause in x.

Rules for Async Exception Propagation

The easy way to explain AIE propagation is with two points:

- An `AsynchronouslyInterruptedException` that is thrown by the `interrupt` method on a `RealtimeThread` object propagates all the way through the thread and causes it to terminate.

- An `AsynchronouslyInterruptedException` thrown by the `fire` method on an AIE object propagates until it reaches the `doInterruptible` for that AIE. There it stops. On the way to the stopping place, the exception will execute every appropriate `catch` block that catches `AsynchronouslyInterruptedException` and every appropriate `finally` clause.

Oblivious catch

Propagation is automatic if the programmer uses standard Java exception processing mechanisms and the `fire` and `doInterruptible` methods on the `AsynchronouslyInterruptedException` object. It can get more complicated if the application reaches into the internals of AIE processing.

An `AsynchronouslyInterruptedException` has special properties, but it is in most respects an ordinary Java-language exception. It can be caught with a specific `catch` clause,

```
catch (AsynchronouslyInterruptedException e){...
```

or a broad `catch` clause, like

```
catch (InterruptedException e){...
```

or even,

```
catch(Throwable t){...
```

In any of these cases the RTSJ runtime will follow this sequence of events:

1. **Fire.** Some thread or async event handler fires the AIE, and the RTSJ runtime uses an internal mechanism to throw an asynchronously interrupted exception aimed at one particular `doInterruptible`.

2. **Schedule.** A thread almost never fires an AIE at itself. That means the first part of the AIE processing takes place in the thread that calls `fire`, and the bulk of the processing takes place in the target thread. The second part of the processing does not take place until the scheduler chooses to execute the target thread.

3. **Locate target stack frame.** The Java runtime locates the target thread and finds the first `catch` clause that matches the exception or the first `finally` clause. Either the thread that calls `fire` or the target thread could do this,

but the best performance will probably come from JVMs that find the target frame before the target thread is dispatched.

> **Finally clauses in methods that throw AysnchronouslyInterruptedException cannot be trusted. They will not be executed if the method is interrupted.**

The behavior of `catch` clauses and `finally` clauses in methods that throw AsynchronouslyInterruptedException is deceptive. The exception never executes those clauses. The AIE would auto-propagate as soon as control entered a method that throws AIE. So when the JVM is propagating an AIE, the JVM only considers `catch` and `finally` clauses in methods that do not throw AIE.

Assume that the first thing the Java runtime finds in looking up the stack is a `catch(Throwable t)` clause in a method that does not throw AIE. The following sequence then occurs:

1. **Transfer control in the target thread.** The Java runtime transfers control to the `catch` clause just as if AIE was an ordinary exception.

2. **Catch.** The `catch` clause executes to completion.

3. **Continue.** The method containing the `catch` clause continues until it executes a `return` or an `athrow` bytecode.

4. **Rethrow.** The runtime support for the `return` and `athrow` bytecodes notices that the AIE has been caught but is still pending. It rethrows the exception without any program involvement, and the exception propagates up the stack to the next matching `catch` or `finally` clause.

Nonmatching doInterruptible

An AIE can pass through any number of `doInterruptible` methods before it reaches its target. Unlike the oblivious `catch`, `doInterruptible` understands the special properties of an asynchronous interrupt. Starting at the point where the AIE reaches the `doInterruptible` method...:

1. **catch.** The AIE is caught in a

       catch (AsynchronouslyInterruptibleException e)

   clause hidden in `doInterruptible`.

2. **interruptAction.** The `catch` clause calls the `interruptAction` method on the `Interruptible` object that was passed to `doInterruptible`. By default, that method does nothing, but it can be overridden to take application-specific action when the `run` method is interrupted.

3. **finally.** The call to the interruptAction method is wrapped in a try/finally construct so that no matter what is thrown from interruptAction, the code in the finally clause will execute.

4. **happened.** The finally clause contains a call to the happened(true) method on the current AIE object. The happened method is designed to determine whether the exception matches this AIE.

5. **propagate.** The happened method detects that the exception is not aimed at this doInterruptible. Since the parameter to happened is true, it will propagate the AIE, which in this case amounts to rethrowing the exception.

Matching doInterruptible

An AIE being caught in its own doInterruptible method proceeds like one in a nonmatching doInterruptible until it calls happened. Starting at that point, the exception is handled differently:

1. **happened.** The finally clause contains a call to the happened(true) method on the current AIE object.

2. **return.** The happened method detects that the exception *is* aimed at this doInterruptible. For this exception it doesn't matter whether the parameter to happened was true or false. The method will return true, which doInterruptible ignores since happened(true) does not return unless the current AIE is the target.

   Control returns from doInterruptible. Since the AIE was handled in this function, the AIE is no longer pending and the return bytecode does not rethrow the AIE. Unless the interruptAction method did something that is visible to the surrounding class, the code that called doInterruptible cannot tell whether the Interruptible method was interrupted or ran to completion.

Internals

The propagation of an AIE depends on a careful interaction of the bytecode interpreter and the catch clause in doInterruptible.

First the bytecodes:

- **areturn, dreturn, freturn, ireturn, and return**

  All of these bytecodes return from one method to another. If the AIE pending flag is set and they are returning to a method that throws AIE, they should immediately throw the pending AIE.

- **monitorexit**

  This bytecode tells the JVM that it has reached the end of a synchronized block. This is affected by a pending AIE just as the return byte codes are.

- **invokeinterface, invokespecial, invokestatic, invokevirtual**

  All of these bytecodes call from one method to another. If the AIE pending flag is set and they are invoking a method that throws AIE, the bytecodes should immediately throw the AIE that is pending.

- **athrow**

  This bytecode has to notice when it being used to throw an AIE. For consistency, throwing an AIE from a context that is not ATC-deferred has to behave as if throwing an AIE was the same as firing it. In a context that is ATC-deferred, the athrow bytecode should act as if it were an ordinary exception, transferring control to the "nearest suitable catch block."

  When athrow finds a finally block or a catch clause that matches the exception, it transfers control to the target code.

  The runtime will ignore catch and finally blocks in methods that throw AIE when it is looking for the matching catch block. This includes narrowly defined catch blocks like:

        catch (AsynchronouslyInterruptedException e)

  and finally blocks

        finally {
        }

  and broadly defined catch blocks like

        catch (Throwable t)

- **monitorenter**

  Save the thread AIE deferred state, and make the thread state AIE deferred.

- **monitorexit**

  Restore the thread AIE deferred state, and throw an AIE if appropriate.

  Next, the runtime reactions to an asynchronously interrupted exception (AIE) (Table 17–1 and Table 17–2):

Table 17-1 Runtime reaction to an AIE

State	Action
Ordinary code: method does not throw AIE	Mark the thread for pending AIE.
Interruptible	Mark the thread for pending AIE. Immediately throw the AIE.
Propagating an exception other than AIE	Mark the thread for pending AIE. Discard the exception and replace it with the AIE.
In a synchronized block	Mark the thread for pending AIE.
Blocked in `wait`, `sleep`, or `join`	Mark the thread for pending AIE and throw the AIE.

Table 17-2 Runtime reaction to a pending AIE

State	Action
Leaving a synchronized block in a method that does not throw AIE	Do nothing.
Leaving a synchronized block in a method that throws AIE	Throw the AIE.
Entering a method that does not throw AIE	Do nothing.
Entering a method that throws AIE	Throw the AIE.
Returning to a method that does not throw AIE	Do nothing.
Returning to a method that throws AIE	Throw the AIE.
In a `happened` method that matches the AIE	Turn off the AIE pending flag for the current thread.
In a `happened` method that does not match the AIE	Throw the AIE if `happened`'s parameter is `true`.

Several methods in `AsynchronouslyInterruptedException` help with propagation:

- **boolean doInterruptible(Interruptible logic)**

  This method is the usual fully automated way to manage asynchronously interrupted exceptions. It catches AIE, which it propagates only if it should.

- **boolean happened(boolean propagate)**

  This is an instance method of `AsynchronouslyInterruptedException`. It atomically decides whether the current exception belongs to it. (It just compares the current exception to `this`. They match if they are the same.) The method then acts on that decision:

```
if(there is no current AIE)
   return false    //What are we doing here?
if(match)
   make the AIE non-pending
   return true
else   // not a match
   if(propagate)
      propagate the exception (throw it)
   else
      return false // leave the AIE pending
```

If we write off the `null` case as some nut calling `happened` just for fun, we're left with the following decision table:

Table 17–3 Decision table for happened method

	propagate==true	propagate==false
match	pending off, return `true`	pending off, return `true`
no match	propagate	return `false`

Note particularly, that if `happened` returns, it will return with the AIE pending flag off.

> ## Careless use of the happened method can lose an AIE.

- **propagate**
  If there is a current/pending AIE, this method throws it. It is intended to be used from `happened` and from hand-coded handlers for AIE. One extremely convenient feature of the `propagate` method is that it does not include `throws AsynchronouslyInterruptedException` in its signature. That means that you can use it without enclosing it in a `try`/`catch` (which would make `propagate` somewhat pointless) or without including `throws AsynchronouslyInterruptedException` in the signature of the method that calls `propagate`.

  Most of the remaining methods on `AsynchronouslyInterruptedException` are helper methods for `doInterruptible`:

- **boolean fire()**
  Normally, `fire` throws the AIE into the target thread, but if the AIE's `doInterruptible` method is not active, `fire` returns `false`.

- **boolean disable()**

  This method is only valid while `doInterruptible` in the AIE is active. It defers this exception. If the AIE is fired while it is disabled, it is deferred until `enable` is called or `doInterruptible` returns.

- **boolean enable()**

  This method is only valid while the `doInterruptible` method in the AIE is active. If the AIE is disabled, this method enables it. If the AIE was deferred by the `disable`, `enable` throws it.

- **boolean isEnabled()**

  This method returns `true` if this AIE is enabled; otherwise, it returns `false`.

  The last method on `AsynchronouslyInterruptedException` is:

- **getGeneric**

  This class method returns an instance of the exception that is thrown when the `interrupt` method on `RealtimeThread` is called with no arguments. (Which is the only visible version of the `interrupt` method.)

Application Handling for Asynchronous Interrupts

The `doInterruptible` method is a convenience, but you can properly handle asynchronous exceptions by putting the right protocol in a catch block. Example 17–2 shows one way to catch the kind of AIE thrown by the `interrupt` method on `RealtimeThread`.

The first two lines in the example collect a reference to the generic AIE exception thrown by `interrupt` (it always throws exactly the same exception ... allocated in immortal memory) and save it in a class variable. Everything in the `run` method is part of a `try`/`catch` construct.

1. **doIt.** A call to `doIt` is enclosed in the `try` clause. If `doIt` throws an AIE, the exception is caught.

2. **generic.** Since `fire` causes the same type of exception as `interrupt`, the `catch` clause will be invoked for exceptions caused by `fire on an AIE` or `interrupt` on the real-time thread. If the AIE does not equal the generic AIE, it was caused by `fire` (or a specific `throw` statement in this thread).

   The problem is that `catch` clauses catch AIEs only temporarily. The exception will reappear as soon as the code makes a transition that notices the pending AIE. (See Table 17–2.)

   This part of the code uses the `happened` method to turn the pending flag off. When its argument is `false` (as it is here), the `happened` method does not

Example 17–2 Handling a nonspecific AIE

```
static AsynchronouslyInterruptedException generic =
     AsynchronouslyInterruptedException.getGeneric();
private int n=0;

public void run() {
  try{
    doIt();
  } catch (AsynchronouslyInterruptedException aie) {
    //If it is generic,
    //make this aie non-pending
    if(generic.happened(false)){
      System.out.println("Run caught it. n = " + n);
    } else {
      System.out.println(
        "Not generic AIE, auto-propagated");
      // let the exception fall out and be re-thrown
    }
  }
}
```

automatically rethrow the AIE if it does not match. Instead, it returns false if the current AIE does not match the AIE on which happened was called. In this case, happened will clear the AIE pending flag and return true if the pending AIE (at the time happened is called) is the generic AIE. If happened returns true, the example announces that it caught an AIE and completes.

3. Not generic. It was not caused by interrupt, so the code continues as nothing happened. (Just to demonstrate the alternative to propagate.) The AIE will automatically be thrown by the RTSJ runtime as soon as control reaches a context that throws AIE.

This sequence sounds ripe for race conditions, so let's look at it more closely.

a.   The happened method acquires a lock on the current thread. The value of the current AIE cannot change while the happened method is executing.

b.   If the current AIE changes before we call happened, the code will branch into the else clause, and the AIE will remain pending It will be rethrown as soon as control enters a method that can throw AIE.

c.   If the current AIE changes after we call happened, it will not see a pending AIE and it will install itself as the current AIE and set the pending flag. The new AIE will be thrown as soon as control reaches a method that can throw AIE.

Example 17–3 contains the doIt method called in Example 17–2. It does not take any measures to manage interrupts. Such management would be pointless since doIt cannot catch an AIE even to execute a finally clause.

Example 17–3 A method that throws an AIE

```
private void doIt()
  throws AsynchronouslyInterruptedException   {

  while(true){
    n += 1;
    try {sleep(1);} catch(InterruptedException e){}
  }
}
```

In most cases, the AIE propagation should be allowed to operate without interference, preferably hidden in the doInterruptible or Timed infrastructure. Sometimes, however, it might be necessary to modify the usual propagation rules. For instance, noninterruptible methods called from doInterruptible may want to catch AIEs intended for the doInterruptible either temporarily or permanently (see Example 17–4).

Use doInterruptible to handle AIEs.

Example 17–4 Permanently catching someone else's AIE

```
/**This method is passed a reference to an AIE
   that is aimed at a function up the stack.
   It will intercept that AIE--not letting it
   propagate up the stack.
*/
public void nest(
    AsynchronouslyInterruptedException pAIE){
  AsynchronouslyInterruptedException aie =
    new AsynchronouslyInterruptedException();

  //...do something that might get an AIE fired
  //at us.
  try {
    nestedAIE();
  } catch (AsynchronouslyInterruptedException cAie){
    if(pAIE.happened(false)){
      //This AIE belonged to the Timed
```

Example 17–4 Permanently catching someone else's AIE (Continued)

```
              //method that called us, but we've
              //grabbed it.  We asked if it happened,
              //and made it non-pending.
              //We could rethrow it with throw pAIE.
              //but we're just going to steal it.
              System.out.println("Stealing");
          } else if(aie.happened(false)){
              //This aie was aimed at us.
          } else {
              //It belongs to someone else.
              AsynchronouslyInterruptedException.
                 propagate();
          }
      }
  }
}

public void nestedAIE() throws
      AsynchronouslyInterruptedException {
    for(int i = 0; i < 30; ++i){
      try{
         Thread.sleep(10);
      } catch (InterruptedException e){}
    }
}
```

Example 17–5 demonstrates a method that catches someone else's AIE, then decides that it should pass the AIE on up to its target.

When the method decides that it wants to let the AIE propagate, it cannot use the propagate method. The AIE is no longer pending, so propagate would not be able to rethrow it. Neither can nest throw the AIE that it caught. The compiler will see that nest does not throw AsynchronouslyInterruptedException and give compile-time errors.

We have two options:

1. Use pAIE.fire. This will throw the exception in a way that the compiler cannot detect. Using fire brings all the mechanism of fire into play: enable/disable and a return value.

2. Have nest throw InterruptedException. Since AIE is a subclass of InterruptedException, the compiler will let us throw it, but since the method does not exactly throw AsynchronouslyInterruptedException, it will not become asynchronously interruptible. (Which would ruin the example since it would not be able to catch an AIE.)

Example 17–5 Catch the AIE, then propagate it

```
/**This method is passed a reference to an AIE
   that is aimed at a function up the stack.
   It will intercept that AIE--and use it, then
   let it propagate up the stack.
*/
public void nest(
    AsynchronouslyInterruptedException pAIE){
  AsynchronouslyInterruptedException aie =
    new AsynchronouslyInterruptedException();

  //...do something that might get an AIE fired
  //at us.
  try {
    nestedAIE();
  } catch (AsynchronouslyInterruptedException cAie){
    if(pAIE.happened(false)){
      //This AIE belonged to the Timed
      //method that called us, but we've
      //grabbed it.  We asked if it happened,
      //and made it non-pending.
      System.out.println("BorrowAIE");
      //Now we want to return it.
      //It is not pending so it cannot
      //auto-propagate, but we can throw it.
      pAIE.fire();
    } else if(aie.happened(false)){
      //This aie was aimed at us.
    } else {
      //It belongs to someone else.
      AsynchronouslyInterruptedException.
        propagate();
    }
  }
}
```

Noninterruptible Code

Some sequences of operations cannot tolerate an asynchronous exception. Consider this code for adding a node at the front of a singly linked list:

```
temp = List.head;
List.head = this;
this.next = temp
```

If the code were interrupted by an AIE between the second and third lines, it would leave the list containing only the new entry. Any contents before the update would be unreachable.

There are three ways to fix this problem.

```
this.next = List.head
List.head = this
```

is probably the best fix. The algorithm is simpler and the intermediate state is safe, but

```
private void listPush(){
   Object temp = List.head;
   List.head = this;
   this.next = temp;
}
```

works too. The first fix works by making the problem go away. The second works by hiding the delicate sequence in a method that is not interruptible because it does not throw `AsynchronouslyInterruptedException`. Since it does not throw the AIE, any async exception that attempts to interrupt the thread will remain pending until the method returns.

Up to this point we've been ignoring the possibility that the list might be shared by multiple threads. If it is, it needs more protection. All the examples up to here can break if two threads try to update the list at the same time. A synchronized block solves both problems.

```
synchronized(List.class){
   Object temp = List.head;
   List.head = this;
   this.next = temp;
}
```

Async exceptions are always deferred during synchronized blocks, so this solution addresses async safety both against concurrent updates and against async exceptions.

The synchronized block is probably the best general method for masking async exceptions. There are certainly cases where a block of code cannot tolerate an async exception but does not need to worry about concurrent access by multiple threads, but that is a special case and should be considered carefully.

Figure 17–1 illustrates the progress of an AIE through a call stack as it inter-acts with various contexts:

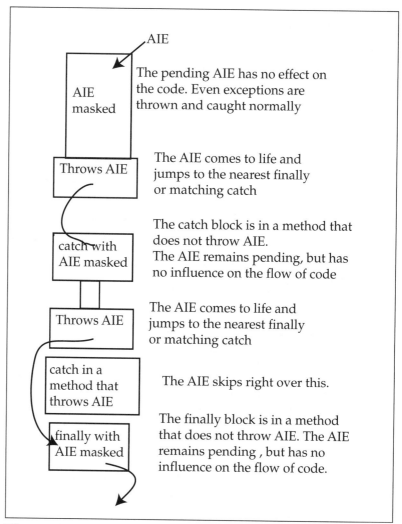

Figure 17–1 An AIE timeline

The Tools.   The following tools and techniques help manage async exceptions:

- **Change the algorithm.** In many cases, an algorithm can be modified so each state in it is safe. This class of algorithm does not need to mask async exceptions.

- **Use a synchronized block.** There are several types of synchronized blocks. All of them defer async exceptions.

  The problem with synchronized blocks is that they may be too powerful for the task. Acquiring a lock can consume significant CPU time and can cause serialization that you do not need.

  The good thing about synchronized blocks is that there is a good chance that the code which needs to be protected against async interruption also needs to be serialized.

- **Enclose the code in a method that does not throw AIE.** This technique protects against async exceptions without automatically acquiring a lock. It is sometimes difficult to phrase an algorithm so it neatly puts the code that must not be interrupted in a `finally` clause, but it is nearly always possible to isolate that noninterruptible code in one or more methods.

- **Disable the AIE.** This is a very specialized tool. It does not prevent async exceptions, and it only masks one AIE. If this limited effect is sufficient, disabling an AIE is preferable to the methods that completely mask async exceptions since disabling an AIE is narrowly focused.

When you consider the design of the system, the time it takes to respond to asynchronous exceptions is likely to be a critical performance metric for some threads. So algorithms that do not need to mask async exceptions are favored.

Special Issues for Synchronized blocks

A synchronized block is not interruptible, but if the synchronized block invokes another method, it needs to pay close attention to the rules.

The synchronized code in:

```
synchronized(object){
    //code
}
```

is simply ATC-deferred, but if `bar` can throw `AsynchronouslyInterruptedException`, the invocation of `bar`—

```
synchronized(object){
    bar();
    //more code
}
```

—opens a window. If an AIE is thrown at the thread while it is in `bar`, or even while it is executing in the synchronized block before it calls `bar`, control will leap past `more code` to a hidden `finally` clause associated with the `synchronized` block, then on to a `catch` for a `finally` clause in some method that does not throw AIE.

Even though the method that encloses the synchronized block may throw AIE, the synchronized block should catch the AIE. For other exceptions, a `catch` clause outside the synchronized block might be a viable way to recover from an exception thrown by a method called from the synchronized block (though it would be inconvenient since the catch block would not be synchronized.) Async exceptions must be caught inside the synchronized block, like this:

```
synchronized(object) {
  try {
    bar();
  } catch(AsynchronouslyInterruptedException e) {
    // deal with the exception.
    // then handle it, propagate it,
    // rethrow it, or ignore it.
    // If we ignore it, it will remain pending until
    // control leaves this synchronized block.
  }
  // More code
}
```

Legacy Code

The quantity of existing code in class libraries and other forms of Java components is one of the great assets of the Java programming language. Since most of this code was not written with any consideration for real-time issues, it needs to be used cautiously, but it would be foolish to insist that RTSJ applications start fresh. That is an important reason for the decision to make methods defer async exceptions by default. It is safe to throw an async exception at a method that was not written to handle it. If the method was coded to poll for the old-style thread interrupt, it will see the interrupted flag. If it was oblivious to interrupts, it will be oblivious to RTSJ interrupt. The only problem is, of course, that the async exception will be delayed.

You can safely use legacy code in real-time threads that are interrupted by AIEs.

Calling legacy code from code that handles AIEs is trivial, but most legacy code cannot use interruptible code without a glue layer. The legacy code does not know about `AsynchronouslyInterruptedException`, so a method that catches AIE and does not throw it must be used to glue the two parts together.

Note that simply catching an AIE is enough to satisfy Java, but it leaves the exception pending. It will reappear as soon as control enters a method that throws AIE.

Use of ATC for Thread Termination

Calling the interrupt method on a cooperative real-time thread will terminate that thread safely and quickly.

If a thread was written to expect AIEs and to behave well in that environment, it will frequently visit methods that throw AIE. Since the exception thrown by the `interrupt` method does not match any AIE on the call stack, the exception will propagate through all appropriate `finally` clauses, `catch` clauses, and `interruptAction` methods back through the thread's runnable method and the thread will terminate.

Nothing happens if an application calls the `interrupt` method on a thread that never calls a method that throws `AsynchronouslyInterruptedException`, never polls its interrupted flag, and never responds to exceptions from blocking calls that signify interrupts. Since that list includes many legacy applications written for the Java platform, `interrupt` is not a reliable general-purpose way to kill threads.

Table 17–4 summarizes some suggestions for thread termination.

Table 17–4 Good behavior for thread termination by means of the generic AIE

Frequently visit methods that throw AIE.

Catching the AIE is OK, but calling `happened` incautiously can cause trouble.

Expect interruptible methods to be interrupted. Use `finally` and `catch` clauses to clean up.

Expect interruption. Use the various mechanisms for making blocks of code noninterruptible to protect code that cannot tolerate interruption.

Chapter 18

Physical Memory

▼ PHYSICAL AND VIRTUAL MEMORY

▼ PHYSICAL MEMORY MANAGER

▼ IMMORTAL PHYSICAL MEMORY

▼ SCOPED PHYSICAL MEMORY

Java programmers are allowed to ignore the fact that the underlying machine is accessing memory that is located at addresses. In many cases, even real-time Java programmers can ignore addresses, but on some embedded real-time systems, the performance attributes of memory cannot be ignored.

There are three places where a real-time program might concern itself with the details of memory access:

- **The memory management unit.** On many processors, the MMU and cache cooperate to set the cache attributes of each page. When there is a large mismatch between the performance of the processor and the memory, the cache-mode of memory can alter the effective performance of the memory by two orders of magnitude or more.

The MMU's primary purposes are the control of read/write/execute access to memory, and the mapping of virtual addresses to physical addresses. These facilities support fundamental operating system services like memory protection and demand paging.

Demand paging affects determinism so strongly that many implementations of the RTSJ simply disable that service for all the memory they use. If they leave demand paging enabled, programmers may want to use the services detailed in this chapter to position key objects in memory that cannot be paged.

Although memory protection is not a real-time issue, it is important and interesting and some Java programs may benefit from limited control of the MMU's memory protection services.

- **The bus.** The connection between the CPU and memory can run at a wide variety of clock rates. The connection can be as little as one bit wide, or it can transfer entire cache lines at a time. It can include features like support for multiprocessor cache coherency that cost performance.

- **The memory itself.** It may not even be memory. I/O devices, coprocessors, even DIP switches can be accessed as if they were memory.

If it is memory, it could be ROM, RAM, nonvolatile memory, flash memory, or other technology. Its speed can range over two orders of magnitude. It can be static or dynamic with a large number of interfaces giving it various streaming and bursting characteristics. It can be protected by ECC or parity.

The point is that whereas many systems have many megabytes of some pretty good memory, a few megabytes of ROM, and maybe a bit of static memory, other systems have a spectrum of useful memory with widely varying performance characteristics.

An application can get a large performance improvement by putting its most-used data in the fastest memory. It can get a performance boost and more deterministic behavior by keeping data off busy shared buses.

For these reasons, the RTSJ includes the physical memory classes. These let it store objects in the right kind of memory.

Physical and Virtual Memory

The raw memory access classes and the physical memory classes dig down to real memory. This is *far* below the level the JVM ordinarily exposes to its users.

Here is one possible path from a Java-language object reference to a memory device:

1. The object reference is converted to the index of an object descriptor.

2. The object descriptor contains the address of the object.

3. The JVM loads a machine register from a field in the object it finds at the address of the object plus (say) 40. This is called a virtual address.

4. To load the register, the CPU places the virtual address on an address bus that carries it from the CPU to the memory management unit (MMU). The MMU basically strips the high-order 20 bits (a page number) off the address that came from the CPU and uses that value as a key to search a data structure called the page table.

5. If the MMU finds the virtual page number represented in a page table entry for the JVM, it checks the access rights for the page. If they include read, the MMU extracts a physical page number from the page table entry.

6. The MMU produces a physical address by concatenating the physical page number with the low-order 12 bits of the virtual address.

7. The physical address goes through logic that converts the physical address into protocols on the traces that connect the processor chip to the memory chip. The memory chip recovers the data stored at that address and returns the data to the CPU (probably on other traces).

The MMU is the part of the above path that separates virtual addresses from physical (or *real*) addresses. If there is an MMU in the system and it is being used for address translation, then the memory that the JVM sees at address `0xff0c1240` may be located at another address altogether.

If an application wants to communicate with a device at `0xf8004000`, it needs access to that physical address. The virtual address that the operating system assigns to that physical address generally does not matter.

Physical Memory Manager

A running RTSJ implementation has a `static` `PhysicalMemoryManager`. It manages allocation of memory to physical memory allocation objects—
`VTPhysicalMemory`, `LTPhysicalMemory`, `ImmortalPhysicalMemory`,
`RawMemoryAccess`, and `RawMemoryFloatAccess`. It implements the notion of memory type and offers minimal support for removable memory.

If the system configuration were fixed before an application was written, the application could specify the memory type by naming the physical address of the memory and providing some data about how the memory should be mapped.

Configurations are seldom that firmly fixed, and code that identifies types of memory by their address is cryptic. The physical memory manager lets the programmer identify memory by its attributes.

The physical memory allocation and raw memory access classes include constructors with memory type parameters. The memory type parameter is always an `Object`. By convention, memory types are specified as `String` values or arrays of `String` values. Memory can usually be specified by address, by type, or by address and type. This information is passed from the constructor to the physical memory manager, as follows:

- *If the constructor only specifies size*, then the physical memory manager finds the amount of free memory that the caller wants and allocates it

- *If the constructor specifies base and size*, then the physical memory manager verifies that the base and size specifies memory that is free. If it is not, the physical memory manager throws `MemoryInUseException`.

- *If the constructor specifies type and size*, then the physical memory manager tries to find enough free memory in the requested type of memory.

- *If the constructor specifies type, base, and size*, then the physical memory manager verifies that the base and size specify memory that is of the requested type and free.

  - If it is of the wrong type, the physical memory manager throws `MemoryTypeConflictException`.

  - If the extent of memory is not free, the manager throws `MemoryInUseException`.

  The RTSJ does not (now) specify precedence for these exceptions, but I would expect `MemoryInUseException` to have the highest priority, then `MemoryTypeConflictException`, and finally `SizeOutOfBoundsException`.

Memory Type

`PhysicalMemoryTypeFilter` objects interpret the memory type objects passed through physical memory constructors.

Memory type filters help handle removable memory, they help find a type of physical memory, and they concern themselves with the attributes and mapping of virtual memory. A single filter can participate in all three of these activities. The primary constraint on filters is that the memory manager will only accept one filter for any given type of memory.

A filter is installed with the following method:

- ```
  static final void registerFilter(java.lang.Object name
                       PhysicalMemoryTypeFilter filter) throws
                       DuplicateFilterException,
                       IllegalArgumentException
  ```

Figure 18–1 illustrates an interaction between a type filter and the physical memory manager.

Figure 18–1 Interaction between the physical memory manager and a filter

Manager	Filter
Wants to find 200 bytes that fit the type of filter	
I have 200 free bytes at 0x00c0d080 `filter.find(0x00c0d080, 200)`	
	That's not my type, but there are at least 200 bytes of my type starting at 0x00d00000. Return 0x00d00000. (The filter is only allowed to counteroffer addresses greater than the one proposed by the manager.)
That's not free, how about 200 bytes starting at 0x00d18000? `filter.find(0x00d18000, 200)`	
	That starts in my type, but it changes to some other type before the end of 200 bytes. How about 0x00d20000? Return 0x00d20000
That is good here. Now the physical address is settled and we can start on the virtual address.	
Can I map your type of memory to 0x00028c00? `filter.vFind(0x00028c00, 200)`	
	Sure, 0x0028c00 sounds fine. Return 0x0028c00

Should I use special attributes to map the memory?
`filter.getVMAttributes()`
`filter.getVMFlags()`	

  ```

Figure 18–1 Interaction between the physical memory manager and a filter (Continued)

Manager	Filter
	No.
	Return 0 to each.

Last chance for you to configure the memory.
 	
`filter.initialize(0x00d20000,`
`0x0028c00, 200)`	

	It is fine. Do nothing.

Requests to allocate memory can come to the physical memory manager with an array of memory types. In this case, the physical memory manager searches for memory that passes all the filters. This means an application can easily request memory that is shared, fast, noncached, and nonvolatile. Asking for memory that is fast or nonvolatile is not easy. The application has to try to construct an object in fast memory, then try nonvolatile if that fails.

Removable Memory

The remaining methods in the filter support removable memory:

- `public boolean contains(long base, long size)`
  Does this filter describe any memory in the specified range?

- `public boolean isPresent(long base, long size)`
  Is all the memory in the specified range present in the system? If any of it has been removed or not yet inserted, return `false`.

  If any of the range of memory is not covered by this filter, throw `IllegalArgumentException`.

- `public boolean isRemovable(long address, long size)`
  Is any memory in the specified range removable?

- `public void onInsertion(long base, long size,`
  `   AsyncEventHandler aeh)`
  Set up an async event so that if any memory in the specified range is inserted, `aeh` will be invoked.

- `public void onRemoval(long base, long size,`
  `   AsyncEventHandler aeh)`
  Set up an async event so that if any memory in the specified range is removed, `aeh` will be invoked.

The filter methods that handle removable memory are mirrored by similar methods in the physical memory manager. The physical memory manager determines which filter (or possibly several filters) controls the address range and then passes the call to the right filters.

Immortal Physical Memory

The RTSJ JVM has the `ImmortalMemory` class and a singleton instance of the class in place when the machine starts. `ImmortalPhysicalMemory` instances have to be created. They can be created with the full flexibility of the physical memory manager. An application can create an immortal physical memory object allocated from a megabyte of memory starting at some base address, it can just ask for the memory to be of a particular type (or array of types), or it can combine those options and specify the address and the type.

In any of those cases, the application will get an object that controls allocations of immortal objects from a particular region of memory.

Except for the constrained address range, immortal objects allocated from an `ImmortalPhysicalMemory` object behave like other immortal objects. They are never freed (or, technically, their lifetime exceeds the lifetime of the application), the garbage collector never tries to free them, they can be used by no-heap threads, and they are governed by the rules for immortal memory in "Assignment rules" on page 180.

The `ImmortalPhysicalMemory` object itself is an ordinary object. It could reside in heap memory, but if a thread cannot reach the object, the thread cannot allocate memory in the object. And if the object is freed, then nobody can allocate from it again (but objects allocated in the memory controlled by the object will remain immortal.) In most cases, `ImmortalPhysicalMemory` objects should be created in immortal memory.

Scoped Physical Memory

There are two types of scoped physical memory: `LTPhysicalMemory` and `VTPhysicalMemory`. Like `ImmortalPhysicalMemory`, these scoped physical memory classes behave like their built-in analogs except for their memory constraints.

Scoped physical memory objects can be created whenever you would create a regular scoped memory object. In particular, they will frequently be created in other scopes. Example 18–1 shows the use of scoped physical memory.

Example 18–1 Using Scoped Physical Memory

```
class Action implements Runnable{
  int j;
  public void run() {
      //  Memory allocated by Integer.valueOf
      //  will be allocated in "fast" memory
    Integer n = Integer.valueOf(args[j]);
    intArgs[j] = n.intValue();
  }
}

  //  Get 8k of fast memory
fast = new LTPhysicalMemory("fast", 8*1024);
Action  action = new Action();

for(int i = 0; i < this.args.length; ++i){
  action.j = i;
  fast.enter(action);
  System.out.println(intArgs[i]);
}
```

Raw Memory Access

- ▼ SECURITY
- ▼ PEEK AND POKE
- ▼ GET/SET METHODS
- ▼ MAPPING
- ▼ THE RAWMEMORYFLOATACCESS CLASS

Programs that run in the Java abstract machine see memory as a stack of primitive data for each thread and a bag of objects. Nothing changes type, nothing even has an address. That is a useful model for computations that do not involve resources outside the Java environment, but it cripples Java for applications that deal with memory-mapped hardware.

Native methods are the traditional workaround for the Java language's inability to use an address. They are usually written in C, and sometimes in assembly language. From a linguistic point of view, native methods open the world of pointers to Java applications. Practically, they are an uncomfortable hack.

None of the security and protection measures incorporated in the Java environment function in native methods. A correct JVM must insist that native methods come from a secure local store. If the machine's operating system can proscribe dangerous native methods, such proscription offers some protection

293

against malicious code, but it offers no protection against trusted native methods that contain dangerous bugs.

The probability of dangerous bugs could be near zero if the native methods contained only the few lines of code required to access one address in memory. They could be written that way, but that would pose an efficiency problem. The JVM expends a surprising amount of time preparing to call a native method. Especially when performance is critical, that overhead discourages trivial native methods. Programmers seldom write separate native methods to read and write each register of a memory-mapped device. They are more likely to code a few native methods that contain the bulk of a device driver for that device.

If the Java platform offered a way to use pointers safely, then the following would ensue:

- Classes that access memory could be downloaded.

- They would operate within the JVM's security and protection envelope.

- In many cases, they would perform better since they would not need to cross between native methods and the JVM.

- Programmers would have less reason to include non-Java components in applications for a Java platform.

Raw memory access is included in the RTSJ mainly to help make it practical to use hardware devices without requiring native methods.

If the RTSJ gives Java applications reasonable real-time performance, then the only architectural issue that prevents Java from extending unbroken from high-level application code all the way to the low-level device is Java's nonsupport for pointers. Raw memory access solves this problem.

There is one other problem. Most I/O hardware uses interrupts to communicate with its driver. Conventional Java has no notion of an interrupt.

... I direct your attention to async event handlers and happenings.

The `RawMemoryAccess` and `RawMemoryFloatAcesss` classes give RTSJ systems a convenient and secure way to access memory through pointers. This gives them direct access to memory-mapped hardware that makes it relatively easy for Java applications to implement device drivers, program flash memory, and perform other operations usually left to operating system internals.

The design of the raw memory access classes lets a programmer define something very similar to a C structure and lay it over physical memory. A crucial omission is that the raw memory access classes do not define a way to load or store references to Java objects. That would have constituted a serious breech in JVM integrity.

Security

Raw memory access is, by its nature, bad for security. The platform may refuse to permit raw access to any memory. It may set aside a pool of memory for raw memory access, or it may find some set of conditions that would qualify a thread for read or write access to memory-mapped devices or even internal operating system data structures.

The operating system (if any) and the JVM (if any) together must ensure that malicious or buggy code cannot damage anything but itself. This doesn't mean that the security system has to prevent bugs. A defective device driver will still be able to bring down the entire computer. The security system only isolates the problems. A defective device driver will not be able to cause a protection violation in the JVM, disturb an object belonging to the JVM, or modify an internal JVM data structure.

It would be unusual for a thread that is not part of the implementation of the JVM to be allowed to touch addresses in the JVM's code or data.

If the supporting operating system has a notion of protection, it will automatically prevent threads in the JVM from accessing addresses in the I/O space or any address ranges that have not been given to the JVM. A JVM that wants to support device drivers written in the Java programming language, will have to come to an agreement with the operating system; this approach will transfer some responsibility for protecting the I/O devices from the operating system to the JVM.

Peek and Poke

Peek and poke are the names for the basic language functions that access memory by address. Peek takes an address as its parameter and returns the value at that address. Poke takes an address and a value as parameters and stores the value at the address. The RTSJ could have created analogs for peek and poke, but that would have required careful checking of the thread's right to access a particular address on every call. That is the best design if the application is not expected to revisit addresses. The RTSJ expects raw memory access to be used for memory-mapped I/O and regions of memory that are shared with software outside the JVM. These applications heavily use a few locations (or small regions) in memory.

The first step in raw memory access is through the security portal. The RawMemoryAccess class can handle situations in which rights to memory locations must be rechecked every time the memory is accessed, but in most cases a thread's access rights will not change over time. A RawMemoryAccess object is bound to a range of addresses when the object is created:

- RawMemoryAccess(java.lang.Object type, long size)
  RawMemoryAccess(java.lang.Object type, long base, long size)

  Both constructors throw SecurityException, OffsetOutOfBoundsException, SizeOutOfBoundsException, UnsupportedPhysicalMemoryException, and MemoryTypeConfictException.

The second constructor is easier to understand:

- **type.** This parameter may be an object or an array of object. It describes the type of memory and the way the JVM should access it. A caller might request that some memory-mapped device memory be mapped for noncached access. The set of supported types is platform dependent.

  In most cases, the type parameter should probably be left blank.

- **base.** This is the starting address in physical memory for the region the caller wants to access.

- **size.** This is the size of the region the caller wants to access.

The first constructor does not have a base address. The system gets to select an address that meets the caller's type and size requirements. This sounds useless, but it may be a cleaner way to request access to a memory-mapped device than the more specific constructor. Consider this:

```
String [] type = new String[4];
type[0] = new String("device");
type[1] = new String("ethernet");
type[2] = new String("Intel");
type[4] = new String("no cache");
RawMemoryAccess eDvc = new RawMemoryAccess(type, 512);
```

The constructor has clearly asked for 512 bytes of memory that maps an Intel Ethernet controller for noncached access. If there is one in the system and the physical memory manager knows about it, this code will create a raw memory access object that points to that controller. The alternative, which includes the physical address of the device, is less portable.

Get/Set Methods

The simplest ways to access raw memory through a `RawMemoryAccess` object
are the primitive get/set methods:

- `public byte getByte(long offset)`
- `public void setByte(long offset, byte value)`
- `public short getShort(long offset)`
- `public void setShort(long offset, short value)`
- `public int getInt(long offset)`
- `public void setInt(long offset, int value)`
- `public long getLong(long offset)`
- `public void setLong(long offset, long value)`

All the methods that read and write multibyte values interact with the
`BYTE_ORDER` static variable in the `RealtimeSystem` class. If `BYTE_ORDER` equals
`BIG_ENDIAN`, then the high-order byte is at the low address; otherwise, the high-
order byte is at the high address.

You use these methods like this:

```
public void init(){
    try {
        //  Hang on to the old value of the control
        //  register
        int ctrlReg = eDvc.getInt(CTRLREG);
        //  Set an initial state
        eDvc.setInt(CTRLREG, 0);
        //  Turn off interrupts
        eDvc.setInt(CTRLREG,
            (ctrlReg & MASK_INT_FIELDS) |
                MY_NOINT_FIELD);
        //  Wait for device to respond
        while(eDvc.getInt(STATREG) != 0);
        //  Set it running
        eDvc.setInt(CTRLREG, INIT_CTRL);
    } catch (SizeOutOfBoundsException e){
        throw new RuntimeException(
            "Size error in init");
    } catch (OffsetOutOfBoundsException e){
        throw new RuntimeException(
            "Offset error in init");
    }
}
```

(This is not real device initialization code. Configuring an Ethernet device would take pages.)

Often it makes sense to represent memory with an array. There is a choice:

- An array of `RawMemoryAccess` objects involves an array object and a `RawMemoryAccess` object per chunk of memory. All those objects give it considerable memory overhead, but it can easily represent noncontiguous regions of memory.

- A set of array get/set methods parallels the primitive raw memory get/set methods. Methods in the former are particularly good at representing large extents of memory; e.g., frame buffers. The other interesting application of the array access methods is redefinition of other primitives.

  - `public void getBytes(long offset, byte [] bytes, int low, int number)`
  - `public void setBytes(long offset, byte [] bytes, int low, int number)`
  - `public void getShorts(long offset, short [] shorts, int low, int number)`
  - `public void setShorts(long offset, short [] shorts, int low, int number)`
  - `public void getInts(long offset, int [] ints, int low, int number)`
  - `public void setInts(long offset, int [] ints, int low, int number)`
  - `public void getLongs(long offset, long [] longs, int low, int number)`
  - `public void setLongs(long offset, long [] longs, int low, int number)`

Using these methods, you can do the following:

- **Access a frame buffer of 16-bit pixels.** This can be done in many different ways, using `getShort` and `setShort` with offsets, `getShorts` and `setShorts` with an array of shorts that covers the entire frame buffer, or `getShorts` and `setShorts` with one entry of an array mapped to different offsets in the frame buffer. The following example does it all three ways:

```
public void clear(){
    try {
        // One way
        for(int offset = 0; offset < BUFFER_SIZE; offset += 2)
            frameBuffer.setShort(offset, BLUE_VALUE);
```

```
        //  Another way
        short [] filler = new short[BUFFER_DIM];
        for(int i=0; i< BUFFER_DIM; ++i)
            filler[i] = BLUE_VALUE;
        frameBuffer.setShorts(0, filler, 0, BUFFER_DIM);
        //  Or yet another way
        for(int i=0; i<BUFFER_DIM; ++i)
            frameBuffer.setShorts(i, filler, 0, 1);
    } catch (SizeOutOfBoundsException e){
        //  Program bug
    } catch (OffsetOutOfBoundsException e){
        //  Program bug
    }
}
```

- **Play games with mapping an array over a longer data type.** Java has no all-purpose mechanism for redefining data, nothing that takes one chunk of data and lets the programmer see that data as different types.

The RawMemoryAccess class does not let programmers peer into the JVM's internal data structures or the heap with a reinterpreting eye, but it does support reinterpretation of memory that can be accessed through RawMemoryAccess.

The following example reads some memory as a short, then accesses the same memory as bytes, and reverses the upper and lower bytes. Finally, it reads the short again. The values in s1 and s2 will differ in the order of their bytes.

```
public void swap(int n) throws OffsetOutOfBoundsException {
    try {
        short s1 = frameBuffer.getShort(n*2);
        byte [] bytes = new byte[2];

        frameBuffer.getBytes(n*2, bytes, 0, 2);
        byte hold = bytes[0];
        bytes[0] = bytes[1];
        bytes[1] = hold;
        frameBuffer.setBytes(n*2, bytes, 0, 2);
        short s2 = frameBuffer.getShort(n*2);
    } catch (SizeOutOfBoundsException e){
        throw new OffsetOutOfBoundsException();
    } catch (OffsetOutOfBoundsException e){
        throw e;
    }
}
```

Mapping

Systems that use an MMU may offer an API that lets processes ask to have blocks of physical memory mapped into their address space. The most general version of this mechanism lets a process specify the address of the physical memory, the size of the mapped region, and the virtual address it should be mapped to.

The `RawMemoryAccess` class includes methods that access these mapping mechanisms. Since these cannot be supported with MMU hardware and may not be supported by the operating system even when an MMU is present, the mapping methods in `RawMemoryAccess` should only be used in code that is clearly platform dependent.

- **public long getMappedAddress( )**

  This method returns the virtual address where the memory mapped by this raw memory access object can be found.

- **public long map( )**
  public long map(long base)
  public long map(long base, long size)

  These three methods all change the virtual address at which the memory accessed by raw memory object appears. If the system does not support mapping memory, these methods all do nothing but return the current address of the backing memory. If the operation is supported, the `map` operations map the backing memory (or part of the backing memory in the case of the method with a `size` parameter) into virtual memory. If there is no base parameter, the system chooses an address.

  If the memory is already mapped into the JVM's address space, the `map` with no parameters does nothing, and `map` methods with a base address remap it to that address.

- **public void unmap( )**

  This method removes the backing memory from the JVM's address space. If possible, the system will make the memory inaccessible to threads in the Java platform. In any case, `get` and `set` methods on the backing memory will fail when the object is not in the mapped state. The object will stay in the unmapped state until it is remapped by one of the `map` methods.

Perhaps the best use of `unmap` and `map` is to disable and reenable a raw memory access object. Whether the underlying system has support for mapping memory or not, a raw memory access object will throw an exception if one of its memory access methods is called when it is in an unmapped state.

The RawMemoryFloatAccess Class

The `RawMemoryFloatAccess` class extends the `RawMemoryAccess` class. It has analogs to the `RawMemoryAccess` constructors:

- ```
  public RawMemoryFloatAccess(java.lang.Object type,
      long size)
      throws SecurityException, OffsetOutOfBoundsException,
      SizeOutOfBoundsException,
      UnsupportedPhysicalMemoryException,
      MemoryTypeConflictException
  ```

- ```
  public RawMemoryFloatAccess(java.lang.Object type,
      long base, long size)
      throws SecurityException, OffsetOutOfBoundsException,
      SizeOutOfBoundsException,
      UnsupportedPhysicalMemoryException,
      MemoryTypeConflictException
  ```

The `RawMemoryFloatAccess` class passes all the base raw memory access methods through without modification and adds methods that get and set float and double values:

- ```
  public double getDouble(long offset)
  ```
- ```
  public void setDouble(long offset, double value)
  ```
- ```
  public void getDoubles(long offset, double [] doubles, int
      low, int number)
  ```
- ```
  public void setDoubles(long offset, double [] doubles, int
      low, int number)
  ```
- ```
  public float getFloat(long offset)
  ```
- ```
  public void setFloat(long offset, float value)
  ```
- ```
  public void getFloats(long offset, float [] floats, int low,
      int number)
  ```
- ```
  public void setFloats(long offset, float [] floats, int low,
      int number)
  ```

Floating-point access to raw memory is an unusual requirement. Normal I/O devices do not communicate with their device driver by floating-point values.

An implementation of the RTSJ is required to implement only `RawMemoryFloatAccess` if the underlying JVM supports floating-point data types (it is optional for the micro edition.)

If the implementation does support `RawMemoryFloatAccess`, the format of the floating-point values remains unspecified. The Java specification requires the values to behave according to the IEEE floating-point specification, but it does not specify the layout in memory of the bits making up the floating-point value. The RTSJ provides for the different byte orderings that might appear in `short`, `int`, and `long` numbers. When it comes to floating point, you are on your own.

`RawMemoryFloatAccess` must be considered a marginal class for applications that value portability.

Chapter 20

Synchronization without Locking

▼ PRINCIPLES OF WAIT-FREE QUEUES

▼ THE WAIT-FREE WRITE QUEUE

▼ THE WAIT-FREE READ QUEUE

▼ THE WAIT-FREE DOUBLE-ENDED QUEUE

▼ NO-WAIT QUEUES AND MEMORY

▼ IMPLEMENTATION NOTES

Priority inversion avoidance mechanisms built into the RTSJ prevent some of the most insidious blocking problems between threads, but the structure of the RTSJ adds some new ones. The wait-free queues offer a programmer a mechanism that clearly exposes interactions between threads that should not engage in priority inversion or one of the automated mechanisms for avoiding inversion.

For instance, if a NoHeapRealtimeThread needs to share data with a heap-using thread, it will probably have the potential to block the no-heap thread over an interval where the heap-using thread could cause garbage collection. That could cause the no-heap thread to block behind the heap-using thread. The scheduler will, of course, boost the priority of the heap-using thread to prevent priority inversion. That could be just what the programmer intended, but it means that the blocked no-heap thread and any other no-heap threads at lower priorities might block for garbage collection. If that is what you want, fine, but why use a no-heap thread if waiting for garbage collection is OK? And, are the other threads and intermediate priorities also prepared for garbage collection delays?

Wait-free queues do just what they say. At least one end of the queue will never cause the thread using it to wait for garbage collection. They can be used for communication between heap-using and no-heap threads without silently bringing garbage collection into the picture.

Wait-free queues look like "hurry up and wait" frozen in software, but it is better to look at them as appropriate laziness. It is much easier to write code for a heap-using thread than a no-heap thread, so good design will use tiny no-heap threads (and async event handlers) connected to heap-using threads that do the bulk of the work.

A wait-free queue would normally be used to couple a no-heap thread to a heap-using thread. This does not make much sense if the producer and consumer are working on the same deadline, but they may be loosely coupled.

Soft Real Time with Hard Real-Time Activities. Picture yourself walking down the sidewalk on a city street. You stroll down the street in no particular hurry. You can stop to look at something or even visit a shop. From time to time you get to a street that you need to cross. This changes the time constraint. It is actively dangerous to loiter in the crosswalk. The principle is illustrated in Figure 20–1.

Hard Real Time Feeding Soft Real Time. Consider an inspection station on an assembly line. It might have two seconds to inspect each part. If it misses that deadline, it either has to hold up the assembly line or let a part go uninspected. If it finds a defect, the rules change. It has to identify the defective part and reject it in the two-second window, but the defective part is shunted to a different timeline. It gets dumped into a bin with other suspect parts. If by some chance, the bin is not there or full, the defective part is dumped on the floor. The assembly line

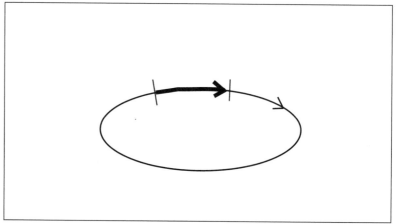

Figure 20–1 Soft real time with a hard real-time interval

doesn't stop because junk is not being cleaned up fast enough. Sooner or later defective parts will be more carefully inspected. The defect will be categorized and logged. It might be repaired and returned to production or recycled as scrap. Meanwhile the inspection will continue on its two-second cycle and process hundreds of thousands of parts. The principle is illustrated in Figure 20–2.

Hard Real Time with Soft Real-Time Input. Consider a train (or a scheduled airplane). In an ideal world, it stays within a few minutes of a published schedule. A stand-by passenger has a more relaxed schedule. If there is an empty seat, he gets it, but he may wait for hours or even days before he gets a ride. From the train's point of view, it picks up the passengers that can get on in the four-minute boarding window, then proceeds to the next station. It doesn't wait for passengers. If they are there, they can get on. If they are not, the train doesn't wait. The principle is illustrated in Figure 20–3.

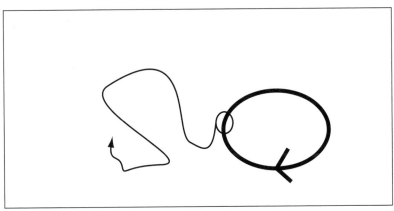

Figure 20–2 Hard real time feeding data to soft real time

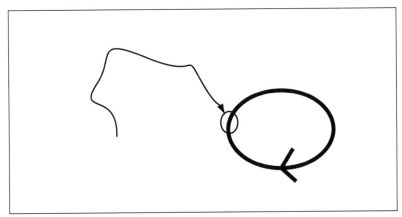

Figure 20–3 Hard real time with no-wait input from soft real time

Principles of Wait-Free Queues

The wait-free queues are slightly unusual versions of ordinary producer/consumer queues.

One end of the queue acts like a typical message queue:

- It is synchronized so multiple threads can safely use it.

- If it is a blocking read, an empty queue will block a read until a write provides data for it to read.

- If it is a blocking write, a full queue will block a write until a read leaves an empty queue entry for the write to use or until the write thread is interrupted.

The nonblocking end of the queue always returns immediately.

A wait-free write queue either enqueues its object and returns `true` or it finds a full queue and returns `false`. A wait-free read queue either returns the object from the head of the queue or it returns a null to indicate that the queue is empty. The wait-free read queue also provides a blocking read that can result in the caller waiting for a lower-priority thread to complete but will not trigger the system's priority inversion avoidance mechanism.

Constructors

The constructors for wait-free queues use similar constructors:

```
public WaitFreeWriteQueue(java.lang.Thread writer,
            java.lang.Thread reader,
            int maximumElements,
            MemoryArea area) throws
                IllegalArgumentException,
                InstantiationException,
                ClassNotFoundExsception,
                IllegalAccessException

public WaitFreeReadQueue(java.lang.Thread writer,
            java.lang.Thread reader,
            int maximumElements,
            MemoryArea memory) throws
                IllegalArgumentException,
                InstantiationException,
```

```
            ClassNotFoundExsception,
            IllegalAccessException

  public WaitFreeDequeue(java.lang.Thread writer,
            java.lang.Thread reader,
            int maximumElements,
            MemoryArea area) throws
                IllegalArgumentException,
                InstantiationException,
                ClassNotFoundExsception,
                IllegalAccessException
```

The specified reader and writer are only hints to the queue implementation since any thread can access either end of the queue.

The maximum number of elements and the memory area are used by the constructor to preallocate a queue of Object references and do other queue initialization.

Common Methods

Some methods are common to the wait-free read and write queues:

```
public void clear( )
```
Empties the queue.

```
public boolean isEmpty( )
```
Returns true if the queue is empty.

```
public boolean IsFull( )
```
Returns true if the queue is full.

```
public int size( )
```
Returns the number of nonempty entries in the queue.

The Wait-Free Write Queue

Objects in this class pass a queue of data from a no-heap thread to a heap-using thread. Its write method never blocks for garbage collection or boosts garbage collection at the consumer end of the queue into the no-heap range.

Methods

```
public java.lang.Object read( )
```
This read method will block if the queue is empty. It removes one entry from the head of the queue and returns it to the caller.

```
public boolean write(java.lang.Object object) throws
        MemoryScopeException
```
This write method cannot block. With an ordinary queue, a thread that tried to add an object to a full queue would block until there was room in the queue for the object. If you wanted to avoid waiting in the write, you would first check the queue to ensure that there was room, then add an entry to the queue only if there was room for it. This method suffers from race conditions. Another thread can add an entry after you check. Now you wait even though you thought you would not.

The nonblocking write is atomic (even though it is not synchronized) so it does not suffer from race conditions.

```
public boolean force(java.lang.Object object) throws
        MemoryScopeException
```
When write returns false, indicating that there is not space in the queue for the new object, the writer has three options:

1. Discard the object it was going to enqueue.

2. Hang onto the object and try to write it to the queue again later. (After a while this turns into a separate no-wait queue feeding the first one. This is almost certainly unjustified complexity. It would have been easier to use a larger no-wait queue than to chain two of them together.)

3. Discard the last object already in the queue by using force.

The force method is not quite as simple as it seems. It always places its payload in the queue, but its effect on the rest of the queue is hard to deduce. It returns true if the queue was full and the last entry was replaced. If the queue was not full, force returns false but it still replaces the last object in the queue. If the queue was empty, force returns false and writes its argument to the queue.

In the last analysis, the writer cannot tell whether it replaced an object unless force returns true. If force returns true, it definitely replaced the last object in the queue. If it returned false, it replaced the last entry in the queue unless the queue was empty.

This only becomes a problem when the writer wants to replace the last entry in the queue. If it is using `force` because it has an object that it urgently needs to place in the queue, the normal ordering of the priorities of the producer and consumer should prevent trouble.

In general, the following execution sequence could occur:

writer	**reader**
`write` returns `false`, indicating that the queue is full.	
	Preempts the writer and reads all the objects in the queue or calls the queue's `clear` method.
Calls `force` to replace the last entry in the queue. `force` returns `false`.	

The writer knows that the queue was no longer full; `force` was called because it returned `false`, but the writer cannot tell whether the queue was entirely empty or just not full … unless the queue is one entry long.

Sharing the Wait-Free Queue

The read operation of a `WaitFreeWriteQueue` and the write operation of a `WaitFreeReadQueue` are sharable. Any number of threads can contend to use the queue at that end. The methods use synchronize blocks to serialize access to their internal state at that end.

Wait-free queues are not designed to have multiple threads using their wait-free end. To support multiple threads at the wait-free end, the wait-free queue class would need to use some sort of synchronized block to protect its data structures. Depending on how it was implemented and used, the synchronized block would certainly cause blocking and might cause serious delays.

This does not mean that the queues cannot be shared at both ends. The wait-free end can be shared by means of a separate synchronized block to serialize access to it, as coded in Example 20–1. The important constraint is that the synchronized block must be completely independent of the other end of the queue.

Example 20–1 Sharing the wait-free end of a wait-free queue

```
WaitFreeWriteQueue queue;

public synchronized boolean write(java.lang.Object obj)
        throws MemoryScopeException {
    return queue.write(obj);
}
```

The Wait-Free Read Queue

WaitFreeReadQueue lets a thread accept input from another thread without waiting for the input.

The code in Example 20–2 shows the main loop in a periodic thread that accepts new period values from a wait-free write queue.

Example 20–2 Using WaitFreeReadQueue for loose coupling

```
RelativeTime newPeriod;
RealtimeThread rt = currentRealtimeThread();

while(true){
    //  ****
    //  Do some work
    //  ****
    //  See if a new period has
    //  arrived on the queue.
    newPeriod = (RelativeTime)queue.read();
    //  If there is a new period,
    //  update the period in our thread
    if(newPeriod != null){
        PeriodicParameters oldParam;
        oldParam =(PeriodicParameters)
            rt.getReleaseParameters();
        oldParam.setPeriod(newPeriod);
    }
    rt.waitForNextPeriod();
}
```

If this were in a real application, it would probably be better to directly set the new period from the thread that generates periods and avoid the added complexity of the queue. The queue might be useful in updating the period if the target thread needed to modify its operation to accommodate the updated period.

The Extra Constructor

WaitFreeReadQueue has a second constructor with an argument that the other wait-free queue constructors do not share:

```
public WaitFreeReadQueue(java.lang.Thread writer,
                java.lang.Thread reader,
                int maximumElements,
                MemoryArea memory,
                boolean notify) throws
```

```
IllegalArgumentException,
InstantiationException,
ClassNotFoundExsception,
IllegalAccessException
```

If the `notify` parameter is `true`, this constructor creates a queue that can support the `waitForData` method. If `notify` is false, the effect of this constructor is no different from the standard `WaitFreeReadQueue` constructor.

Methods

```
public java.lang.Object read( )
```
The `read` method does not block, so if there is no data in the queue, `read` must return null.

```
public void waitForData( )
```
If the queue was created with `notify` enabled (see the special constructor above), `waitForData` blocks the calling thread until at least one object is in the queue.

The trick is that `waitForData` does not cause the priority of the producer to be boosted. It is a form of priority inversion, but the implementation uses a no-heap async event handler between the producer and consumer. The scheduler does not see the priority inversion and so does not invoke a priority inversion avoidance mechanism.

This is a suitable mechanism for the type of "soft real-time with hard real-time activities" situation mentioned in the first part of this chapter.

```
public boolean write(java.lang.Object object) throws
            MemoryScopeException
```
This is an ordinary `write` method. It will block if the queue is full. There is no reason it would fail to place its argument in the queue, but if somehow `write` returned without placing its argument in the queue, it would return `false`.

The Wait-Free Double-Ended Queue

The wait-free double-ended queue is just a class that composes a wait-free write queue with a wait-free read queue. This is strictly a convenience class. It offers no facilities that you would not get from the two separate components.

The correct use of a `WaitFreeDequeue` would be to have the higher-priority end of the double-ended queue use `force`, `nonBlockingRead`, and `nonBlockingWrite`. The lower-priority end of the double-ended queue should use `blockingRead` and `blockingWrite`.

Methods

```
public java.lang.Object blockingRead( )
```
Performs a read on the constituent WaitFreeWriteQueue.

```
public boolean blockingWrite(java.lang.Object object) throws
            MemoryScopeException
```
Performs a write on the constituent WaitFreeReadQueue.

```
public boolean force(java.lang.Object object)
```
Performs a force on the constituent WaitFreeWriteQueue.

```
public java.lang.Object nonBlockingRead( )
```
Performs a read on the constituent WaitFreeReadQueue.

```
public boolean nonBlockingWrite(java.lang.Object object)
            throws
            MemoryScopeException
```
Performs a write on the constituent WaitFreeWriteQueue.

No-Wait Queues and Memory

Assignment rules and the reference rules for no-heap threads are important to wait-free queues. The queue object itself is created in some memory area. The queue itself is created in the same memory area as the queue object. The object references passed through the queue can be in any area allowed by the reference rules.

If all objects are in heap memory, there is no problem. But a major application for wait-free queues is communication with no-heap threads. A no-heap thread would be unable to reference the queue object or any of its contents if they were in heap.

If all objects are in immortal memory, the queue will work without a hitch and can be used by any type of thread. The problem here is that all resources consumed by the wait-free queue, including all the objects sent through the queue, must reside in immortal memory. That works easily, but it turns the queue and all the objects that are passed through it into a preallocated, static resource.

The queue can be placed in scoped memory. The most convenient system is to construct the queue and all the objects that will pass through it in a single, scoped memory area. The thread that created the queue can use it, and it can let other threads it creates inherit access to the scope containing the queue. As with immortal memory, the objects passed through the queue cannot be dynamically allocated carelessly, but the memory is freed when all the threads leave it.

In every case except a no-wait queue in heap memory, the application must implement a system for recycling the objects passed through the queue. The easiest way to build a recycling system is to create a second no-wait queue that holds objects for recycling, as shown in Algorithm 20–1.

Algorithm 20–1. Object recycling

```
Create the a wait-free queue q,
    and n objects of type T to go in it
  construct the wait-free queue as required
  construct the recycling queue, r. An n-entry wait-free
    queue with its wait on the end opposite to q.
  for(i = 0; i < n; ++i)
    r.write(new T());
Use the recycling queue after every q.read
  obj = q.read();
  r.write(obj);
and before every q.write
  obj = r.read();
  //copy data into obj
  q.write(obj)
```

Since the recycling queue is big enough to contain every object created for the queue, no write to the recycling queue will ever block or fail to add its data to the queue.

Preloading the recycling queue as illustrated in Algorithm 20–1 keeps use of the queue consistent. It also stores references for all the preallocated objects in one convenient structure.

Implementation Notes

Implementors of wait-free queues may find that synchronized blocks are required to protect the queue data structure. Synchronized blocks are acceptable provided that the code in the synchronized blocks is brief and never allocates an object or does anything else (like calling System.gc) that could cause garbage collection. The synchronized block could cause the priority of the heap-using thread to be boosted to the level of the no-heap thread, but since the synchronized block will not run garbage collection, the priority boosting will be brief.

Recommended Practices

▼ POWERFUL AND EASY-TO-USE FEATURES OF THE
   RTSJ

▼ VERY POWERFUL AND DANGEROUS FEATURES OF
   THE RTSJ

▼ VERY POWERFUL AND FINICKY FEATURES OF THE
   RTSJ

▼ SELECTION OF PRIORITIES

Ideally this chapter would be full of sage advice developed over years of experience with the Real-Time Specification for Java. It is not. I wrote this book while the RTSJ and its reference implementation were solidifying into a final specification. I have the "advantage" of having spent many hours struggling with features that did not make it into the final specification, and I know why the features of the RTSJ were included.

The RTSJ enhances the Java platform in some fundamental ways, but it is still the Java platform. The naming conventions, object-oriented design guidelines, and appropriate use of language features do not change. Even applications that make heavy use of the real-time extensions are Java programs.

Powerful and Easy-to-Use Features of the RTSJ

Most of the features of the RTSJ are safe. Any application can benefit from them, and applications that use multiple threads can benefit greatly.

Real-Time Threads

Everything that uses a thread can use a real-time thread, though the program has to contend with the more restricted set of constructors offered for the RealtimeThread class. Real-time threads offer priorities that really work, periodic scheduling, and priority boosting. (Briefly, in case you haven't read Chapter 5, this removes some obnoxious problems from interactions between threads at different priorities.)

Periodic Threads

In its simplest form, without resource limits or miss handlers, a periodic thread runs a piece of code at regular intervals. Whether you need to sample and save a voltage level 30,000 times a second or run a tape backup once a week, periodic threads are a simple, powerful tool for the job.

Asynchronous Event Handlers

Do not let the name mislead you. AsynchronousEventHandler is a long, complicated way to say reusable thread.

The RTSJ allows, and encourages, the implementation to reduce the startup cost of asynchronous event handlers.

High-Resolution Time

Nanosecond resolution may not do much for you this year, but a time class that can represent either an interval or an absolute time and easily converts an interval into a date and time is certainly a convenience.

Happenings

Happenings are name for events that take place outside the Java environment. The RTSJ provides a general interface between external events and asynchronous events inside the Java environment.

Happenings give an implementation of the RTSJ a standard way to "see" asynchronous events outside the Java environment. User interface APIs already have a special-purpose ability to detect events. They use mechanisms like AWT events to notify an application of keystrokes and mouse activity. An interface like the RTSJ happening interface is already in the implementation of the GUI classes. Some part of AWT converts external GUI events into internal events.

Happenings are a good way to communicate with devices that do not fit into one of the other I/O systems supported by a Java platform.

Very Powerful and Dangerous Features of the RTSJ

Immortal memory is the deadly seducer of the RTSJ. It is seductive because it is as easy to use as heap memory, but it works anywhere, and never causes garbage collection. It is dangerous because it is a limited resource and it runs out after you are committed to it.

There's so much, no one will miss the little I need

Many systems have a little bit of battery-backed static RAM. It is useful stuff because it is as fast and easy to use as ordinary RAM, but data stored there will survive through power failures. Unfortunately, it costs much more than ordinary RAM.

The system designer tells the hardware engineer that the system will need some amount, say, 2421 bytes of nonvolatile RAM. The hardware engineer rounds that up to some standard part; say, 4096 bytes. That leaves 1675 bytes free.

If there are three software design teams, each will hear that there is more than a kilobyte of uncommitted nonvolatile RAM. Each team will soon require at least 1675 bytes of nonvolatile RAM beyond their original requirements. This leaves software requiring 3350 more bytes of nonvolatile RAM than the system has.

Unit tests don't show the problem since each software team can run by itself.

This situation sounds unlikely, but it happens again and again. It requires software teams that work separately, maybe in different time zones. It also depends on a sort of denial. Perhaps the developers in each team don't want to mention the "extra" nonvolatile RAM to the other teams for fear that they would want to share it if they knew about it.

Immortal memory has a lot in common with nonvolatile RAM. Someone needs to keep and enforce a budget.

Simple

Any object can contain a reference to immortal memory, any thread or asynchronous event handler can use immortal objects, and the only connection between garbage collection and immortal memory is that the garbage collector includes objects in immortal memory in its root set.

A chunk of code that uses only immortal memory is nearly as easy to write as code that uses only the heap. Code that restricts itself to immortal memory can forget garbage collection and reference rules

Leaky

Objects allocated in immortal memory last at least as long as the application that created them. There is no garbage collection for immortal objects. If you can confidently analyze a block of code and state the number of objects it will allocate over the life of the application, that code is a candidate for immortal memory. Whether it is a good candidate depends somewhat on just how many objects it will use.

If the number of objects a block of code will allocate is a function of some variable, the block is not a good candidate for immortality. It is likely to exhaust immortal memory. That is an acceptable state only if the application has allocated everything it intends to store in immortal memory and can run to completion without creating another immortal object.

The normal and proper use of immortal memory is to allocate all immortal objects early in an application's execution. If all immortal objects are allocated from a single method, the implementor can easily analyze the consumption of immortal memory. It is also easy to test. If the method that allocates immortal objects returns without throwing an error, there is enough immortal memory.

Viral

Immortal memory cannot contain references to scoped memory. If an application attempts to mix scoped and immortal memory, the inclination will be to keep moving objects into immortal memory until the application stops taking memory reference exceptions. Careful, and sometimes awkward, programming can prevent all objects from migrating into immortal memory, but it is so easy to just swat each reference exception bug by moving the offending object into immortal memory.

There is no easy way to blend scoped and immortal memory. The best approach is to build a small, clean interface between objects in immortal memory and scoped objects and then maintain the boundary.

Other features of the RTSJ have as much destructive potential as immortal memory, but they are hard to use. You know you are working with a tricky tool.

Very Powerful and Finicky Features of the RTSJ

The features listed in this section are not dangerous, but they are hard to use.

Scoped Memory

Scoped memory is a type of memory that can be used to allocate temporary objects but that does not require garbage collection. The bytecode interpreter and the scoped memory classes work together to ensure that objects allocated in scoped memory can be allocated and freed quickly without risking violations of referential integrity.

Scoped memory is an important factor in making many standard Java class libraries accessible to code that cannot tolerate garbage collection. The object allocations that take place in the standard methods are contained within the scope. It needs to have enough memory to hold all the objects allocated during an invocation of a method, but they are all discarded after the method returns. By use of the techniques from Chapter 13, values can be passed into and out of a standard method. Methods that maintain state by storing objects off static variables will not work. They will get an assignment error when they try to store a reference to a scoped object in a static variable.

No-Heap Asynchronous Event Handlers

A no-heap asynchronous event handler is the kind of Schedulable that moves the problem of reusing thread objects into the implementation of the JVM.

No-Heap Real-Time Threads

If a no-heap thread is rooted in immortal memory, it has all the difficulties of immortal memory but it can use scoped memory. That is somewhat harder to use than immortal memory, but it is less dangerous.

No-heap real-time threads and no-heap async event handlers can both be scheduled without consideration of the garbage collector. This can make them vastly more responsive.

Asynchronously Interrupted Exceptions

Asynchronously interrupted exceptions are a carefully crafted way for a thread or async event handler to reach into another thread and throw an exception.

This exception is a good tool for aborting computations that have timed out, for stopping a progressive algorithm when its budget is expired, for killing a thread, for notifying a thread of an urgent fault, or for any other task that requires some entity in the system to abruptly change the logic of a thread.

Asynchronously interrupted exceptions that use the `doInterruptible` mechanism are easy to use. The most difficult part is writing interruptible methods knowing that they can be interrupted so thoroughly that even `catch` and `finally` clauses in the method are skipped on the way to the next method that does not throw AIE.

Asynchronously interrupted exceptions are harder to use if the application requires something that `doInterruptible` does not offer.

Selection of Priorities

The schedulable objects in an RTSJ system can be divided into three groups:

1. Ordinary threads

2. Real-time threads and asynchronous event handlers

3. No-heap real-time threads and no-heap asynchronous event handlers

The ordinary threads have only ten priorities available to them, and those priorities are lower than the priorities available to real-time threads.

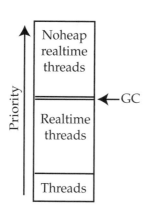

The priorities of real-time and no-heap real-time threads can be scattered in any order through the space of real-time priorities, but the platform is designed under the assumption that no-heap real-time threads will be given higher priorities than heap-using real-time threads.

If priorities are assigned to threads, as shown on the left, no-heap threads and event handlers will not block for garbage collection.

The platform will allow heap-using threads to be given priorities above no-heap threads, but that causes distressing garbage collection behavior.

The garbage collector does not actually have a priority above real-time threads. If there is a background garbage collection, it runs at a priority below any thread, even non-real-time threads. Demand garbage collection runs at the priority of the thread that needs memory. It is shown at a priority between real-time and no-heap threads as a memory aid. When no-heap threads are all given priorities higher than other threads, the system works "as it should" from the point of view of no-heap threads.

A no-heap thread is coded in that demanding environment because that thread has tight timing requirements that cannot tolerate delay caused by garbage collection. If a heap-using thread has higher priority than the no-heap thread, the timing of no-heap thread will be impacted by garbage collection in the higher-priority thread. If GC delays were tolerable, the thread could have been coded to use heap memory.

Garbage collection delays can also sneak into the no-heap priority range. If a no-heap thread waits for a resource held by a heap-using thread, it can be exposed to garbage collection. This is a particularly unfortunate race condition because the destructive case may be so rare that it never occurs under test.

The no-heap thread may not realize that a heap-using thread is sharing a synchronized method with it. If the method is brief, the disruption caused by the low-priority thread will be minimal unless it allocates a new object and happens to run out of memory. Unless the allocated object is exceptionally large or the garbage collector is an incremental garbage collector that uses a little time on each allocation, the chances of triggering garbage collection on a random object allocation is low. The no-heap thread could easily run for years, occasionally blocking and boosting the low-priority thread on the synchronized method. Garbage collection will hit perhaps one in a million of those rare occasions in which the high-priority thread blocks on the synchronized method.

For better or worse, priority boosting applies even when it boosts the priority of garbage collection above a no-heap thread. Figure 21–1 shows garbage collection in a heap-using thread delaying a no-heap thread that is interacting with it and another no-heap thread that is an innocent bystander.

Strategies for managing "strange" interactions between heap and no-heap threads include the following:

1. If the highest-priority activity has to allocate heap objects, try to make sure there is plenty of empty heap when it runs. This is a fragile situation, but you have no choice.

Figure 21–1 Priority boosting garbage collection

Low priority heap-using thread	mid-priority no-heap thread	High priority no-heap thread
Enters a synchronized method		
	Preempts and starts a computation	
		Preempts and starts a computation
		Calls the method locked by the heap-using thread and blocks. The sheduler boosts the heap-using thread to this priority
Boosted. Runs and uses new to allocate a heap object. Runs out of memory and calls the garbage collector		

2. If a no-heap thread must share a synchronized method with heap-using threads, avoid allocation of heap objects in that method. If the object does not allocate heap objects, it cannot trigger demand garbage collection. The no-heap thread will block for up to the duration of the method, but the execution time used for analysis will not need to include worst-case garbage collection time.

3. Use nonblocking mechanisms, like the nonblocking queues discussed in Chapter 20, for communication between heap and no-heap threads.

4. Separate heap and no-heap threads. Do not put the runtime in a position where it has to boost a heap-using thread to the priority of a no-heap thread.

Index

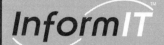